THE CHILD'S

Other Solid Ground Children's Books

Almost from the beginning of our ministry Solid Ground has been searching for books to minister to the young. Some of the very best are listed below:

Bible Animals: *Lessons Taught by Them for Children* by Richard Newton
Bible Jewels: *Lessons Taught by Them for Children* by Richard Newton
Bible Models: *Shining Lights of Scripture* by Richard Newton
Bible Promises: *Sermons for Children* by Richard Newton
Bible Warnings: *Sermons for Children* by Richard Newton
My Brother's Keeper: *Letters to a Younger Brother* by J.W. Alexander
The Child at Home by John S.C. Abbott
The Child's Book on the Fall of Man by Thomas H. Gallaudet
The Child's Book on Repentance by Thomas H. Gallaudet
The Child's Book on the Sabbath by Horace Hooker
The Child's Book on the Soul by Thomas H. Gallaudet
Early Piety Illustrated: *Memoir of Nathan Dickerman* by Gorham Abbott
FAMILY WORSHIP for The Christmas Season by Ray Rhodes
FAMILY WORSHIP for the Reformation Season by Ray Rhodes
FAMILY WORSHIP for the Thanksgiving Season by Ray Rhodes
Feed My Lambs: *Lectures to Children* by John Todd
Heroes of the Early Church: *Lessons for the Young* by Richard Newton
Heroes of the Reformation: *Lessons for the Young* by Richard Newton
Jesus the Way: *Child's Guide to Heaven* by Edward Payson Hammond
The King's Highway: *10 Commandments for the Young* Richard Newton
Life of Jesus Christ for the Young (2 volumes) by Richard Newton
Little Pillows and Morning Bells by Francis Havergal
A Manual for the Young: *Exposition of Proverbs 1-9* by Charles Bridges
Morning Stars: *Names of Christ for His Little Ones* by Frances Havergal
Nuts for Boys to Crack: *Spiritual Truth in Earthly Dress* by John Todd
Old Paths for Little Feet by Carol Brandt
The Pastor's Daughter by Louisa Payson Hopkins
Rays from the Sun of Righteousness by Richard Newton
Repentance & Faith: *Explained to the Young* by Charles Walker
Safe Compass and How it Points: *for Children* by Richard Newton
Scripture Biography for the Young: Vols. 1 - 5 by T.H. Gallaudet
Scripture Biography for the Young: *King Josiah* by T.H. Gallaudet
The Scripture Guide: *Lessons for the Young* by J.W. Alexander
Small Talks on Big Questions by Helms & Thompson-Kahler
Tract Primer: *First Lessons in Sound Doctrine* by American Tract Society
The Truth About Christmas by Peter Jeffery
Truth Made Simple: *Attributes of God for Children* by John Todd
Young Ladies Guide by Harvey Newcomb
Young People's Problems by J.R. Miller
Youth's Book on Natural Theology by Thomas H. Gallaudet

THE CHILD'S PREACHER

A Series

of

Addresses

on

Systematic Theology

to the Young

Alexander Fletcher
Lowther J. Barrington
John Crawshaw
Lyman A. Eddy
John Charles Ryle

SOLID GROUND CHRISTIAN BOOKS
BIRMINGHAM, ALABAMA USA

Solid Ground Christian Books
6749 Remington Circle
Pelham AL 35124
205-443-0311
mike.sgcb@gmail.com
www.solid-ground-books.com

THE CHILD'S PREACHER
A Series of Addresses on Systematic Theology to the Young

Alexander Fletcher
Lowther J. Barrington
John Crawshaw
Lyman A. Eddy
John Charles Ryle

Taken from the 1855 edition by *Carlton & Phillips*, New York

First Solid Ground edition in June 2011

Cover design by Borgo Design
Contact them at borgogirl@bellsouth.net

ISBN- 978-159925-257-5

Introductory Essay
Charles H. Spurgeon

CHILDHOOD AND HOLY SCRIPTURE

PAUL TAUGHT YOUNG TIMOTHY the gospel himself: he made him not only hear his doctrine, but see his practice. We cannot force truth upon men, but we can make our own teaching clear and decided, and make our lives consistent therewith. Truth and holiness are the surest antidotes to error and unrighteousness. The apostle said to Timothy, "Continue thou in the things which thou hast learned and hast been assured of, knowing of whom thou hast learned them."

He then dwelt upon another potent remedy which had been of great service to the young preacher—namely, the knowing of the Holy Scriptures from his earliest childhood. This was to young Timothy one of his best safeguards. His early training held him like an anchor, and saved him from the dreadful drift of the age. Happy young man, of whom the apostle could say, "From a child thou hast known the Holy Scriptures, which are able to make thee wise unto salvation through faith which is in Christ Jesus"!

To be prepared for the coming conflict, we have only to preach the gospel, and to live the gospel; and also to take care that we teach the children the Word of the Lord. This last is specially to be attended to, for it is by the mouth of babes and sucklings that God will still the enemy. It is idle to dream that human learning must be met by human learning, or that Satan must cast out Satan. No. Lift up the brazen serpent wherever the fiery serpents are biting the people, and men shall look to it and live. Bring the children out, and hold them up, and turn their little eyes towards the divinely ordained remedy; for still there is life in a look—life as against the varied venoms of the serpent which are now poisoning the blood of men. There is no cure after all for midnight but the rising sun;

no hope remains for a dark world but in that light which lighteneth every man. Shine forth, O Sun of Righteousness, and mist, and cloud, and darkness must disappear. Keep to the apostolic plans, and rest assured of apostolic success. Preach Christ; preach the Word in season and out of season: and teach the children. One of God's chief methods for preserving His fields from tares, is to sow them early with wheat.

The work of God's grace in Timothy commenced with early instructions—"From a child thou hast known the Holy Scriptures."

Note the time for instruction. The expression, "from a child," might be better understood if we read it, "from a very child;" or, as the Revised Version has it, "from a babe." It does not mean a well-grown child, or youth, but a child just rising out of infancy. From a very child Timothy had known the sacred writings. This expression is, no doubt, used to show that we cannot begin too early to imbue the minds of our children with Scriptural knowledge. Babes receive impressions long before we are aware of the fact. During the first months of a child's life it learns more than we imagine. It soon learns the love of its mother, and its own dependence; and if the mother be wise, it learns the meaning of obedience and the necessity of yielding its will to a higher will. This may be the keynote of its whole future life. If it learn obedience and submission early, it may save a thousand tears from the child's eyes, and as many from the mother's heart. A special vantage-ground is lost when even babyhood is left uncultured.

The Holy Scriptures may be learned by children as soon as they are capable of understanding anything. It is a very remarkable fact, which I have heard asserted by many teachers, that children will learn to read out of the Bible better than from any other book. I scarcely know why: it may, perhaps, be on account of the simplicity of the language; but I believe it is so. A Biblical fact will often be grasped when an incident of common history is forgotten. There is an adaptation in the Bible for human beings of all ages, and therefore it has a fitness for children. We make a mistake when we think that we must begin with something else and lead up to the Scriptures. The Bible is the book for the peep of day. Parts of it are above a child's mind, for they are above the comprehension of the most advanced among us. There are depths in it wherein leviathan may swim; but there are also brooks in which a lamb may wade. Wise teachers know how to lead their little ones into the green pastures, beside the still waters.

I was noticing, in the life of that man of God whose loss presses very heavily upon many of our hearts—namely, the Earl of Shaftesbury—that his first religious impressions were produced by a humble woman. The impressions which made him—Shaftesbury—the man of God, and the friend of man, were received in the nursery. Little Lord Ashley had a godly nurse who spoke to him of the things of God. He tells us that she died before he was seven years of age; clear proof that early in life his heart had been able to receive the seal of the Spirit of God, and to receive it by humble instrumentality. Blessed among women was she whose name we know not, but who wrought incalculable service for God and man by her holy teaching of the chosen child. Young nurses, note this.

Give us the first seven years of a child, with God's grace, and we may defy the world, the flesh, and the devil to ruin that immortal soul. Those first years, while yet the clay is soft and plastic, go far to decide the form of the vessel. Do not say that your office, you who teach the young, is in the least degree inferior to ours, whose main business is with older folks. No, you have the first of them, and your impressions, as they come first, will endure last; oh, that they may be good, and only good! Among the thoughts that come to an old man before he enters Heaven, the most plentiful are those that aforetime visited him when he sat upon his mother's knee. That which made Dr. Guthrie ask for a "bairn's hymn" when he was dying,[1] is but an instinct of our nature, which leads us to complete the circle by folding together the ends of life. Childlike things are dearest to old age. We shuffle off a portion of the coil that doth surround and hamper us, and go back again to our more natural selves; and therefore the old songs are on our lips, and the old thoughts are in our minds. The teachings of our childhood leave clean-cut and sharp impressions upon the mind, which remain after seventy years have passed. Let us see that such impressions are made for the highest ends.

It is well to *note the admirable selection of instructors.* We are not at a loss to tell who instructed youthful Timothy. In

---

[1] See the following page for a fuller description of this incident.

the first chapter of this epistle Paul says, "When I call to remembrance the unfeigned faith that is in thee, which dwelt first in thy grandmother Lois, and thy mother Eunice; and I am persuaded that is in thee also." No doubt grandmother Lois and mother Eunice united in teaching the little one. Who should teach the children but the parents? Timothy's father was a Greek, and probably a heathen, but his child was happy in having a venerable grandmother, so often the dearest of all relatives to a little child. He had also a gracious mother, once a devout Jewess, and afterwards also a firmly believing Christian, who made it her daily pleasure to teach her own dear child the Word of the Lord. O dear mothers, you have a very sacred trust reposed in you by God! He hath in effect said to you, "Take this child and nurse it for Me, and I will give thee thy wages." You are called to equip the future man of God, that he may be thoroughly furnished unto every good work. If God spares you, you may live to hear that pretty boy speak to thousands, and you will have the sweet reflection in your heart that the quiet teachings of the nursery led the man to love his God and serve Him. Those who think that a woman detained at home by her little family is doing nothing, think the reverse of what is true. Scarcely can the godly mother quit her home for a place of worship, but dream not that she is lost to the work of the church; far from it, she is doing the best possible service for her Lord. Mothers, the godly training of your offspring is your first and most pressing duty. Christian women, by teaching children the Holy Scriptures, are as much fulfilling their part for the Lord, as Moses in judging Israel, or Solomon in building the temple.

"Give Me a Bairn's Hymn"
by Theodore Cuyler

I have just been reading—through eyes brimming with tears— the narrative of Dr. Guthrie's last hours. They were all in perfect keeping with his noble and beautiful life. For three score years and ten Guthrie had been patterning after Jesus, who "went about doing good." To the last he was the same simple-hearted, genial, child-like creature, in genius a full-grown man, in simplicity a child.

His love of children was a passion with him. He had eleven of his own; one of whom, Johnnie, had gone home to heaven in his infancy. For the poor outcast lads and the lasses of the wretched "Cowgate" in Edinburgh, Dr. Guthrie's heart went out in tenderest compassion. He visited them in their miserable whisky-cursed homes. He organized for them the first "ragged school" ever established in Scotland. And, among all his printed productions, his "Plea for Ragged Schools" is the most characteristically touching and eloquent.

When the great pulpit-orator came to die, he grew more and more like a child himself. He felt like a babe on the bosom of Jesus. The sight of a little grandchild who came into his dying chamber brought a smile over his pale face, and he whispered
"PUT HER UP."
When lifted on the bed, she crept up to him and kissed him, and he nodded his head, and said sweetly, "My bonnie lamb!"

During those last hours he found great solace in the singing of dear old favorite psalms and "spiritual songs." But of none was he so fond as of the simple Sunday-school melodies. When they asked him on one of the last nights of his life, "What shall we sing for you?" he answered quickly, *"Give me a bairn's [2] hymn."* So they sang for the veteran pilgrim, "Jesus, tender Shepherd, hear me," and " There is a happy land, far, far away."

Glorious old hero of the Cross! His theology was all narrowed down to one word, *Christ.* His faith was the faith of a little child. When asked, "Have you that Savior now?" he promptly answered, "Yes; I have none else." Then he was heard to murmur to himself, "Over on the other side," and kept ejaculating the words, "Happy, happy, happy." and so he fell asleep in Jesus, without a struggle or a sigh. The last of earth was the beginning of the everlasting weight of glory. Today Scotland weeps over the silence of her most gifted tongue. But the voice has passed into the memories of heaven, and Guthrie is singing 'a bairn's hymn' before the throne!

---

[2] Bairn – a Scots and Northern English word for a child.

EDITOR'S PREFACE.

For several years we have contemplated the publication of a work like the present, and have been making a collection of the various volumes and pamphlets of sermons, addresses, and lectures to the young issued from the English press.

Unwilling, however, to compile the work wholly from foreign sources, we waited until furnished with a supply of similar matter from the pen of one of our own American ministers, who kindly consented that his productions might be incorporated in the present volume at our discretion. That we have not similar contributions from other American preachers is not because we have failed to solicit them. The truth is that American ministers have as yet written but few sermons for children ; and, indeed, have preached quite too few.

One important object of the present volume is to furnish practical hints, which may serve to encourage young ministers, and others who imagine it a difficult thing to preach to children, to make the attempt more frequently. It will be found that the variety of texts and subjects which may be adapted to children's capacities is almost endless.

The great requisites, in order to interest children, are plainness of speech and fertility of illustration. When these are employed, low and silly expressions are worse than useless, and trifling thoughts and foolish imaginations are a positive offense. It is perfectly practicable to adapt every essential, or strictly important religious topic, not only to the capacity, but even to the tastes of children; yea, to interest them deeply in such subjects, and at the same time to preserve dignity of expression and purity of thought. How vastly important, therefore, is it for every minister to qualify himself for, and to habituate himself to, preaching the Gospel to children.

Besides, there are numerous Sunday-school superintendents, visitors, and teachers who need good models of religious addresses to the young, either to read directly to those under their care, or to serve as hints and helps to their own efforts.

Finally, while we would deem it unwise to fill our Sunday-school libraries with volumes of sermons, we do not think it out of place to furnish one such volume among hundreds on other topics. While some Sabbath scholars may prefer lighter reading, we do not doubt that large numbers will gladly and earnestly peruse the solid and edifying, but at the same time vivacious and life-like addresses of which the Child's Preacher is composed.

The greater number of these sermons are from the pen of that distinguished preacher to children, the late Rev. Alexander Fletcher, D. D., of London; one is from a volume by the Hon. and Rev. L. Barrington; two are from the pen of Rev. J. C. Ryle; two are from a series by the Rev. John Crawshaw, Wesleyan minister; several are by an anonymous author; and for the remainder we are indebted to the Rev. L. A. Eddy, of Cazenovia, New-York.

CONTENTS.

Illustrations.

———◆———

CHILD'S PREACHER.

CREATION.

In the beginning God created the heaven and the earth.—
Gen. i, 1.

LITTLE children, you have often read or heard these words, and yet have not thought much about them; but if you know what they mean, you know more than many men, who have been called both great and wise in times past, have been able to find out. They unfold to us a great secret, when they tell us that "God created the heaven and the earth."

It is very sad to think how many people there have been in God's world who have lived and died without knowing anything about him. And there are

still many who are ignorant of him;
some because they have never heard of
him, and some because they do not like
to keep him in mind! Yet he is very
good, and is always doing good to us; we
could not live or move without him, so
that it seems strange that any one should
forget him. But, my children, if we had
not the Bible, we should know as little
about God as the poor heathen do: nay,
though we have it, it too often happens
that he is not in our thoughts.

Do you know why it is called the
Bible? It is so kind of God to give it to
us! But why is it called the Bible? I
will tell you. "Bible" means "book."
The Bible is the book which God has
given us to read, to learn, to think about.
It is "the book" that tells us what we
ought to do, what we ought to pray for,
what we ought to hope for. Other books
may be true, my children; but the Bible
is "the truth, the whole truth, and nothing but the truth." From the first verse,
which tells you that "God created the
heaven and the earth," to the very last, it

is all true; there is nothing false in it at all. "The book," then, is the best of all books ; it is "the book" of God. Do you think, now, my children, that you understand why it is called "the Bible?" But how is it God's book? Did he write it? I will tell you. It was "given by inspiration of God," (2 Tim. iii, 16;) that is, it was not written by him with pen, and ink, and paper, but he taught some good men by his Holy Spirit what to write. So some parts of "the book" were written by Moses, some by David : (you have often heard of these good men, have you not?) Then there were prophets, and the writers of the Gospel, and St. Paul, and other holy men who wrote and spoke what God commanded, that we might know and do his will. I hope to tell you more about this another time, "if the Lord will;" but one thing I ask of you—pray God, for Jesus Christ's sake, to give *you* his Holy Spirit, or else I shall preach to you in vain, and you will hear in vain.

Let us, then, now see a little more about

this text. "In the beginning God created the heaven and the earth." We will try and understand something, 1st, about "the beginning;" 2d, about "creation;" and 3d, about "God."

First, as to "the beginning." You cannot carry your thoughts back for many years, because you are very young; and even if you had been very old—more than a hundred years old—you would still be very, very far from "the beginning." "The beginning" here means the first of everything in the world; and that was about six thousand years ago. Before that there was nothing in the world; there was no world such as we now see. There were angels in heaven, there was God. He made the angels before "the beginning" of the world; we do not know how, or when; but He himself is without beginning. He made the world "in the beginning," almost six thousand years since, before which there were none of those things which afterward appeared. Did you ever think, when you walk along the pleasant green fields, and gather the

yellow cowslips, or search in the hedge-
banks for the sweet blue violets, or weave
your May garlands, that once there were
no flowers to twine? It was not, my
children, because the cold frost and snows
of winter came and chilled them in the
bud, for there was no winter, no summer,
no green grass, no bright blossom, nor
any ground to till; there was nothing for
any one to plant or sow; there was no
man; there was nothing! Still there was
God above; and there may have been
many beautiful and glorious beings singing his praise without ceasing, and other
worlds far away with the shining stars in
the sky; but there was nothing belonging
to this world, till in "the beginning God
created the heaven and the earth." Now,
perhaps you will think it very strange
that there should be nothing in "the beginning," and nobody; so it is, and more
and more wonderful the more we think
about it. We can understand better that
there were no trees, no flowers, no houses;
but the rocks and the mountains, the
hills and the valleys, the sea and the dry

land, seem as if they must have been forever.   If they were not so, how could they
ever be ?

Think a little, my children; think of
the text—what are the words?   "In the
beginning God *created* the heaven and
the earth."   This brings us to consider,
secondly, the meaning of creation.

Second. Tell me, then, what did God
do in the beginning?   He "*created* the
heaven and the earth."   Very well.
Now, then, children, what do you understand by that?   I will try and explain it
to you.   It means to make something
without anything to make it of.   You
cannot do so ; nor could the wisest man
that ever lived do such a thing.   We
may make a great many things, as you
may see by looking round you.   The pulpit was made by some man ; the windows
of this church were made by men, and
the benches on which you sit ; but then
they had all that was wanted to make
them of.   The carpenter not only has his
tools to use, but the wood to fashion into
the thing he wants ; and all other trades-

men have first their tools, and then their
stuff; but though they may *make* many
curious and beautiful things, they cannot
create a thing so small as a pin's head.
Do you now understand the difference between making and creating? God need-
ed nothing in his work; " He created the
heaven and the earth," which means that
everything both there above and here below were made by him alone; so he is
called the Creator.

If you have got "the book," and can
read, open it at the first chapter, and see
how all things are there set in order before
us, and how each was created in turn as
the earth was ready to sustain them.
First, there was day and night, then the
sky, then the dry land and the sea. After
these, the green grass, and herbs, and
fruits, and trees; then the sun and the
moon; then the birds and fishes; then
creeping things and cattle; and last of all
man himself, for whose use all these
things were made.

Third. Before we finish, let us see,
thirdly, what is known of him who created

all these things. What does "the book"
tell us of his nature? It says "God is a
Spirit," (John iv, 24,) and where is he?
He is everywhere. The book says, "If
I ascend up into heaven, thou art there:
if I make my bed in hell, behold, thou art
there. If I take the wings of the morning, and dwell in the uttermost parts of
the sea; even there shall thy hand lead
me, and thy right hand shall hold me."
Psalms cxxxix, 8–10. He is the God of
heaven and earth. His glory and majesty
are seen in heaven; his power and goodness are shown to us on earth. But besides this, "the book" tells us a great
many things about God, and the best that
it tells us is that "God is love." 1 John
iv, 16.

Dear children, your parents love you
very much; they would be sorry if you
were hurt, and so sorry if you should be
sick, or if you were to die! But God
loves you more tenderly, for he "so loved
the world that he gave his only-begotten
Son, that whosoever believeth in him
should not perish, but have everlasting

life." John iii, 16. I cannot now speak
to you of that; I have a great many
things to tell you of "the book," but I
should not be able to speak of them now,
if you could listen to them. But as God
has done a great deal for you, I wonder
whether it has ever come into your minds
to think what you ought to do for him?
Perhaps you think you have done enough
when you have knelt upon your knees and
said your prayers; but I want you to "love
him with all your heart, with all your
soul, and with all your mind," (Matthew
xxii, 37,) and then you will serve him as
dear children. He has said in "the
book," "I love them that love me; and
they that seek me early shall find me:"
(Prov. viii, 17:) there is the little child's
promise for you, which shows that God
cares for children. If you do not love
him, shall I tell you what to do? Pray
this little prayer very often: "O God,
give me thy Holy Spirit for Jesus Christ's
sake, to make me love thee!" God will
hear and answer little children's prayers;
so when you ask him to be kind to you

and your dear parents, and all your family, add this little prayer. Try and remember it, and let me hear that you say it sometimes. If you love God, you will not forget him. He will never forget you; and I hope you may so remember him, that he may take you to heaven. You see in the text that both heaven and earth are mentioned; and why? Is it not to remind you of the *end* as well as "the beginning?" Look up, then, my children! for Jesus has promised "where I am, there shall my servant be." John xii, 26. O, how happy they will be who get to that place; it is the Christian's home! Let us try, then, to follow Jesus; and you may be quite sure that he loves those who walk in his steps too well to shut the door when they seek to enter into his presence and kingdom!

GOD'S WISDOM.

O the depth of the riches of the wisdom of God!—
Rom. xi, 33.

MAY my young friends never speak, or hear, or read, or think of Christ, without remembering that he is GOD as well as *man*. It is said of Christ, in Col. ii, 3, " In him are hid all the treasures of wisdom and knowledge." This cannot be said of any angel, or of the greatest of archangels; and it could not be said of Christ if he were not very God, as well as man. I wish you particularly to observe the words, " treasures of wisdom." What does the word "treasures" intimate? It clearly shows that true wisdom is true wealth. It shows that there is nothing in the whole earth worthy to be compared with wisdom. Gold and silver, pearls and diamonds, are only useless as chaff compared with the wisdom of Christ. The heavens and the earth, the sun, the moon, and the stars, all belong to Christ. What treasures!

But I tell you the truth when I say, that all these are insignificant, yea, nothing, compared with the treasures of wisdom and knowledge which are hid in Christ!

May your young minds be impressed with this—that there is nothing you can desire so valuable as wisdom. A poor child, blessed with divine wisdom, is richer than foolish kings, who can boast of their scepters, their crowns, and their palaces. Solomon was both the wisest and the richest king that ever lived on earth. What does he say of wisdom? He says, what the Spirit of God taught him to say, and what he knew to be true, Prov. iii, 15: "Wisdom is more precious than rubies: and all the things thou canst desire are not to be compared unto her."

If wisdom is so precious when placed in the heart of man, what must the perfection of wisdom be in the mind of God? What must it be in all its boundless treasures, laid up and hid in Christ? "O the depth of the riches of the wisdom of God!"

May the Holy Spirit impress the minds of my young friends with what I shall now, by his gracious help, endeavor to say of the wisdom of God!

I. I shall endeavor to show what we understand by the wisdom of God.

1. Wisdom is one of the perfections of God. Do you know, my young friends, what a perfection is? It is something very excellent. It is something so excellent that it cannot be *more* excellent. The wisdom of God and of Christ is one of God's excellences. It cannot be more excellent than it is. God cannot be wiser than he is, for his wisdom is infinite. Mark that word infinite. This cannot be said of any excellence in the best of men, or in the greatest of angels. Their wisdom is not infinite; but the wisdom of God is infinite. Therefore it is a glorious perfection. "O the depth of the riches of the wisdom of God!"

2. God's wisdom is that perfection by which he forms the best and wisest plans. Every plan God contrives, or makes, or forms, must be the wisest, must be the

best. Before a house is built, there is
first a plan, beautifully and skillfully
drawn out on paper. God gave David
the king a most wonderful plan of the
temple. Sir Christopher Wren first formed a plan of St. Paul's. The wisdom of
the builder shines in the wisdom of his
plans. Without a wise plan, a good convenient house can never be built. We
must always look first to the plan. If we
compare all things to a building, God is
the builder of all things: and he first
made a wise plan. There are three wise
and wonderful plans God has made. There
is the plan of creation: the wisdom of that
plan is perfect. There is the plan of providence: that plan is perfect. There is the
plan of redemption: that plan is perfect.
None of them could be more perfect;
none of them could be more complete.
" O the depth of the riches of the wisdom
of God!"

3. The wisdom of God is that perfection
by which he does everything in the best
manner. Two scholars at school are both
employed doing the same thing: how dif-

ferent the manner! How different the doing of the wise boy, and of the foolish! The manner of the doing of the one marks wisdom, that of the other marks folly. Let us now look to God's manner of doing things, and we shall see that it is not only good, but the very best. Does he make a sun? he has made it in the best manner. Has he made a Bible? it is in the best manner. Has Jesus made a righteousness for our salvation? it is in the best manner. It is a robe which cannot be more complete, which cannot be more glorious. Has God made a heaven for his saints? it cannot be more complete, it cannot be more blessed. " O the depth of the riches of the wisdom of God!"

4. Wisdom is that perfection by which God does everything for the best end. Let me ask you, What is the best end, or best purpose, for which God can make all things, and preserve all things? If you have been religiously educated, you will answer at once, and without any difficulty, "His own glory." Now everything God does shows his glory. The

glory of his wisdom shines in all his works. Yes, in every one of them, from the formation of a particle of sand to the formation of a mountain, whose summit reaches the clouds. Yes, from the formation of a little winged insect, to the formation of an archangel before the glorious throne above! Why did he make the heavens and the earth? To declare his glory, and to make man and angels blessed. Why did he make his Bible? O mark the following answers! He made it to make known himself, that we might love him and serve him. He made it to make known salvation, and persuade us to receive it. He made it to make known the way to heaven, and to teach us to walk in it. "O the depth of the riches of the wisdom of God!"

II. We will now endeavor to show wherein, particularly, God's wisdom appears. Already we have shown this in part; but we will proceed a little further in this glorious and delightful field.

1. God's wisdom shines in creation. Psa. civ, 24: "O Lord, how manifold

are thy works! in wisdom thou hast made
them all: the earth is full of thy riches."
What a prospect we have now before us!
It consists of the manifold works of God.
Let us look on these manifold works, and
admire the wisdom which God's manifold
works display. Look above to the sun,
moon, and stars; then say, " O Lord, in
wisdom thou hast made them all!" Look
on the earth beneath, on its grass, and
corn, and herbs, and flowers, and shrubs,
and trees; then on the birds of the air, the
fishes which swim in the waters, on the
beasts of the field, on the cattle upon a
thousand hills, and on the human race of
all nations, and kingdoms, and color, and
language. Then say with the Psalmist,
" O Lord, in wisdom thou hast made them
all!" Wisdom contrived them all; power
made them all, directed by wisdom. How
true the saying of the wise man, Proverbs
iii, 19: "The Lord by wisdom hath found-
ed the earth; and by understanding hath
he established the heavens."

2. God's wisdom shines in providence.
God's daily acts of his providence furnish

daily displays of his wisdom. A wise father shows his wisdom in the daily provision he makes for his children and family. To provide one day, and to leave them to want another, would show both folly and cruelty. Apply this to God, and see how wise God is. Every day God supplies the wants of every living thing. What a provision! The table of his providence he richly covers every day. The provision is not only most abundant but most suitable. He feeds all creatures " with food convenient" for them. Prov. xxx, 8. From that providential table, birds, beasts, fishes, creeping things, insects, and human beings, receive their daily food.

God has a providential wardrobe as well as a providential table. From that wardrobe, which is well stored, he supplies all his creatures with clothing convenient for them. Some with wool, others with fir, others with scales spangling like burnished gold, and others with the richest feathers, lovely, like the glowing colors of the rainbow.

Providence shows the gracious wisdom of God in the daily blessings he confers upon his people. Every day he comforts them with his goodness, protects them with his power, and guides them with his wisdom. The regularity, constancy, and abundance of these spiritual blessings proclaim, in loudest, sweetest language, the wisdom and goodness of God. May God the Spirit enable you and me to utter the following words with hearts overflowing with wonder, thankfulnesss, and love! Psa. lxiii, 7: "Because thou hast been my help, therefore in the shadow of thy wings will I rejoice." Psa. lxviii, 19: "Blessed be the Lord, who daily loadeth us with his benefits."

3. God's wisdom shines in Redemption. In contriving the plan of redemption, there were two things necessary to be considered. The plan must meet these two things fully and perfectly; if it did not, our race must have perished forever. Young friends, think seriously on these two things. The first is this: — A plan must be contrived by which offended jus-

tice must be satisfied. The second is this :— A plan must be contrived by which guilty sinners may be saved; a plan must be contrived by which God may be reconciled to men; a plan must be contrived by which guilty, rebellious sinners may be reconciled to God. Now, if all the angels of heaven had sat down in council for thousands of years, they never could have contrived a plan by which these two could have been gained. But God, by his infinite wisdom, contrived the plan. Thus, God did what none but God could do. And what plan did God's wisdom contrive? It was this : That his own Son, the Second Person of the Trinity, should come into the place of fallen man; that he should become man; that he should take upon him the sins of men; that he should obey the law for men; that he should suffer for men; and that he should die for men. To show the wisdom and perfection of the plan, Jesus became all this. He became man. He obeyed. He suffered. He died! Then, justice was satisfied, fully satisfied; then,

God was reconciled to man. And when divine grace is applied to the poor sinner's heart, and to the young sinner's heart, he is reconciled to God. He loves the God he once hated.

How infinitely wise is God in contriving a plan by which all this is done, and without which it could never have been done! So wise is this plan, that it is called the "manifold wisdom of God." Eph. iii, 10, 11 : "To the intent that now unto the principalities and powers in heavenly places might be known by the Church the manifold wisdom of God, according to the eternal purpose which he purposed in Christ Jesus our Lord." "O the depth of the riches of the wisdom of God!"

CONCLUSION.

1. Young friends, take Jesus for your wise and merciful teacher. O put yourselves under his care, and he will teach you the most blessed lessons of wisdom, gentleness, meekness, and holiness. What a privilege, what an honor is this, to have Jesus, the only wise God, for your teacher!

2. Hear his loving voice, Matt. xi, 28, &c.: "Come unto me, all ye that labor, and are heavy laden, and I will give you rest. Take my yoke upon you, and learn of me: for my yoke is easy, and my burden is light."

-----◆-----

GOD'S OMNIPRESENCE.

Whither shall I go from thy Spirit? or whither shall I flee from thy presence?—PSALM cxxxix, 7.

WHAT is the meaning of the word omnipresence? It means to be present in every place, and everywhere at the same time. This is true of God. He is present in every place, and in every place at the same time. He is as much present in one place as in another. Yes, as much present in a desert as in a lovely garden. He is as much present in a cottage as in a palace, and as much in a school-room of young scholars as he is in the most splendid sanctuary filled with adoring worshipers.

What, then, is omnipresence? We answer, It is one of the attributes or perfections of God the Father, Son, and Holy Ghost, ONE GOD. This glorious perfection can belong to none but God; it can belong to no creature, to no angel. It belongs only to God. God is infinite, and therefore must be omnipresent. To be infinite is to be without bounds and limits; such is God. He is without bounds, he is without limits; therefore he must be everywhere present. Zophar thus spake to Job of God as infinite, and therefore as omnipresent, Job xi, 7: "Canst thou by searching find out God? canst thou find out the Almighty unto perfection?" Verse 8: "It is high as heaven; what canst thou do? deeper than hell; what canst thou know?" Verse 9: "The measure thereof is longer than the earth and broader than the sea."

> Can creatures to perfection find
> Th' eternal uncreated mind?
> Or can the longest stretch of thought
> Measure and search his nature out?
> 'T is high as heaven, 't is deep as hell,
> And what can mortals know or tell?
> His glory spreads beyond the sky,
> And all the shiny worlds on high.—WATTS.

I.—WHERE GOD IS PRESENT.

1. *He is present in heaven.* Is the sky or the firmament called heaven? He fills the sky or the firmament. Is the vast space where the stars twinkle and shine called heaven? He fills that vast space. There is another heaven still; it is called the third heaven, and the heaven of heavens. The sky, the first heaven, is glorious; the second, or the starry heaven, is more glorious than the first; the third heaven, the heaven of heavens, is infinitely more glorious than the other two. And that heaven, God the Father, Son, and Holy Ghost, one God, fills with his presence, and fills with his glory. Thus Solomon speaks of God in heaven, Eccles. v, 2: "God is in heaven, and thou upon earth, therefore let thy words be few." The prophet had a blessed view of God as present in heaven, and he gives the following account of what he saw, Isa. vi, 1: "I saw also the Lord sitting upon a throne, high and lifted up, and his train filled the temple." Verse 2: "Above it stood the seraphims: each one had six

wings ; with twain he covered his face, and with twain he covered his feet, and with twain he did fly." Verse 3: "And one cried unto another, and said, Holy, holy, holy, is the Lord of hosts: the whole earth is full of his glory."

O what blessedness it must be to enter heaven, and see God filling heaven with his glory! Little children when they die see that glory; they see Jesus the Lamb in the midst of the throne. Then they cast their golden crowns at his feet, and sing hosannahs of sweetest praise :—

> "There is beyond the sky
> A heaven of joy and love;
> And holy children when they die
> Go to that world above."

2. *God is present on earth.* He is as much present in the wilderness as in the city, and in the forest as in the fruitful valleys, beautified with villages and hamlets. The believer has this comfort, that if he crosses mighty seas and goes to distant lands, his gracious God is near. As a child of God, he can say with holy joy, "If I take the wings of the morning, and

dwell in the uttermost parts of the sea, even there shall thy hand lead me, and thy right hand shall hold me." Psalm cxxxix, 9, 10. Happy indeed is that child who can say, "Wherever I go, my God and Saviour is there. If I go to Africa, he is there; if I go to India, he is there; if I go to the islands of the great Pacific Ocean, he is there: yes, my God and Saviour is there. I may be removed far, far from my kind father and my loving mother; but I cannot be removed from my Saviour and my God. Wherever I may go, or to whatever distant land I may be removed, even there shall the hand of my God lead me, and the right hand of my Saviour hold me."

The prophet Isaiah had a delightful view of God's omnipresence when he said, chap. vi, 3, "The whole earth is full of his glory." Zechariah felt similar joy and delight when he thus wrote of God's gracious, powerful, and defending presence with his Church and people, chap. ii, 5: "For I, saith the Lord, will be unto her a wall of fire round about, and will be the glory in the midst of her." May the following lines express the holy wish and earnest prayer of all our hearts!

> Lord, let thy grace surround me still,
>   And like a bulwark prove,
> To guard my soul from every ill,
>   Secured by sovereign love.—WATTS.

3. *God is present in hell!* Little children may ask, How is God present in that place of misery and despair? For what purpose is he present there? He is present there in his justice. He is present there to punish his impenitent enemies. He is present there to punish those who despised his mercy on earth; who refused Christ, and neglected his great salvation. He is present on earth as a loving father in the midst of his Church: he is present in hell, in the midst of his enemies, as an angry judge.

Dear young friends, think of this, and send your earnest prayer to Jesus, to save you from that dreadful hell where God is present, not to save, but to punish; present, not to give a cup of pleas-

ure, but a cup of anguish and of wrath.
O may the following lines, by God's
Spirit, most deeply touch your youthful
hearts!

> In heaven God shines with beams of love,
>   With wrath in hell beneath:
> 'T is on his earth I stand or move,
>   And 't is his air I breathe.—WATTS.

II. — WITH WHOM GOD IS GRACIOUSLY
PRESENT.

1. *He is graciously present with all his
Church.* How clearly this is stated in
God's holy word! The whole Church is
taught to sing, (Psa. xlvi, 11,) "The Lord
of hosts is with us; the God of Jacob is
our refuge." Is the Church a flock?
God is ever present with his whole flock.
Is the Church a family? God is ever
present with his whole family. Is the
Church an army? Jesus, as the captain
of salvation, is ever present at the head
of his army. Is the Church a kingdom?
He is ever present with them as their
king, to rule them by his love, and defend them by his power. He says to
them, "Lo, I am with you alway, even

unto the end of the world." Matthew
xxviii, 20.

2. *God is graciously present with each
individual saint.* He is as much so as if
there were only one saint on the face of the
earth. How remarkable is this! How
delightful, how encouraging is this! God
is graciously present with every pious minister and every pious hearer. He is graciously present with every pious parent
and every pious child. He is graciously
present with every pious teacher and every
pious scholar. Jesus dearly loves the
lambs of his flock. Each lamb—yes, each
lamb—"he gathers with his arms." Each
lamb—yes, each lamb—"he carries in his
bosom." Wonderful! Surely this is sufficient to make every pious child shout
and sing for joy, "Hosanna to the Son
of David, who cometh in the name of the
Lord to save us; Hosanna in the highest."
Matt. xxi, 9.

3. *God is graciously present with his
people at all times.* This being the case,
he is present with them in all *circumstances.* He is present with them in

childhood and youth; he is present with them in manhood and old age. See that dear little child on his way to heaven. Who is that by his side, and always at his side? It is his Saviour and God. He is graciously present with his people in all his ordinances. He is present with them in the secret closet of prayer. The pious child is praying in the closet, and Jesus is there. He is present with the pious family in their abode, when they meet to worship the name of God. He is present with his people in the sanctuary, in his public courts. This teaches them to sing —and sweetly to sing—

> How lovely is thy dwelling-place,
>   O Lord of hosts, to me!
> The tabernacles of thy grace,
>   How pleasant, Lord, they be!
>   SCOTCH PSALMS.

It is in the holy sanctuary and in the public courts that holy children meet with Christ. There he is seen, there he "is known in her palaces for a refuge." Psa. xlviii, 3. Beloved young friends, if you wish to see Christ and know Christ, go to

the palaces of his ordinances, for his ordinances are his palaces. There you will
see the King. There you will see King
Jesus in his beauty.

God is graciously present with his people in all their afflictions: yes, in every
one of them. No matter what their affliction is, he is never absent. Others
may be absent, but he is always present;
others may not be near, he is always
present there. Hear his own word, hear
his own promise, Isa. xli, 10 : "Fear thou
not; for I am with thee : be not dismayed;
for I am thy God." What lovely words
are these : "Fear thou not, for I am with
thee !" May the Holy Spirit engrave them
on your youthful hearts !

God is always graciously present with
his people in their dying hour. Many
pious children I have seen in that solemn
hour. I have seen them happy and blest.
I have seen the smile upon their cheek,
and I have seen their eye bright with the
beam of heavenly hope. O! what made
them so happy and blest? Christ, their
Saviour and their God, was with them in

the hour of death.   When passing through
the valley and shadow of death, Jesus was
with them there.   This is the secret of
their joy,—this is the secret of their hope,
—Jesus was with them there!

There is a lesson which Christ can
teach you.   It is more valuable than a
thousand worlds.   My beloved young
friends, may Jesus teach you that blessed
lesson now!   It is, that you may utter
and sing with the heart the following
lines :—

> Though I walk through the gloomy vale
>   Where death and all its terrors are,
> My heart and hope shall never fail,
>   For Christ my Shepherd 's with me there.
>
> Amid the darkness and the deeps
>   Thou art my comfort, thou my stay;
> Thy staff supports my feeble steps,
>   Thy rod directs my doubtful way.—WATTS.

CONCLUSION.

1. God's omnipresence should teach us
to be *afraid of offending God*.   Are children afraid to sin in the presence of their
earthly parents?   O, how much more,
my young friends, should you be afraid

of sinning in the presence of your heavenly Father! When you are tempted to sin, may you feel what young Joseph felt when he uttered these striking words, Genesis xxxix, 9 : "How can I do this great wickedness, and sin against God?"

2. God's omnipresence should encourage us in *the discharge of every duty.* He is ever present to assist little children who love him. When they engage in prayer or praise, he is near them to help them. When they engage in hearing the everlasting Gospel, he is near them to help them, and to apply to their youthful hearts the word of life. When entering on any duty, and on every duty, he says, "My grace is sufficient for thee." 2 Cor. xii, 9.

3. God's omnipresence should encourage us *to flee to Jesus for mercy.* He is not only able to save, but he is near to save. Dear young friends, he is near you, he is beside you. O, cast yourselves at his feet, and pray, "Lord Jesus, save our souls!" Then he will come and save. Amen.

GOD'S OMNISCIENCE.

Thou knowest all things.—JOHN xxi, 17.

BELOVED young friends, never forget that Christ is God as well as man. He is God and man, in one person. O, how wonderful is God! Everything about God is wonderful. We cannot think or speak of anything belonging to God which is not wonderful. He is everywhere. How wonderful! A king cannot be in two places at one time. Even an angel can only be present in one place at one time. But God is in every place at once, and all places are filled with his presence.

Jesus is wonderful! As man he is wonderful. As God he is wonderful. As God and man in one person he is wonderful. How amazing is the love of Christ! What brought him from heaven to earth, —to obey, to suffer, and die for little children? It was his love. What wonderful love! His knowledge, also, is wonderful, and as amazing as his love.

He knows all things. And he knows all things because he is God. Peter knew he was God as well as man. When Jesus said to Peter the third time, "Lovest thou me?" Peter answered, "Lord, thou knowest all things; thou knowest that I love thee." Here Peter acknowledged two things: first, that Jesus was omniscient, that is, knew all things; second, that Jesus was God. For Peter was certain of this—that Jesus was God—because he knew all things.

I intend, my young friends, to show, first, What we understand by the omniscience of God; secondly, Mention some things which God knows; thirdly, Show some wonders connected with God's knowing all things; and lastly, Point out some lessons which the omniscience of God teaches.

I. What is the omniscience of God? The word omniscience signifies the knowledge of all things. When we say God is omniscient, we mean this—that God knoweth all things. To be omniscient is not merely to know much, or to know more than would fill all the books of all the libraries of the world. To be omniscient is not to know more than an angel, or an archangel, or all the angels of heaven. If one knew as much as all the men on the face of the earth, or as much as all the angels in heaven, even then he is not omniscient. But if he even knew a million of times more than all the holy angels before the throne of God, still he does not know all things. There is much he does not know; yea, there is more he does not know than what he does know. Therefore, he is not omniscient.

O, how wonderful is God! He knows all that ever man knew; he knows all that ever angels knew. He knows all which men cannot know, and can never know. He knows all which angels cannot know, and which they can never know. He knows all things; he is omniscient! O, how wonderful! Does Jesus know all things? He does. Then he is more than man; he is more than angel. He is God and man in one person. He is the omniscient God!

II. We now proceed, trusting in divine help, to mention some things which God knows.

1. *He knows himself.* When you look upon the sky in a very clear night, and when no moon shines, what do you see? You see countless stars. But these stars are few in number compared with the wonders which are in God. The angels and saints in heaven are constantly seeing new wonders in God; that is, wonders which they never saw before. And this will be the case forever. They shall ever see new wonders in God; yes, wonders which they never saw before.

Now, God knows perfectly, and sees perfectly, all the wonders of his being. We may know many things we do not understand. Even a very little child knows what a watch is. He knows the use of a watch. He knows that the hands of the watch show the hours of the day. But he does not understand how all this is done. Thus it is one thing to know a watch, but a very different thing to understand it. Now God perfectly knows all the wonders of his being, and he perfectly understands them all. How true the following beautiful passage, Psalm cxlvii, 5: "Great is the Lord, and of great power: his understanding is infinite." We cannot measure what is infinite. The earth can be measured—the ocean can be measured—the sun can be measured. But God's understanding cannot be measured. It has no bounds. It has no limits. It is infinite. Pause, young friends, and think! His understanding is infinite! O, how wonderful! God perfectly knows, God perfectly understands himself. His boundless self—his infinite self—he fully knows, he fully understands. O, my young friends, think with wonder, adoration, and love upon that glorious God—that glorious, that lovely Jesus, who fully knows, and perfectly understands himself—his infinite, his boundless self! O, say and sing—

"This awful God is ours,
    Our Father and our Love;
He will send down his heavenly powers
    To carry us above."

2. *God knows all things on earth.* Think seriously on the following passage, commit it to memory, and may the Holy Spirit engrave it on your youthful hearts! Heb. iv, 13: "But all things are naked and open before the eyes of him with whom we have to do." Everything on earth God knows, perfectly knows. We may know many things, and not know one of them perfectly. God knows all things on earth, and perfectly knows them all.

Let us come to particulars. Christ, as God, knows every man, woman, and child on the face of the earth. Everything about them he knows, and more perfectly than they can know themselves. He knows every little child in Europe, Asia, Africa, America, and Australia. He knows the parents, the color, the temper, and the faults of every child. Yes, and he knows, too, the sufferings and the afflictions of every child—of every dying child! He knows where every little child lives, what it says, what it does, what it suffers, and what it enjoys.

He knows every beast, every fish, every

bird, every worm, every creeping thing, and every butterfly. He knows every tree, and plant, and shrub, and flower, and herb, and every blade of grass. Even a poor little sparrow cannot fall to the ground but he knows it, Matt. x, 29; Luke xii, 6. He knows every mountain and valley, every river and stream, every fountain and lake, every ocean and sea. Dear children, this shows what omniscience is. When you think of Christ's omniscience, wonder and adore. Observe what the Bible says of the omniscience of God. Job xxxiv, 21: "His eyes are upon the ways of man, and he seeth all his goings." Mark these words: "His eyes?" These are the eyes of his omniscience. What wonderful, what bright, what penetrating eyes! Let us hear farther what the Bible says. Psa. xxxiii, 13: "The Lord looketh from heaven; he beholdeth all the sons of men." Solemn truth! May you feel its importance! Now, God is looking down from heaven on us; yes, and on every man, woman, and child upon the face of the earth.

Omniscience! What an astonishing eye! Let us hear other testimonies of God's omniscience from Scripture. Psa. cxxxix, 2: "Thou knowest my down-sitting and mine up-rising, thou understandest my thoughts afar off." He knows when the little child lies down on his bed, or rises in the morning, and begins the day without prayer. David felt this when he said, verse 3: "Thou compassest my path and my lying down, and art acquainted with all my ways." David was convinced that God knew his very words, verse 4: "For there is not a word in my tongue, but, Lord, thou knowest." God knows all the ways and actions of little children. Prov. v, 21: "The ways of men are before the eyes of the Lord, and he pondereth over all their goings." Chap. xv, 3: "The eyes of the Lord are in every place, beholding the evil and the good." This is not all. God knoweth the very thoughts of the hearts of little children. Psalm xciv, 9: "He that formed the eye, shall he not see?" Ver. 11: "The Lord knoweth the thoughts of man."

3. *God knoweth all the stars of the sky.*
Psa. cxlvii, 4: "He telleth the number of
the stars, he calleth them all by name."
Jesus made them all, he therefore knows
them all. He also preserves them all, and,
therefore, he knows them all. Have you
never looked upon the sky, and gazed upon
the countless stars sparkling in their loveliness? Have you not wondered as you
gazed? But if you ever looked at the stars
through a telescope, you may remember
you saw a far greater number than those
you observe with the naked eye. If your
father was by your side, you very likely said,
"Father, father, what a great many more
stars I now see. But, I assure you, my
young friends, the multitude you saw is
small in number compared with what you
did not see. Consider, then, how wonderful is Jesus. He knows each one of these
stars better than you know your brothers
and sisters. He has a name for them all.
You can call your sisters and brothers by
name. But how amazing is the omniscience of Jesus! He calleth the countless
stars by name, and they obey him. May

you love this wonderful Jesus! then he will come to you when you die, and he will call you by name, and take you to glory.

4. *God knoweth all the angels of heaven.* None can tell the numbers of the angels in heaven. To you and to me they are without number. Not so to Christ. He can count them one by one with greater ease than you and I can count the smallest sum. What is more, he knows each one, and that most intimately and perfectly. If a shepherd had a flock of some thousand sheep, and if he knew every one of them, his knowledge would fill you with surprise. It is said that the great Cyrus, the king of the Medes and Persians, knew every soldier in his numerous army. If this really was the case, his knowledge was wonderful indeed. But what are numerous flocks, what are numerous armies, compared with the angels of heaven, who are "an innumerable company of angels?" Heb. xii, 22. There are millions of millions of angels, and Jesus knows them all. He can call each one of them by name. When he wishes to

send an angel on some message to our
world, he need only call his name, and
instantly he comes out from the midst of
myriads of angels, and waits his Lord's
commands.

The holy Daniel saw the multitude of
angels before the throne of heaven. And
what does he say? Dan. vii, 10: "Thousands of thousands ministered unto him,
and ten thousand times ten thousand
stood before him." What must be the
knowledge of Jesus? for he intimately
knows them all; and (how kind!) he
sends his angels to watch over and defend little children who love him. Psa.
xci, 11, 12: "He shall give his angels
charge over thee, to keep thee in all thy
ways. They shall bear thee up in their
hands, lest thou dash thy foot against a
stone."

5. *God knows all things, past, present,
and to come.* All that ever lived; all that
has ever taken place in heaven, earth,
and hell; all that is now going on in all
places, cities, and nations; and all that
ever shall take place throughout the vast

universe, he knows, and as perfectly as if only one thing or one person were present before his eye. Pause, and wonder! think, and adore! Open your Bible, and read the proof of what I have now said. Thus God speaks in his majesty and truth. Isaiah xlii, 9: "Behold, the former things are come to pass, and new things do I declare; before they spring forth I tell you of them." Chap. xlvi, 9, 10: "I am God, and there is none else; I am God, and there is none like me, declaring the end from the beginning, and from ancient times the things which are not yet done."

III. The manner in which God knows all things is truly wonderful.

1. He knows all things at once. Much we may know, but it is not at once before our thought. At once we only see distinctly one thing, or one person, or one word. But all God knows is at once before his eye! How wonderful is this!

2. God never forgets anything he knows. All he knows forever remains

in his boundless mind, clearer than the brightness of the sky.

3. God knows all things without fatigue, uneasiness, perplexity, or pain. Many things may very soon trouble and perplex the wisest and the greatest of men. This is impossible with God. "All things are naked and open before the eyes of God, with whom we have to do." Heb. iv, 13.

CONCLUSION.

1. May we learn the humble lesson of our own ignorance, when we look upon the glorious brightness of the divine omniscience.

2. Does Jesus know all things? Then let us learn the becoming lesson of studying to please Jesus in all things.

3. May the Spirit teach us the lesson of joyful confidence in Jesus, since he knows all our wants, our necessities, our dangers, and our sorrows. He knows our wants, and is willing to supply them. He knows our necessities, and is willing to relieve them. He knows our dangers,

and is willing to defend us. He knows
our sorrows, and is willing to comfort us.
He knows our sinfulness, and is willing to
save us.

Blessed, blessed is the child who can
say in faith, "This omniscient Jesus is
mine, and I am his!" Amen.

--------◆--------

GOD'S LOVE.

God is love.—1 JOHN iv, 8.

How true; the Bible is all wonderful!
Every star in the sky is wonderful. God's
glory shines in every rolling star. So
every part of the Bible is wonderful.
Do you ask me, What is the most wonderful sentence in the Word of God? I
answer at once, It is our *text*—"GOD IS
LOVE!" This short sentence only consists
of three words, "God—is—love." But
never were three words put together containing so much as these three. Never
were three words so wonderful as these
three. It is not said, "God is loving," or

" ever loving." This is a glorious truth. It is not said, "God's love overflows, and ever flows." This is indeed a glorious truth. All this is as delightful as it is true. All this is as wonderful as it is delightful. Our text contains much more than this. " God is love." This is the most delightful of all. It is the most wonderful of all. It is the most comprehensive of all. What does a pious child see in this text? He sees the whole Gospel of Christ. He sees the whole plan of salvation. He sees the whole covenant of grace with all its promises, with all its blessings, with all its treasures. What a sight!

By the assistance of the Holy Spirit we proceed to consider the love of God under various names. I wish you particularly to observe that God's love receives different names according to its different acts. It is called complacency, good-will, grace, mercy, condescension, and long-suffering. There are six different ways in which God shows the love, the benevolence, the kindness, and the goodness of his nature.

While we are considering the love of God under these various delightful names, may love to God fill our hearts! May the fire of sacred love burn in our bosoms, never to be extinguished!

I. DIVINE DELIGHT, OR COMPLACENCY.

Complacency signifies the delight one person takes in another. This is called "a love of complacency, or delight." Look to the love of a mother to her babe. This love is a love of complacency. Her delight in her babe is love tender and pure. The love which one dear friend shows to another is a love of complacency or delight. Such was the love of David to Jonathan. Such was the love of Jonathan to David. They loved each other, and they delighted in each other.

There may be love without delight. I will explain this. A father has an only son. This son is exceedingly wicked. He is breaking his father's heart. He is bringing down his gray hairs with sorrow to the grave! His father loves him. But he has no delight in him. He can have no delight in him. It is impossible. There is really nothing in him in which he can delight. It is all the other way.

God delights in pious children. By nature, they have nothing in which God can delight. In the day of conversion he gives them the beauties of holiness. He gives them the lovely graces of the Holy Spirit, and then he delights in them. He loves them with a love of complacency and delight. Jesus foreseeing from all eternity the lovely graces of holy children, says in Proverbs viii, 23, 30, 31: "I was set up from everlasting, from the beginning, or ever the earth was. Then I was by him, as one brought up with him: and I was daily his delight, rejoicing always before him; rejoicing in the habitable part of his earth; and my delights were with the sons of men." Thus the prophet speaks of the great delight God takes in his people. Young immortals, may you live to know that God delights in you! Isaiah lxii, 4, 5: "Thou shalt no more be termed Forsaken; neither shall thy land

any more be termed Desolate : but thou
shalt be called Hephzi-bah, and thy land
Beulah : for the Lord delighteth in thee,
and thy land shall be married. And as
the bridegroom rejoiceth over the bride,
so shall thy God rejoice over thee."
When pious children think of Christ de-
lighting in them, and loving them with a
love of complacency, they can say with
wonder and with thankfulness—

> "Defiled and loathsome as we are,
> He makes us white, and calls us fair;
> Adorns us with that heavenly dress,
> His graces and his righteousness."

II. God's Love is seen in his Good-
will.

There are many to whom we can show
no love of delight. There is nothing in
them in which we can delight. Still, we
may show toward them a love of good-will.
This love of good-will may be so sincere,
and so strong, that we may do much for
the benefit and salvation of those in whom
at present we see nothing to love, but
much to hate, and even to abhor. God is

so holy, so perfectly holy, that he cannot feel any love of delight to wicked, rebellious sinners. But he can and does show them a love of good-will. Jesus has shown this love in the most marvelous way.· He has shown it in the most marvelous degree. He has shown it by the most marvelous acts. He became poor, that rebellious sinners might be made rich. There is his love of good-will. He shed his blood, that sinners might be washed from their pollution. There is his love of good-will. He died that sinners might live. There is his love of good-will. We have a very striking account of God's love of good-will in Ezekiel xxxiii, 11: "As I live, saith the Lord God, I have no pleasure in the death of the wicked; but that the wicked turn from his way and live : turn ye, turn ye from your evil ways; for why will ye die, O house of Israel?"

III. God's Love is called Grace.

Grace is kindness shown to one who is unworthy. Grace is kindness shown to one who does not deserve the least kindness from God's hand. Angels in heaven never offended God. God constantly shows them kindness. This kindness we do not call grace. We call it love. They are worthy of God's love. They are not unworthy. The love which God showed in sending his well-beloved Son into our unworthy world, is the greatest, the most astonishing display of grace the eyes of angels ever beheld. John iii, 16: "God so loved the world, that he gave his ONLY-BEGOTTEN SON, that whosoever believeth in him should not perish, but have everlasting life." Thus, the apostle calls by the name of grace that kindness shown to the unworthy by the gift of Christ. Rom. v, 15: "For if through the offense of one many be dead, much more the grace of God, and the gift by grace, which is by one man, Jesus Christ, hath abounded unto many."

My young friends, are you saved by grace? Do you believe, do you feel that you are saved by grace? Then you can sing, then you can pray:—

" Come, thou Fount of every blessing,
  Tune my heart to sing THY GRACE;
Streams of mercy never ceasing
  Call for songs of loudest praise.
Teach me some melodious sonnet
  Sung by flaming tongues above;
Praise the mount—O fix me on it,
  Mount of God's unchanging love."

IV. GOD'S LOVE IS SEEN IN HIS MERCY.
What is mercy? It is kindness shown to the miserable. God's heart is full of mercy. He looked upon poor, miserable sinners. His mercy moved within him. Then he felt a desire to save them, a desire infinitely strong. His mercy moved him to contrive a plan by which a miserable world could be saved.

Endeavor, my young friends, to meditate with holy interest on the mercy of God, as mentioned in the following passages of Scripture. Psalm c, 5: "For the Lord is good; his mercy is everlasting." That shows God never tires in showing mercy. In everlasting mercy God has everlasting delight.

God's glory shines in all his perfections.

But his mercy shines with peculiar glory, as peculiarly showing his goodness. Therefore the holy Psalmist says, Psalm cxxxvi, 1, 23: "O give thanks unto the Lord; for he is good: for his mercy endureth forever. Who remembered us in our low estate: for his mercy endureth forever."

So peculiarly glorious is the mercy of God, that the Psalmist speaks of it as being above all his works. Psalm cxlv, 9: "The Lord is good to all: and his tender mercies are over all his works."

Then, young friends, think of the delight which God has in his mercy. He has delight in all his acts. But he delights in the acts of his mercy as he does not delight in any other acts. Hear the words of the prophet, and may they be to your ears and hearts as the music of heaven! Micah vii, 18: "Who is a God like unto thee, that pardoneth iniquity, and passeth by the transgression of the remnant of his heritage? he retaineth not his anger forever, because he DELIGHTETH IN MERCY." O what encouragement is this for little

children to flee to Jesus for mercy! See
how willing he is to show mercy, and
see how he delights to perform acts of
mercy. Let us then proclaim aloud, and
sing sweetly the honors of his mercy:—

"Give to our God immortal praise;
Mercy and truth are all his ways;
Wonders of grace to God belong,
Repeat his mercies in your song.

"He sent his Son with power to save
From guilt, and darkness, and the grave:
Wonders of grace to God belong,
Repeat his mercies in your song."

V. God's Love is seen in his Condescension.

How does God show his condescending
goodness? He does it by the delight
which he takes in holy children, however
poor, or mean, or neglected. It is condescension in Christ to show kindness to a
young prince clothed in robes. And it is
great condescension to take delight in a
pious little child covered with rags. It is
great condescension in a king or queen
to come from their royal palace, and visit

a poor woman living in an humble cottage in a retired spot in some wood or forest. This, however, is nothing compared with the loving condescension of Christ, mentioned in the following passage. Isaiah lvii, 15: "For thus saith the high and lofty One that inhabiteth eternity, whose name is Holy; I dwell in the high and holy place, with him also that is of a contrite and humble spirit, to revive the spirit of the humble, and to revive the heart of the contrite ones."

God shows his condescension in hearing and answering prayer. O what merciful condescension, to hear the prayers of a little child! Psalm xci, 15: "He shall call upon me, and I will answer him."

Christ's taking up little children into his arms, and blessing them, was a most blessed instance of condescension. Matthew xix, 14: "Jesus said, Suffer little children, and forbid them not, to come unto me: for of such is the kingdom of heaven." Let each child pray, "O may Jesus clasp me in his arms, and lay me in his bosom!"

VI. God's Love appears in his Patience and Long-Suffering.

There are three words applied to God, and they all signify the same thing. They are Patience, Forbearance, and Long-Suffering.

How does God show his forbearance and patience? He bears long with sinners. He allows them to live, though they offend him. He keeps them alive, though they displease him. He waits to be gracious toward them. He sends his ministers to plead with them, to entreat them to forsake their sins, to flee from the wrath to come, and to receive Christ as their Saviour and their all.

Beloved young friends, one of the greatest sins which you can commit is to despise God's patience, forbearance, and long-suffering. O beware of this sin, this dreadful, this soul-destroying sin! Hear, and may the Holy Spirit make you feel what the apostle said to the Roman Church, Romans ii, 4–6: "Or despisest thou the riches of his goodness, and forbearance, and long-suffering; not knowing that the goodness of God leadeth thee to repentance? But after thy hardness and impenitent heart treasurest up unto thyself wrath against the day of wrath, and revelation of the righteous judgment of God; who will render to every man according to his deeds."

O, earnestly pray that you may be filled with love to God, and that Jesus, the brightness of his glory, may ever reign upon the throne of your hearts! Amen.

GOD'S TRUTH.

Who keepeth truth forever.—PSALM cxlvi, 6.

IF I ask you, my young friends, the three following questions: What two things differ most from each other? What two things are most unlike each other? What two things are most opposed to each other? very likely you will answer at once, Truth and falsehood. They cannot be made to resemble each other. They cannot be made to conclude peace together. They cannot be made to act together. I will ask three similar questions: What two beings are most unlike each other, and most opposed to each other, and who hate each other with the most perfect hatred? You will answer at once, God and Satan. What is God called? He is called the God of Truth. Deut. xxxii, 4: "A God of truth and without iniquity, just and right is he." What is Satan called? Our Saviour thus describes him in John viii, 44: "He was a murderer from the beginning, and abode not in the truth; because there is no truth in him. When he speaketh a lie, he speaketh of his own: for he is a liar, and the father of it."

WHAT THE TRUTH OF GOD IS.

What is the truth of God? It is one of his glorious perfections. It is one of his moral attributes. There can be no morality without truth. Satan lost his morality when he lost his truth. Because morality in God is most perfect, truth in God is

most glorious. God cannot cease to be
true. God's being would as soon cease as
his truth cease to be. He is necessarily
and eternally true.

The truth of God is that attribute by
which he does whatever he says he will
do. Does God promise? Because he is
true, he fulfills all he promises. Does
God threaten? Because he is true, he
fulfills all his threatenings, if men continue wicked, hardened, and impenitent.

What I propose to do in this sermon,
in dependence upon divine aid, is, to present before you a choice number of texts
of Scripture, where particular mention is
made of God's truth. What shall we see,
dear young friends, when we look on these
texts? We shall see the loveliness of God.
The eye of the body can see many lovely
things in nature ; but the eye of the body
can see nothing so lovely in nature,
as what the eye of the mind sees in
God's truth. The truth of God is lovelier
than the loveliest and most fragrant flowers. It is infinitely lovelier than the richest collection of pearls, of diamonds, or

rubies. It is infinitely more glorious
than the stars of the firmament—than the
sun shining in his meridian strength!
May the eyes of our mind be open to behold! may our hearts be opened to admire the attribute of divine truth!
Blessed is that child who can exclaim
in holy adoration, "O how lovely, how
glorious, is the attribute of divine
truth!"

1. Moses speaks of God as "abundant
in truth." When Moses prayed that God
would show him his glory, God answered
his prayer and said, "I will proclaim the
name of the Lord before thee." Exodus
xxxiii, 19. The name of God proclaimed
to Moses may be compared to a glorious
diadem, and each attribute may be compared to a bright jewel shining in that
diadem. The attribute of truth is one of
the bright jewels. Exodus xxxiv, 5, 6:
"And the Lord descended in the cloud,
and stood with him there, and proclaimed
the name of the Lord. And the Lord
passed by before him, and proclaimed, The
Lord, The Lord God, merciful and gracious,

long suffering, and abundant in goodness and truth." How is God abundant in truth? He is abundant in the promises he makes. His promises are abundant in the rich blessings they contain. Never was the honeycomb fuller of honey than the promises of God are full of blessings. Besides, God is abundant in the fulfillment of his promises. O what rich fruit is produced by the tree of God's promises! O what refreshing showers descend from the cloud of the divine promises! Then think of the immense multitude to whom God gives his promises, so great and so precious; and then acknowledge, in accents of praise, that God is indeed "abundant in truth :"—

> "The sacred truth his lips pronounce,
>   Shall firm as heaven endure ;
> And if he speak a promise once,
>   The eternal grace is sure."

2. David, in his song of praise, speaks of the paths of God as mercy and truth. Psalm xxv, 10 : "All the paths of the Lord are mercy and truth unto such as

keep his covenant and his testimonies."
Precious promises are given to holy children, who love God's laws, and who observe God's ordinances. These promises
are only given to such as are holy and
pious. Wicked children expose themselves to God's threatenings, and cut
themselves off from God's promises. Because God loves holy children, he gives
them a rich inheritance of promises; and
because he loves them he fulfills what he
has promised. Thus, "the paths," or doings "of the Lord are mercy and truth to
such as keep his covenant and his testimonies." Then, let us sing with joyful
hearts:—

> "The dealings of his hand
>   Are truth and mercy still,
> With such as to his covenant stand,
>   And love to do his will."

3. David, in another song, speaks of
God's truth as reaching unto the clouds.
Psalm lvii, 10: "For thy mercy is great
unto the heavens, and thy truth unto the
clouds." The truth of God is presented
before us as a monument. Look at it.

Two things will strike your youthful minds. One is, it is a monument of great height. O how lofty! It is high as the clouds. A second thing will strike you; that is, its astonishing strength. Great is the height of the Alps. But their height is nothing to the height of God's truth. Great is the strength of the Alps. But their strength is nothing when compared with the monument of divine truth. It is a monument which no storms can injure, which no earthquake can shake, and which no lightnings can rend.

Dear young friends, what a refuge is God's truth to pious children! Jesus is called the Truth! He is the Truth. He is a true refuge. Holy children flee to him and are safe. They who flee to him he will never give up to the will of their enemies. His love is too fervent, and his truth too sure, ever to cast them off. He cannot, he will not. O be persuaded to flee to Jesus, who is the way, the truth, and the life! Then you shall be safe, forever safe. Then you can sing to the honor of divine mercy and truth:—

" High o'er the earth his mercy reigns,
And reaches to the utmost sky;
His truth to endless years remains,
When lower worlds dissolve and die."

4. David introduces to our notice, in one of his inspired songs, mercy and truth meeting together. Psalm lxxxv, 10: "Mercy and truth have met together; righteousness and peace have kissed each other." Here we have before us a meeting, a happy, joyful meeting, a loving meeting of old, unchanging friends. Who are these friends? They are four attributes or perfections of the divine nature. They are mercy and truth, righteousness and peace. These friends never differed. It was impossible they ever could differ. How comes it, then, that these friends are meeting so intimately, and embracing each other so affectionately? The reason is this. They all meet in Christ, who, by his obedience and death, has brought great glory to all these perfections. By Christ, justice, or righteousness, is satisfied. By Christ, peace is established between God and man, between heaven and

earth. By Christ, mercy is delighted by the myriads saved through his blood. And by Christ, the purposes of mercy and of truth are accomplished. By Christ, all the promises of truth are most faithfully fulfilled. Mark this, young friends! Jesus, agreeably to eternal purposes of truth, and promises of truth, came from heaven to earth, and accomplished a great salvation. Mercy is delighted. Truth rejoices. Righteousness is delighted. Peace triumphs, and sings the sweetest jubilee. Thus, mercy and truth are said to meet together. Thus, righteousness and peace are said to embrace each other. May the following lines be the joyful expressions of our hearts!

"Mercy and truth on earth are met,
    Since Christ the Lord came down from heaven:
By his obedience so complete
    Justice is pleased, and peace is given."

5. In another sacred song, David speaks of truth as a herald going before the face of God to proclaim his glory. Psalm lxxxix, 14: "Justice and judgment are the habitation," or establishment, " of thy

throne : mercy and truth shall go before thy face." Here observe that Christ's throne is a strong throne. No rebellion of man or of angels can shake or endanger his throne. The mutiny of countless angels did not affect his throne when Satan and his legions rebelled, and were cast out of heaven. They could no more shake God's throne than an insect could overturn a mountain. What makes God's throne so sure? It is established by justice and judgment, by mercy and truth. What a blessed, what a durable throne is Christ's! It rests on four sure foundations. Justice, judgment, mercy, truth, are its four foundations. If one of these were removed, his throne could not stand for one hour. But they never can be removed. They are immutable as God's being. They are eternal as God's nature.

I see a beautiful inscription on the throne of Christ. No letter of burnished gold ever shone so bright and glorious. What is the inscription? It is this: Justice and judgment, mercy and truth.

Beloved children, look and wonder! Look and love! Hear, and believe, what God the Father says of the government of his Son :—

> "My truth shall guard him in his way,
>   With mercy on his side;
> While in my name, through earth and sea,
>   He shall in triumph ride."

6. David sings of divine truth as the defense of the children of God. Psalm xci, 4 : "He shall cover thee with his feathers, under his wings shalt thou trust: his truth shall be thy shield and buckler." Doves are in danger from birds of prey, such as hawks, owls, and eagles. They are also in danger of being caught or shot by fowlers. The souls of little children are in danger from enemies more to be feared than devouring tigers or sharks. Who are they? We answer, The corruptions of their own heart, the world and its snares, Satan and his wiles. Who is the fowler that lays nets to ruin souls, who shoots at them his destroying darts, and waits for their ruin? It is Satan. O, the myriads of souls he has caught!

Alas, the myriads he has destroyed; yes, destroyed forever! Beloved children, flee to Jesus, who is the truth, and you are safe, forever safe. He will cover you with the shield of his truth, and then you shall be invincible.

> "Then you can laugh at Satan's rage,
> And face a frowning world."

7. David sings sweetly of the eternal duration of God's truth. Psa. c, 5: "For the Lord is good; his mercy is everlasting; and his truth endureth to all generations." The Pyramids of Egypt, which were built before Abraham's day, shall not last forever. The time will come when Paris, and Vienna, and Rome, and London shall be no more. Even the mountains shall not continue forever as they now are. At the last day they shall melt with fervent heat, as drops of lead melt when they fall into a furnace of fire. Not so the truth of God.

> " Wide as the world is thy command,
> Vast as eternity thy love ;
> Firm as a rock thy truth shall stand,
> When rolling years shall cease to move."

GOD'S JUSTICE.

Just and right is he.—DEUT. xxxii, 4.

THERE are seven things said of God in this verse, from which we have chosen the words of our text. What is the first? "He is the Rock." Truly Jesus is a rock of strength. He is a rock of duration— the Rock of ages. He is a rock of defense to little children, who flee to him for refuge from the wrath to come. What is the second? "His work is perfect." His work of creation, his work of providence, his work of redemption, are all perfect. "O Jesus, the mighty Saviour, thou hast finished the work the Father gave thee to do!" What is the third? "All his ways are judgment." Everything he does is righteous, good, wise, and just. What is the fourth? "A God of Truth." "He is not a man, that he should lie." Numbers xxiii, 19. In himself he is the true God. In his word he is true to his promises. What is the fifth? "Without iniquity."

No sin stains his nature, or his word, or his actions, or his government. O how pure! What is the sixth? "He is just." What inscription is that I see written with bright colors on his throne? It is justice. What is the seventh? "Right is he." That is, infinitely good, infinitely perfect. He cannot be tempted to sin, neither tempteth he any man. James i, 13.

By the assistance of the Holy Spirit, we now proceed to consider the attribute of justice. Come and behold it. Come and admire it. Let the wicked tremble when they look upon it, and see its dreadful frowns. Let pious children look upon it, and rejoice when they behold its lovely smiles.

First, consider what the justice of God is, and then, secondly, point out some of those ways in which he has shown his justice.

I. WHAT IS THE JUSTICE OF GOD?

1. Justice is that attribute of God by which he infinitely loves what is right. And it is also that attribute by which God

infinitely hates all that is wrong. What did good King Jehoshaphat say to the judges of Israel? He said: "Wherefore now let the fear of the Lord be upon you: take heed and do it: for there is no iniquity with the Lord our God." 2 Chron. xix, 7. What does Elihu say respecting the justice of God? Job xxxiv, 12: "Yea, surely God will not do wickedly, neither will the Almighty pervert judgment." What do the redeemed before the heavenly throne say and sing respecting the justice of God? Rev. xv, 3: They say and sing, "Great and marvelous are thy works, Lord God Almighty; just and true are thy ways, thou King of saints."

How different the wicked child is from God! How unlike is the wicked child to God! What is just and right the wicked child refuses to love, refuses to speak, refuses to act. Beloved young friend! may God change your heart, and teach you to love, and speak, and act what is right! Then you will resemble your heavenly Father, of whom it is said, "Just and right is he."

2. Justice is that attribute by which God gives just and good laws. Bad lawgivers show their injustice by their unrighteous laws. God is an infinitely good lawgiver, and he shows the perfect justice of his nature by the justice of his laws. David exceedingly admired the just and wise laws of God, the just and wise lawgiver. Hear and observe the loving manner in which he speaks of the just laws of the just Lord. Psa. cxix, 1 : "Blessed are the undefiled in the way, who walk in the law of the Lord." Bad laws can never make happy and blessed; but they who love and obey God's righteous laws must be blessed. Verse 2 : "Blessed are they that keep his testimonies, and that seek him with the whole heart." O how affectionately good children, redeemed by Jesus's blood, speak of God as a just and a merciful God! Isaiah xxxiii, 22 : "For the Lord is our judge, the Lord is our lawgiver, the Lord is our king; he will save us." Blessed in time and in eternity are those children who can say with the heart—

"His laws are just and pure,
His truth without deceit:
His promises are ever sure,
And his rewards are great."

3. Justice is that attribute by which God dispenses justice. When a king, sitting upon his throne, punishes the wicked and rewards the good, he dispenses justice. When a father, at the head of his family, does what is right among his children, he dispenses justice. God, as a just God, will and must punish the wicked if they live and die in their wickedness. Every day they are offending God. Every day God is angry with them. Psalm vii, 11: "God is angry with the wicked every day." Dear young friends, only think how shocking it is, how dangerous it is, to be under God's anger every day!

God sometimes punishes the wicked in this life, but not always. O remember, that if they escape punishment in this life, they shall not escape punishment in the life to come! If they die refusing to receive Christ; if they die Christ's enemies, O what a punishment awaits them in the life to come! Psalm xi, 6: "Upon the wicked he shall rain snares, fire and brimstone, and a horrible tempest: this shall be the portion of their cup." These, my young friends, are matters awfully true, serious, solemn, and affecting. May God the Spirit most deeply impress them on your youthful hearts!

Does God, by his justice, dispense punishments among the wicked? He also dispenses rewards among the righteous; but we must always remember, and never forget, that these rewards are not rewards of merit, but rewards of grace. They are just rewards through what Christ has done and suffered. These rewards are a stream flowing to the righteous through a just and righteous channel. Every holy child most readily confesses that he is not worthy of the rich rewards given him by a just and gracious God. The pious child can say, in the language of holy, pious Jacob, Gen. xxxii, 10: "I am not worthy of the least of all the mercies, and of all the truth, which thou hast shown unto thy servant."

What does David say of the gracious rewards which God, as a just God, dispenses among his people? Hear his own words. Psalm xix, 11: "In keeping thy commandments there is great reward." Also, he says, Psalm lviii, 11: "Verily there is a reward for the righteous: verily he is a God that judgeth in the earth."

Pious children have rich rewards of grace here, and rich rewards of glory hereafter.

> "They are like plants of generous kind,
>   By living waters set,
> Safe from the storms and blasting wind,
>   Enjoy a peaceful state.

> "Green as the leaf, and ever fair
>   Shall their professions shine;
> While fruits of holiness appear,
>   Like clusters on the vine."

" Verily there is a reward for the righteous!"

II. THOSE WAYS BY WHICH GOD SHOWS HIS JUSTICE.

1. God showed his justice *in casting our first parents out of Eden.* They sin-

ned by eating the forbidden fruit. They were able to keep the first covenant; they broke it. They believed and obeyed the devil rather than God. O how melancholy, how affecting, how grievous! And what happened to them? God drove them out of Eden,—lovely Eden, happy Eden,—where they walked with God, holy, blessed, and happy! He drove them out, and placed an angel with a flaming sword at Eden's gate, that they might enter that lovely paradise no more forever. Gen. iii, 23, 24: "Therefore the Lord God sent him forth from the garden of Eden. So he drove out the man: and he placed at the east of the garden of Eden cherubims, and a flaming sword which turned every way, to keep the way of the tree of life." It is a great calamity for wicked children to be sent away from their native land, in a convict-ship, and to be banished never to return; but this is nothing compared with the just punishment inflicted on our first parents, when they were banished from Eden to return no more!

2. God showed his justice *in destroying the old world by a flood of waters.* Very likely there were two thousand millions of human beings on the face of the earth before the awful flood. They were almost all wicked. What a world it must have been! Bad as the world has been since, it is nothing compared with what it was then. So bad were the people at that time, that out of all the hundreds of millions of human beings, there were only eight persons who had any profession or appearance of religion. Who were they? They were Noah, his wife, his sons, and his sons' wives. Only eight persons! Noah was a preacher of righteousness. He faithfully preached to the people; he warned them of their sin, and of their danger. They laughed at him; they mocked him, and called him a foolish old man. At last the flood came, and the hundreds of millions of human beings were all destroyed! None were saved, except eight persons! Genesis vii, 23: "And every living substance was destroyed which was upon the face of the ground:

and Noah only remained alive, and they that were with him in the ark!" O, what an awful display of God's justice was this! Beloved children, seek grace to flee from sin, and stand in awe of the justice of God. For "who can stand before him if once he is angry?" Psalm lxxvi, 7.

3. God showed his justice *in the punishment of the Egyptians.* You know that their treatment of the Israelites was most cruel and barbarous; for more than three hundred years their cruelty continued. The longer it lasted the worse it became. Then the time arrived when God poured out his fury upon them. Ten calamities followed, each one close upon the heels of another. Then came the destruction of the first-born of man, and even of cattle. The destroying angel flew quicker than lightning over all the land of Egypt. He entered every habitation; yes, from the cottage to the palace. There was a dead corpse in every house! and there was weeping and wailing over all the land of Egypt! None escaped the awful calamity except the people of God. This

dreadful judgment was followed by the destruction of the whole army of the Egyptians in the Red Sea. May God sanctify to us these awful displays of divine justice, and make us afraid of displeasing a God so just and so mighty!

4. God showed his justice *in Christ's sufferings and death.* Jesus suffered, the just for the unjust; yet his sufferings were just. He put himself most willingly in our room and stead. We deserved for our sins the infinite wrath of God. He became our surety. And what does his becoming our surety mean? It means this—that he engaged to bear the wrath of God, which we deserved, in our room and stead. As it is just to require a man to pay the debt of another, because he bound himself to do it; so it was just in God to punish his own Son because he bound himself and engaged to suffer and die for us. On this account, what did justice say? It said this, Zech. xiii, 7: "Awake, O sword, against my Shepherd, and against the man that is my fellow, saith the Lord of hosts: smite the

Shepherd." And what did justice do? Isa. liii, 10: "Yet it pleased the Lord to bruise him; he hath put him to grief." What can pious children say when they think of this wonderful display of justice, the most wonderful that has ever been given, and the most wonderful that shall ever be given, throughout an endless eternity? They say this, Isa. liii, 5: "But he was wounded for our transgressions, he was bruised for our iniquities; the chastisement of our peace was upon him; and with his stripes we are healed."

CONCLUSION.

Young friends, do you wish to escape from the wrath of offended justice? Do you wish? You can only escape by fleeing unto Jesus. As the doves flee to their windows, may you flee to the bosom of Christ's love. Then you will be safe, forever safe. Take with you words, turn to Jesus, to Jesus flee and say:—

> "Jesus, full of all compsssion,
>   Hear thy youthful suppliant's cry;
> Let me know thy great salvation;
>   Save me! else, I faint and die!"

GOD'S HOLINESS.

Who is like unto thee, O Lord, among the gods? who is like thee, glorious in holiness?—EXODUS xv, 11.

A HOLY child is more comely in the eye of angels, and in the eye of God, than a king upon his throne, arrayed in robes of royal purple, and having on his head a crown of purest gold. Even if the child is poor, covered with rags, and living in the meanest cottage, that little child is more comely in the eye of God than the unholy children of princes, dwelling in palaces, and sparkling with jewels. Holiness is the loveliest thing on earth. Holiness is the loveliest thing in heaven. What is it which makes angels so beautiful? Holiness. What is it which makes heaven so blessed? Holiness. What is it which makes God so glorious? Holiness. Is this the case? then let each dear child say, in the words of Moses in our text, and say with adoring reverence and love, "Who is like unto thee, O Lord? who is like thee, glorious in holiness?"

"Holy Spirit, mercifully give thy gracious help, while we consider what the holiness of God is, and while we show in what the holiness of God especially appears. O, while we behold as in a glass the holiness of God, may little children be changed into the same image. Graciously hear our prayer, for Jesus's sake. Amen."

I. WHAT IS THE HOLINESS OF GOD?

To this very important question we give three answers.

1. Holiness is that attribute by which God is infinitely free from all sin. Remember, my young friends, the meaning of an attribute. When applied to God, it means any excellence or perfection belonging to God; as, for example, wisdom, power, justice, love, and holiness, are all excellences belonging to God, and therefore they are attributes. Now, holiness is that attribute by which God the Father, God the Son, and God the Holy Ghost, one God, is perfectly and infinitely free from all sin. There are black spots even in the sun. The best child, and the holi-

est saint on earth, have their blemishes and their black spots of sin. One says, that even the very heavens are not clean in God's sight. Job xv, 15. But there can be no blemishes, no dark spots of sin in God. Joshua, before he died, strongly exhorted Israel to serve God, because he is a holy God. Joshua xxiv, 19. For the same reason, David calls upon us sweetly and joyfully to sing the praises of God, Psalm xcix, 9: "Exalt the Lord our God, and worship at his holy hill; for the Lord our God is holy."

2. Holiness is that attribute by which God infinitely hates and abhors all sin. Dear children, you cannot conceive how much, how intensely God hates, loathes, and abhors all sin. Yes, all sin, and the very least of all sins. Hear what. God said to Israel of old. Hear, and observe how earnestly God entreated them as their Father not to commit sin, because he hated sin so much, Jer. xliv, 4: "How-beit I sent unto you all my servants the prophets, rising early and sending them, saying, O do not this abominable thing

that I hate." May each one of you feel and believe that this counsel, this warning, is delivered by God, as your Father, to you, when you are tempted to any sin. When you are tempted to lie, or to utter sinful words, or to profane the Sabbath, or to keep company with wicked children, may you hear God thus counselling you, thus warning you: "O do not this abominable thing that I hate." Blessed, blessed is that child who avoids sin because God hates it. Blessed indeed is that child who can say, "It grieves me to the heart to commit sin, because it is so hateful to my God and my Saviour."

3. The holiness of God consists of all his moral excellences. There are four attributes or perfections of God, which are in a peculiar sense his moral excellences. Wisdom, justice, love, and truth are these four. Let us look at them. When we look, may the Holy Spirit teach us to love and adore! That is a happy child who can look upon God's perfections and love them.

We then observe, WISDOM is a moral

excellence of God, and is a part of his holiness. There can be no holiness without wisdom. What is wisdom? It is to wish and to purpose to do good things by good means. God is infinitely wise, for he purposes to do the very best things by the very best means. Without this he could not be perfectly holy and good. Because he is perfectly wise, he is perfectly holy. Young friends, seek wisdom; that wisdom "which cometh from above." James iii, 17.

JUSTICE is a moral excellence of God. God is so just, that he can injure no one if he does not deserve it. God is so just, that he must punish the wicked who die without repentance. He is so just, that he delights graciously to reward the righteous. He is so just, that he can do nothing wrong. Thus it is said by the prophet, (Isaiah xlv, 21,) "He is a just God, and a Saviour."

LOVE is a moral excellence of God, and therefore a part of his holiness. God's nature is overflowing with love, therefore overflowing with holiness. Satan has no moral love, therefore he has no holiness. He is the most hateful and the most hating of beings, therefore he is the most unholy and the most sinful. God is infinitely holy, because he is infinitely loving. 1 John iv, 8 : "GOD IS LOVE." Dear children, may your hearts be filled with love to Jesus, who in himself is love—

"Whose heart o'erflows with love."

TRUTH is a moral excellence of God, and therefore is a part of his holiness. There can be no holiness without truth. The worst thing you can say of a child is this : "He has no truth in him." Satan is a liar, the greatest of liars, and the father of liars. Because he is the worst of beings, he is called "the father of liars." John viii, 44. God is infinitely holy, because he is infinitely true. Psa. lxxxix, 14 : "Justice and judgment are the habitation of thy throne : mercy and truth go before thy face."

Pray fervently, my young friends, that you may know, love, and adore these moral excellences of God. There is nothing the eye ever beheld so lovely as the holiness of God, which consists of his wisdom, his justice, his love, and his truth. Lovely is the rainbow with its seven colors. Without all the seven colors, there could be no rainbow; and without these four excellences, there could be no holiness in God.

We naturally admire the colors of the rainbow. I never knew a child who did not like to look upon the rainbow in its loveliness. May we all spiritually love the excellences of wisdom and justice, of love and truth, of which God's holiness consists! Whenever you begin to admire the holiness of God, I tell you this for your comfort,—" Grace has begun in your heart." Can you say from the heart, I love Christ because he is holy? Then I tell you that you are, you must be, the children of God; you are born again; you are among the redeemed of God; you are clothed with the robe of the righteousness of Christ. I pronounce you blessed in the name of the Lord. You shall be blessed forever.

II. In what God's Holiness appears.

1. God's holiness especially appears in God's Son. What a mystery!—Christ, the Son of God, appeared on earth in human shape. He appeared as a child, as a youth, and as a man. As the sun shines in the sky, so holiness shone in Christ. As the light of the sun fills the sky, so the brightness of divine holiness filled the life of Christ. The angel Gabriel, in speaking to Mary of Jesus, calls him that HOLY THING. Luke i, 35: "That HOLY THING which shall be born of thee shall be called the Son of God." O how holy he was when a little child! Therefore he is called, in Acts iv, 27, "The Holy Child Jesus." Like him, may you be made by the Holy Spirit holy children. Then you will have the loveliness of angels—you will have the loveliness of heaven.

When Jesus grew to manhood, holiness shone with greater glory in his life than ever stars sparkled in the sky. Think of this, my young friends, and then say what the apostle said, and feel what the apostle felt, Heb. vii, 26: "For such a high priest became us, who is holy, harmless, undefiled, separate from sinners, and made higher than the heavens." May the eyes of your mind be opened to see and admire the holiness of God, which shone in Christ when he appeared on earth as a child, as a youth, and as a man.

May the following lines be the language of your hearts:—

> " Jesus, in thee our eyes behold
> A thousand glories more
> Than the rich gems of polish'd gold
> The sons of Aaron wore!"

2. God's holiness shines *in his Word*. We had never known the holiness of God but by the Word of God. The wisest of heathen philosophers knew nothing scarcely of the holiness of God. Why? Because they were without the Word of God. The Bible is, by way of eminence, the Holy Bible. Every part of it is holy. What does Solomon say? Prov. xxx, 5: "Every word of God is pure: he is a shield to them that put their trust in him." The Word of God is a pure stream, flowing from Christ the pure fountain. It is

pure light, proceeding from Christ, the glorious Sun of righteousness.

3. God's holiness shines *in his laws.* God's law is a lovely, holy picture. Of what is it the picture? It is the picture of God's holiness; it is the picture of his lovely moral excellences. God drew the picture, and it is the exact resemblance of his holiness. The ten commandments are ten suns, shining in the firmament of the Bible in all the beauty and in all the brightness of their holiness. David sweetly sung of the holiness of God's law when he said, Psalm xix, 7–9: "The law of the Lord is perfect, converting the soul. The commandment of the Lord is pure, enlightening the eyes. The fear of the Lord is clean, enduring forever." It is the wish of my heart that you may be able to say respecting God's law, in which his holiness shines, (Psalm cxix, 97:)—

"O how I love thy holy law!
'Tis daily my delight;
And thence my meditations draw
Divine advice by night."

4. God's holiness shines *in his Gospel.*

The Gospel may be compared to a beautiful mirror, or looking-glass; and what glorious beams of light are seen shining on this mirror? We answer, The holiness of God. The Gospel teaches us by the Spirit two things: first, it shows what the holiness of God is; and, secondly, it shows how we may be made holy. On this account the apostle declares his admiration of the Gospel in the following words, Romans i, 16: "For I am not ashamed of the Gospel of Christ: for it is the power of God unto salvation to every one that believeth; to the Jew first, and also to the Greek." May we feel the holy effects of this holy Gospel!

5. God's holiness shines *in his ordinances.* Prayer, praise, reading, preaching, and hearing divine truth, are the chief ordinances of God's appointment. They must be holy, for they are appointed by a holy God. They are holy, for they are appointed for holy purposes and ends. They are holy, for they are the means which God employs and blesses for making the souls of little children holy. The

ordinances are holy wells, where pious children drink the waters of salvation. The ordinances are holy, pleasant ways, where pious children walk, and become more and more holy. Therefore it is said of holy Zacharias and Elizabeth, Luke i, 6: "They were both righteous before God, walking in all the commandments and ordinances of the Lord blameless."

6. God's holiness shines *in his saints.* They are lovely; but they are lovely in Christ's loveliness. The holiness of pious children consists of the graces of the Spirit. These graces are the beauties of holiness. Saints appear very comely in those graces; therefore, it is said of the saints in the following words, Psa. xlv, 13: "The King's daughter is all glorious within: her clothing is of wrought gold." It is in heaven where saints, where pious children shine most gloriously and perfectly in the beauties of holiness. Holy John saw them in vision, and said, Rev. vii, 14: " Who are they arrayed in white robes?" The angel answered, "These are they who have come out of great tribula-

tion, and have washed their robes in the blood of the Lamb."

Lord Jesus, make us holy. Say to us, in thy · mercy, "I will ; be ye holy." Amen.

THE WORD OF GOD.

When ye received the word of God which ye heard of us, ye received it not as the word of men, but, (as it is in truth,) the word of God.—1 THESS. ii, 13.

MY DEAR CHILDREN,—Have any of you a father who is gone to sea or into a foreign country?

*Yes.**

Does he sometimes write, and thus let you know his wishes and his will concerning you?

Yes.

No doubt you feel that it is very kind of him thus to write, and you attentively

---

* This lecture was delivered in a sea-port town. The answers to the questions, which are printed in italics, were given by the children.

read and highly prize his letters. Is it proper for you to do this?

Yes.

To be sure it is, because he loves you, and wishes you well. You have another, a heavenly Father, who also loves you and wishes you well: and he has given you a revelation or statement of his will in that precious book called the Bible, about which I am going to talk to you to-day.

I shall try to show you,—

I. That the Bible is the word of God.

II. That it is the most valuable of all books.

III. How you ought to read it.

I. THAT THE BIBLE IS THE WORD OF GOD.

You have been taught that it is impossible for anything to have made itself; everything must have a maker. This is true in reference to an atom as well as to a world; it is equally true in reference to a book—to the Bible.

Angels, being good spirits, could not have made it, because it professes to have been written by God. Good spirits could never have done a work themselves and then said that God had done it, for that would be false.

Satan neither could nor would write the Bible. He has not the power. But, if he could, he never would have written such a book; no, no, he is too cunning to write a book full of condemnation against himself;—a book, whose chief aim is to guard mankind against his temptations, and to prevent his designs;—a book, which has done more toward pulling down the strongholds of Satan and overthrowing his kingdom than all other books besides. There is something foolish in the thought of evil producing good—of Satan writing the Bible.

For the same reason that angels could not write the Bible, good men could not write it.

For the same reason that Satan could not write the Bible, bad men could not write it.

There are other reasons why no man, or number of men, and, indeed, why no mere creature, whether good or bad, could write the Bible. The work is too great for them; it is altogether beyond their power. There are in it things in reference to the future which neither angels, nor men, nor evil spirits could know, and therefore they could not write them.

Can you tell what will come to pass in a thousand years from this time?

No.

In a hundred years?

No.

Can the wisest man living tell?

No.

Can GOD tell?

Yes.

There are a number of things foretold in the Old Testament on many subjects, but especially about our Saviour, which came to pass many hundreds of years afterward, and a particular account of them is contained in the New Testament. Then there are some things foretold in the New Testament which have lately taken place, and which are taking place to this day.

As none but God can know the future,

none but God could write a book in which the future is foretold. Truly did St. Peter say, "The prophecy came not in old time by the will of man: but holy men of God spake as they were moved by the Holy Ghost." 2 Peter i, 21. When you grow a little older you will find the prophecies a very interesting and useful study.

If I were to tell the people in Portsmouth that I divided the sea last week from here to the Isle of Wight, and took them all over on dry ground, would they believe me?

No.

If I were to say that I did it twenty years ago, would they believe me?

No.

No, of course they would not, for many persons who are now living here were here then, and they would say, "I was in Portsmouth last week, and also twenty years ago, and I know the sea was not divided." I should not be believed, because the testimony of living men would be against me.

But suppose I were to write a book, and

say the sea was divided, and all the people taken over dryshod a hundred, or five hundred years ago, would they believe my book?

No.

No, indeed, because then all history would be against me. There would be no reference to it in any other book or history, and therefore everybody would say I had written a falsehood; the book would not, could not be believed.

There are many miracles, and other important events mentioned in the word of God, and the people living at the time did not deny them. For instance, when St. Matthew, Mark, Luke, John, Paul, Peter, and others, wrote in the gospels and epistles that our Saviour lived and preached in Judea, that he performed many miracles, that he was tried before Pilate, that he was crucified, that he was buried, that he rose from the dead, that he ascended into heaven, that he sent down the Holy Ghost, and that many believed in him, the people then living did not deny it. Why? Because it was true, and, therefore, they could not. So you see the persons living at the time that the word of God was written bore witness to its truth.

Various histories and other books were written which referred to some of those miracles and other important events, especially to those which were of the most public kind, so that hundreds of years after, down even to this day, history bears testimony to the truth of the word of God, and also to the fact that God put his own seal upon it, by causing miracles to be performed at the time that it was delivered or written, thus showing that the pure doctrine which it contained was from him.

Many plans have been tried, and many books have been written, in different ages of the world, by wise men called philosophers, in order to improve the condition of mankind. But the doctrines and precepts contained in them have been so imperfect and so impure, that it was evident to all that they were mere human inventions, and they have all failed in their effects. You have heard of Hume, a clever man, but an infidel. He is said to have expressed himself in sentiments like the following:—"I am afraid and confounded by that forlorn condition in which I am placed by my philosophy. When I look abroad, I foresee on every side dispute and contradiction. When I turn my eye inward, I find nothing but doubt and ignorance. Where am I? or what? To what causes do I owe my existence, and to what state shall I return? I am confounded with these questions, and begin to fancy myself in the most deplorable condition, surrounded with the deepest darkness." In such feelings Hume was not alone: every man who rejects the word of God is in a state of doubt, darkness, and misery.

There are in the Bible doctrines so pure, precepts so perfect, directions so heavenly, truths so all-important, revelations so wonderful, that it "bespeaks its author God." As truly as you see the footsteps of God in creation, or, as the Psalmist says, "His handy work," just so truly do you see HIS WORK in the Bible. The

Bible is, and can but be, the work of GOD.

Then how wonderful are its effects! It does what no other book ever did, or ever can do; it makes men good, it makes them happy, it prepares them for heaven. Well might the Psalmist say, "The law of the Lord is perfect, converting the soul: the testimony of the Lord is sure, making wise the simple. The statutes of the Lord are right, rejoicing the heart: the commandment of the Lord is pure, enlightening the eyes: the fear of the Lord is clean, enduring forever: the judgments of the Lord are true and righteous altogether. More to be desired are they than gold, yea, than much fine gold: sweeter also than honey and the honey-comb. Moreover by them is thy servant warned: and in keeping of them there is great reward." Psa. xix, 7–11.

II. THAT THE BIBLE IS THE MOST VALU- ABLE OF ALL BOOKS.

It is true that some persons of infidel principles have spoken lightly of the

Bible, and even denied its truth; but they are generally persons who have not properly thought about it, and always persons who have not properly prayed about it.

Sir Isaac Newton was inclined to infidelity in early life: he afterward studied the word of God, and received the truth in earnest. It is said that Dr. Edmund Halley was once speaking to him in favor of infidelity, when Sir Isaac replied, "Dr. Halley, I am always glad to hear you when you speak about astronomy, because that is a subject you have studied, and well understand; but you should not talk of Christianity, for you have not studied it. I have, and am certain that you know nothing of the matter." That was a just and cutting reproof, and would be very suitable to many foolish persons who speak against the Bible now.

1. The Bible is a *very old* book. The first five parts, generally called the five books of Moses, were written by that great and good man Moses more than three thousand years ago.

The other parts of the Old Testament

were written afterward, at different times and by different persons, but all acting under the inspiration of the Holy Spirit.

The New Testament was written at a much later date, about eighteen hundred years ago; but even that is a long, long time!

Many attempts have been made, at different times, by mistaken and wicked men, to destroy the Bible, but still it is preserved. There is something very wonderful in this, something that reminds us of God's watchful care over it.

2. The Bible is the *most wonderful* of all books. The fact just referred to, its preservation amid so many attempts to destroy it, is wonderful. The fact that so many men in different ages, and in diffent places, should have written with as perfect an agreement as though they had met and consulted together, is wonderful. The prophecies recorded in the Old, and fulfilled in the New Testament, are wonderful. The prophecies which are now being fulfilled, (take those about the Jews, for instance,) are wonderful. The sim-

plicity with which it presents to us the plan of salvation, is wonderful. The revelations which it contains respecting a future state of existence, are wonderful. Indeed, it is full of wonders! Well might the Psalmist say, " Open thou mine eyes, that I may behold wondrous things out of thy law." Psa. cxix, 18.

3. The Bible is the *most precious* book to those who properly understand it. Hear what David says : " The law of thy mouth is better unto me than thousands of gold and silver." Psa. cxix, 72. Again he says, "How sweet are thy words unto my taste! yea, sweeter than honey to my mouth!" Verse 103. Again he says, "I love thy commandments above gold ; yea, above fine gold." Verse 127. There are many not only good men and women, but good children too, who, like David, love the word of God. It is stated that Mr. Hone, the author of the "Every-Day Book," was traveling in Wales on foot, before he was convinced of the truth of the Bible, " and being tired and thirsty he stopped at the door of a cottage where was a little girl

seated reading. He asked her if she would give him some water. 'O yes, sir!' she said, 'if you will come in, mother will give you some milk and water;' upon which he went in and partook of it, and the little girl again sat down to her book. After a short stay in the cottage he came out, and said to the child at the door, 'Well, my little girl, are you getting your task?' 'No, sir,' she replied; 'I am reading the Bible.' 'But,' said Mr. Hone, 'you are getting your task out of the Bible.' 'O no, sir! it is no task to me to read the Bible: I love the Bible.' 'And why do you love the Bible?' said he. The simple and beautiful answer was, 'I thought everybody loved the Bible!'" It is said that this had such an effect upon Mr. Hone that he began to read, and then to love the Bible.

The Bible is *precious* to the good man for many reasons.

Because it tells him *about* GOD. The God of Abraham, the God of Isaac, and the God of Jacob; "theirs, and ours!" O pleasing and important knowledge, both for young and old! As God is our creator, our preserver, and as he will shortly be our judge, it is of great importance for us to know all that can be known about God. This knowledge can only be obtained from his own word.

Because it tells him *about* CHRIST. "Search the Scriptures," said our Saviour to the Jews, "for in them ye think ye have eternal life: and they are they which testify of me." John v, 39. In the Old Testament there is much about Christ; but in the New there is more. How sweetly does Dr. Watts sing on this subject!

> " Here would I learn how Christ has died,
>   To save my soul from hell;
> Not all the books on earth beside
>   Such heavenly wonders tell.
>
> "Then let me love my Bible more,
>   And take a fresh delight,
> By day to read those wonders o'er,
>   And meditate by night."

Because it tells him *how he may be saved.* One of the greatest and best men of the last century said: "I am a creature of a day, passing through life as an arrow

through the air. I am a spirit come from
God, and returning to God. I want to
know one thing—the way to heaven—
how to land safely on that happy shore.
God himself has condescended to teach
me the way; for this very end he came
from heaven. He hath written it down
in a book! O, give me that book! At
any price give me the book of God! I
have it: here is knowledge enough for
me. Let me be a man of one book!"

Because of its *important directions* and
precious promises. In whatever state a
person may be, he may always find something in the word of God just as suited to
his case as though it had been written
and sent down from heaven expressly for
him. I have read an interesting little
story about a deaf and dumb boy who
had proved the truth of this. Some gen-
tlemen visited the school in which he was.
" One of them asked him who made the
world? The boy took his slate and wrote
the first verse in the Bible, ' In the beginning God created the heaven and the
earth.' He was then asked, ' How do

you hope to be saved?' He wrote, 'This
is a faithful saying, and worthy of all
acceptation, that Christ Jesus came into
the world to save sinners.' The last question was, 'How is it that God has made
you deaf and dumb, while all those around
you can hear and speak?' The poor boy
seemed puzzled for a moment, and perhaps a thought of unbelief entered his
mind; but quickly recovering himself, he
wrote, 'Even so, Father, for so it seemeth
good in thy sight.'" That boy had attentively read his Bible, and no doubt
its instructions and promises were a comfort to him in his affliction. Yes! yes!
If a person, whether young or old, sincerely serve God, the promises of God's
word will often be powerfully applied to
his mind. Many tempted Christians,
many afflicted sufferers, many heart-
broken widows, many fatherless children,
have been comforted by the precious
promises of the word of God. Read the
Bible! love the Bible! It will cheer you
in the darkest day; it will support you in
the deepest trouble.

Because it teaches him *the way to* HEAVEN. A minister of the Gospel was one day visiting a pious old woman who was in the poor-house. "She had passed her threescore years and ten; had long been known as 'an Israelite indeed;' and was just on the verge of the eternal world: 'the outward man was perishing, but the inward man was renewed day by day.' While in conversation with her on the comforts, prospects, and rewards of religion, the minister saw an unusual luster beaming from her countenance, and the calmness of Christian triumph glistening in her eye. Addressing her by name, he said, 'Will you tell me what thought it was that passed through your mind which was the cause of your appearing so joyful?' The reply of the 'old disciple' was, 'O, sir, I was just thinking what a change it would be from the poor-house to heaven!'"

Where, or from what book, do you think that good woman learned the way to heaven?

From the Bible.

Yes, indeed! from the Bible; and the more you read it, the better you will understand the way to heaven.

As the Bible is so valuable, so wonderful, so precious, what a mercy it is that we have such a large supply of Bibles, and that they can be bought so cheaply. This was not always the case. "In the reign of Edward I., the price of a fair-written Bible was thirty-seven pounds. The hire of a laborer was three cents a day; the purchase of a copy would, of course, have taken from such a person the earnings of four thousand eight hundred days, not reckoning the Sundays; rather more than fifteen years and three months of constant labor would be required to obtain a single copy of the word of God." It was not until the year of our Lord one thousand five hundred and thirty-five, that the whole Bible was printed in the English language. It was completed under the direction of a good man called Miles Coverdale, and a copy was placed in each of the churches; so that persons who wished to read it might have an opportunity of doing so. Historians tell us that there was great joy on that occasion; and no wonder. But Bibles were so scarce and so valuable, that they were kept chained in the churches to prevent them from being lost or taken away. How different is it now! We have Bibles in abundance!

III. How you ought to read the Bible.

1. *With seriousness.* When you remember the Author of the Bible—the subjects on which it treats—the designs for which it was given—the effects which it will produce—in a word, when you remember that it is God's will made known to man, you must feel that seriousness of spirit becomes you when you read it.

2. *With attention.* With such attention that you may both understand and remember it; if you do so, your love for it will increase, and with the poet you will often be ready to sing:—

> " Here are my choicest treasures hid,
> Here my best comfort lies;
> Here my desires are satisfied,
> And hence my hopes arise."

A popish priest once took a New Testament from a little boy and burned it, telling him that it was not a proper book for him to read. The little boy cried; but after a while he dried up his tears and began to smile. "Why do you smile?" said the priest. The boy replied, "Because I was just thinking that you cannot burn those chapters which I have got off by heart." No, no; those were his own, and could not be taken from him. With the Psalmist he could say, "Thy word have I hid in my heart." Psa. cxix, 11.

3. *With prayer.* Some good men have regularly read the Bible on their knees, praying that God would enable them to understand it. Whether you adopt this plan or not, read it with prayer. Pray earnestly that the Holy Spirit may enlighten your mind, that you may see and understand the truth; and you will often feel that a ray of light will dart across your otherwise dark mind, and you will see a depth, a richness, and a beauty in the word of God that you had never seen before. How sweet and

how important are the sentiments of the hymn :—

"Father of all, in whom alone
    We live, and move, and breathe,
One bright, celestial ray dart down,
    To cheer thy sons beneath.

" While in thy word we search for thee,
    (We search with trembling awe!)
Open our eyes, and let us see
    The wonders of thy law.

"Now let our darkness comprehend
    The light that shines so clear;
Now the revealing Spirit send,
    And give us ears to hear."

4. *With faith.* If the word of God be not read with faith, the powerful motives to obedience which it contains will not produce their right effect. If it be not read with faith, its consoling truths and cheering promises will not be properly enjoyed. The promises may be in the Bible, and may be just suited to our particular case; but we cannot be benefited by them as we ought to be, unless we receive them in faith. Take an instance of

what I mean. I have read of a widow who sat weeping by her lonely fireside the morning after the death of her dear husband, "when her little son, a boy of five years of age, entered the room. Seeing the distress of his mother, he stole softly to her side, and placing his little hand in hers, looked wistfully into her face and said, 'Mother, mother, is God dead?' Soft as the gentle whisper of an angel did the simple accent of the dear boy fall upon the ear of the disconsolate and almost heart-broken mother. A gleam of heavenly joy lighted up for a moment her pale features. Then snatching up her little boy, and pressing him fondly to her bosom, she exclaimed: 'No, no, my son, God is not dead! He lives, and has promised to be a father to the fatherless, and a husband to the widow. His promises are sure and steadfast, and upon them I will firmly rely.' Her tears were dried, and her murmurings forever hushed." And God proved himself to be according to his word. Now there was no difference in the outward circumstances of this widow when she was bowed down with sorrow and when she was filled with comfort. The difference was here: in the one moment she neglected the promises of the word of God; in the next, she received them in the exercise of faith. From this act of faith she received greater comfort than she could have done from any human being, or from any earthly source. Yes, yes; the sincere servant of God, who reads the Bible with faith, is more cheered by one promise of God to help, than cast down by ten thousand difficulties.

> " Faith, mighty faith, the promise sees,
>   And looks to that alone ;
> Laughs at impossibilities,
>   And cries—' It shall be done!' "

5. *With a determination to practice what you read.* If one of you boys were to receive particular directions from your father about something that he wished you to do, and then to neglect to do it, would your father be pleased or displeased with you?

Displeased.

To be sure he would, and properly so. If you merely read and understand God's word, and neglect to practice it, will God be pleased with you?

No.

No, indeed! You remember what St. James says: "Whoso looketh into the perfect law of liberty, and continueth therein, he being not a forgetful hearer, but a doer of the work, this man shall be blessed in his deed." James i, 25. One greater than James has said, "If ye love me, keep my commandments." Again, our Saviour says: "If a man love me, he will keep my words; and my Father will love him, and we will come unto him, and make our abode with him." John xiv, 15, 23.

If you read, believe, love, study, pray over, and practice the word of God, you will become, under God's blessing, useful men—useful women. You will not only be useful but happy; happy in life, happy in death, and happy throughout eternity. What need to pray when we read the Bible!

"Do thou, O Lord, my heart incline
To love—to study—every line;
And more than all, my spirit lead
To PRACTICE WHAT I DAILY READ."

THE HOUSE OF GOD.

I went with them to the house of God, with the voice of
joy and praise, with a multitude that kept holyday.—
PSALM xlii, 4.

No doubt you have noticed that the place
in which God's servants meet for public
worship is sometimes called in Scripture
"God's house," or the "house of God."
Is there any house which will contain or
hold God?

No.

No, indeed! You have read the words
of Solomon: "But will God in very deed
dwell with men on the earth? Behold,
heaven and the heaven of heavens cannot
contain thee; how much less this house
which I have built!" 2 Chron. vi, 18.

No creature can be present in more
than one place at the same time; but God
can be, and is present everywhere; and

he has particularly promised to be so where his servants meet to worship him. "Where two or three are gathered together in my name, (says our Saviour,) there am I in the midst of them." Matt. xviii, 20. We are met once more to worship God, on his own day, and in his house. Now, pay all the attention you can while I talk to you,—

I. About the duty of public worship.

II. About the way in which you should attend to it.

I. THE DUTY OF PUBLIC WORSHIP.

1. *It is a reasonable duty.* You told me in a former lecture who made you: now, tell me again.

God.

Yes, God not only made you, but he keeps and supports you; all you have comes from him. You are more dependent upon God than any child can be upon its parents: you will have to give a more strict account to God than any servant ever gave to his master. As you are thus dependent upon God, and must give an

account to God, do you not see that you
ought to worship him?

Yes.

Yes, truly does the poet say—

> "Meet and right it is to sing,
> In every time and place,
> Glory to our heavenly King,
> The God of truth and grace."

2. *It is an important duty.* Do you
remember in what place the children of
Israel worshiped God in the wilderness?
Was it a house, or a tabernacle, or what?

A Tabernacle.

You are right; now let me see how attentive you can be while I tell you something about the tabernacle. It was a kind
of tent which could be set up and taken
down at pleasure. Can any of you tell me
whether the Israelites took the tabernacle
with them, or left it behind, when they
journeyed from place to place?

Took it with them.

Who directed them to do this?

God.

Yes, in the twenty-fifth and following
chapters of the book of Exodus, you will

find that God gave particular directions to
Moses about preparing and putting up the
tabernacle; and, in giving these directions,
God also repeated the commands, which
he had before given, about keeping holy
the Sabbath-day; thus reminding them
that there is a particular connection between keeping the Sabbath-day and public
worship.

When the tabernacle was finished, God
carefully watched over and guarded it.
A cloud rested upon it by day, and "fire
was on it by night." When this cloud
was taken up, the Israelites went on their
journey. Moses says, " A cloud covered
the tent of the congregation, and the glory
of the Lord filled the tabernacle. And
when the cloud was taken up from over
the tabernacle, the children of Israel went
onward in all their journeys : but if the
cloud were not taken up, then they journeyed not till the day that it was taken
up. For the cloud of the Lord was
upon the tabernacle by day, and fire
was on it by night, in the sight of all the
house of Israel, throughout all their jour-

neys." Exod. xl, 34, 36–38. Thus you see, that during the long time, about forty years, that the children of Israel were in the wilderness, God took care that they should have a place for public worship. O! it must have been a grand and interesting sight to see "the cloud of the Lord" which "was upon the tabernacle" arise, and then to see the Israelites prepare for their journey, and at once march forward, some before, and some behind, and "the holy things" of their beloved tabernacle carefully guarded in the midst. For, whatever else was forgotten, the house of God, as they sometimes called it, must not be neglected.

You elder boys and girls will remember that Moses, who had taken so much interest in the tabernacle, died before the Israelites entered the land which God had promised them; but Joshua took the tabernacle over Jordan, and set it up at a place called Gilgal: there it remained until the Israelites had conquered the inhabitants of Canaan. It was then removed to a place called Shiloh, afterward

to Nob, and at last to Gibeah. At Gibeah
it remained till the beautiful temple was
built by Solomon upon Mount Moriah,
sometimes called Mount Zion; then the
ark and holy things, about which I may
tell you more at another time, were removed into the temple, and there the
Israelites worshiped God. O! great,
great was the joy of the Lord's people
when the temple, the "house of God,"
was opened for public worship : many had
been their days of gladness, but never had
they a day like that! The Lord also was
pleased. It is written, when " the house
of the Lord was finished," " then Solomon
assembled the elders of Israel, and all the
heads of the tribes, the chief of the fathers
of the children of Israel, unto Jerusalem,
to bring up the ark of the covenant of the
Lord. And they brought up the ark, and
the tabernacle of the congregation, and
all the holy vessels that were in the tabernacle, these did the priests and the Levites
bring up. It came even to pass, as the
trumpeters and singers were as one, to make
one sound to be heard in praising and

thanking the Lord; and when they lifted up their voice with the trumpets and cymbals and instruments of music, and praised the Lord, saying, For he is good; for his mercy endureth for ever: that then the house was filled with a cloud, even the house of the Lord; so that the priests could not stand to minister by reason of the cloud: for the glory of the Lord had filled the house of God." 2 Chron. v, 2, 5, 13, 14.

After many years that temple was destroyed, and then rebuilt; so that, when our Saviour appeared upon earth, the Israelites still had their beloved temple in which to worship God. You have read with what zeal our Saviour drove out the persons who bought and sold in the temple, and with what deep feeling he called it his "Father's house."

Now, my dear children, you have been very attentive, and I am glad you have, for this makes me hope that you have understood what has been said. Perhaps you have been wondering why I have told you so much about the tabernacle and the temple. Now think, while I ask you a question or two, and try to answer properly; then, perhaps, you will understand. All this has been said to show you how important the duty of public worship is. You have heard what particular directions God gave about the tabernacle, and how he watched over it, that while the children of Israel were in the wilderness they might always have a place to worship in. If the duty of public worship had not been a very important one, do you think God would have done this?

No.

You have heard also what particular directions God gave about the building of the temple, so that when the Israelites were settled in Canaan they might still have a place in which to worship. If the duty of public worship had not been very important, do you think God would have done this?

No.

Of course he would not. When our Saviour was upon earth the Jews had other places of worship besides the temple, called synagogues. In these Jesus united with those who worshiped God, so also did the apostles, thus showing us by their example the importance of this duty.

3. *It is an interesting duty.* O how interesting and how pleasing to see a whole congregation, having laid aside the things of the world, engage in the services of God's house! All, from the gray-headed old man down to the little child, bowing before God in prayer, or singing his praises, or listening to his word. No wonder that Dr. Watts should have felt so strongly and written so sweetly on witnessing such a sight:—

" Lord, how delightful 'tis to see
A whole assembly worship thee!
At once they sing, at once they pray;
They hear of heaven and learn the way.

" I have been there, and still would go,
'Tis like a little heaven below;
Not all my pleasure and my play,
Shall tempt me to forget that day."

4. *It is a profitable duty.* You cannot engage in public worship in a proper manner and in a proper spirit without being better for it. When you pray, sin-

cerely trusting in Jesus Christ, God has promised to hear and answer you. When you sing the praises of God in the manner taught in his word, your praises will be received, your souls will be blessed. When you listen to God's word in a proper spirit you will be instructed, and thus you will become better able to understand the truth. No wonder that good men should so greatly delight in this duty, and so sincerely love the house of God. You know how feelingly the Psalmist speaks about this. "How amiable are thy tabernacles, O Lord of hosts! My soul longeth, yea, even fainteth for the courts of the Lord; my heart and my flesh crieth out for the living God." "Blessed are they that dwell in thy house; they will be still praising thee." "For a day in thy courts is better than a thousand. I had rather be a door-keeper in the house of my God, than to dwell in the tents of wickedness." Psa. lxxxiv, 1, 2, 4, 10.

II. THE WAY IN WHICH YOU SHOULD ATTEND TO THE DUTY OF PUBLIC WORSHIP.

1. *Sincerely.* Taking care that you *really mean* what you say and do. You, no doubt, remember the interesting and important conversation of our Saviour with the woman of Samaria at Jacob's well. "The hour cometh, and now is, when the true worshipers shall worship the Father in spirit and in truth: for the Father seeketh such to worship him. God is a spirit; and they that worship him must worship him in spirit and in truth." John iv, 23, 24. Search your hearts, my dear children, and take care that you be sincere, that you worship God in spirit and in truth; pray also that God would enable you to do this. We have all, whether we are young or old, great need to be careful in this matter; with the poet we may well sing:—

> "We bow before thy gracious throne,
> And think ourselves sincere;
> But show us, Lord, is every one
> Thy real worshiper?"

A father one day said to his son, that at a certain time he must attend to a particular work, which was named: that he must prepare for it, according to directions which were given, and that he must do it well. The time came, and the boy went to the work; but he made no preparation for it, and he did it so carelessly that any one might know he was not thinking of what he was doing. Was that boy sincerely trying to please his father?

No.

Of course he was not. Had he been sincere he would have prepared for the work as his father told him, he would have done it heartily and well, thinking of what he was about. Now, if you go triflingly to the house of God, and sit there in a thoughtless and careless manner, do you think you can be sincere?

No.

No, indeed! If you are sincere, you will prepare for public worship by laying aside all worldly thoughts, and by bowing before God in private, and asking him to help and bless you. If you are sincere, you will go up to the house of God in a thoughtful and serious frame of mind, thinking of the solemn duty in which you

are about to engage. If you are sincere,
you will behave while in the house of God
with all possible seriousness and attention.
If you are sincere, you will return quietly
home, thinking of the truth that you have
heard, and praying that God would enable
you to practice it.

I knew a boy, some years ago, who always used to retire after public worship
for meditation and prayer : and I have
frequently heard him say, that when many
of his own age were taking what they
called their walks of pleasure, he was
often so happy while engaged in praying
that God would bless the services of the
Sabbath to his soul, that he was almost
ready to say with St. Paul, " Whether in
the body, I cannot tell; or whether out of
the body, I cannot tell." 2 Cor. xii, 2.
That youth continued this practice till he
became a man, and he is now a minister
of the Gospel. Go, my dear children, and
do likewise.

2. You should attend to this duty *thankfully*—feeling thankful that you have an
opportunity of worshiping God in his

house, and fervently praising him for the mercies with which he has blessed you. Praise is an important part, both of private devotion and of public worship. In order to praise God aright, you must *think* of his mercies, and try to feel how much you owe to God. I will tell you how a pious mother, of whom I have read, taught her child a lesson of thankfulness. "One morning she heard her little boy say to his sister, who had just been dressing him in an adjoining room, 'No, I don't want to say my prayers—I don't want to say my prayers.' Soon after the child came to the parlor door and said, 'Mother, I am going to get my breakfast.' 'Good morning, my child,' said his mother; 'stop a minute, I want you to come to me first.' She laid down her work, and took him up. He kneeled in her lap, and laid his face upon her shoulder, with his cheek against her ear. The mother rocked her chair slowly backward and forward, and said in a gentle tone, 'Are you pretty well this morning?' 'Yes, mother,' answered the boy, 'I am very well.' 'I am glad you are,' said she; 'I am very well too; and when I awoke this morning and found that I was well, I thanked God for taking care of me.' 'Did you?' said the boy in a low tone, half a whisper. He paused. His conscience was at work. After a minute of silence his mother said, 'Did you ever feel my pulse?' At the same time taking him down and placing his fingers on her wrist. 'No,' he answered, 'but I have felt mine.' 'Well, don't you feel mine now? How it goes beating, beating?' 'Yes,' said the boy. 'If it should stop beating I should die.' 'Should you?' said he. 'Yes; and I can't keep it beating.' 'Who can?' asked the child. 'God!' There was a silent pause. 'You have a pulse too,' said his mother, 'which beats in your bosom here, and in your arms, and all over you; and I cannot keep it beating, nor can you; nobody can but God. If he should not take care of you, who could?' 'I don't know,' said the child, with a look of anxiety; and there was another pause. The boy's thoughtful countenance showed that his heart was reached. 'Do n't you think,' said his mother, 'that you had better ask him yourself?' 'Yes,' said he readily. He kneeled again in his mother's lap, and uttered, in his simple language, a prayer for the protection and blessing of heaven."

Being thus led to think of God's goodness, he was brought to feel it. O think, often think, of the goodness of God toward you! Remember, not only that he keeps you alive, and gives you health, and strength, and food, and clothes, and shelter, and every blessing that is needful for the body; but remember the spiritual mercies with which he has favored you. Think of the gift of God's word, of his Sabbaths, of his house, of his ministers, of his Spirit, of his Son! Think, till your heart overflows with gratitude! till with the Psalmist you are ready to say, "Praise waiteth for thee, O God, in Sion." Psa. lxv, 1. We wait, we long to go up to thine house to offer praise. O happy, happy they whose hearts thus overflow, and who come up to God's house sincerely to offer praise! Such persons can not only sing, but feel while they sing—

> " Praise God, from whom all blessings flow ;
> Praise him, all creatures here below ;
> Praise him above, ye heavenly host ;
> Praise Father, Son, and Holy Ghost !"

3. You should attend to this duty *regularly ;* never staying away from the house of God when you have an opportunity to go, and always striving to be there at the proper time. There are some persons who, by their late attendance, appear as if they thought that the mere listening to the sermon was enough, and that the singing of God's praise, the reading of his word, and uniting with the congregation in prayer, were matters of small importance. Such persons dishonor God, rob themselves of many blessings, and disturb the worship of others. A pious woman who was always seen in her place at the proper time, when questioned about it, said, that it was " a part of her religion not to disturb the devotion of others." Strive not only to be present, but to be there *in time.*

Take care, also, that you do not let any playfellow, or any work, or any pleasure, or anything else, keep you from the house of God when you can possibly be there; for you know not at which service God may bless you most; you know not which service may be your last. An account which was given by a young man at a church-meeting in America, may perhaps help you to remember this, and also cause you to feel its importance. He spoke as nearly as possible in the following words:—

"About a year ago," said he, "I set out in company with a young man to seek the salvation of my soul. For several weeks we went on together, and often renewed our promise never to cease till we obtained the religion of Jesus. But suddenly he neglected to attend public worship, turned his back on all the means of grace, and grew so shy of me that I could scarcely get to speak to him. His strange conduct gave me much pain of mind, but still I felt resolved to obtain the salvation of my soul. After a few days a friend informed me that my companion had received an invitation to attend a ball, and was determined to go. I went to him, and with tears in my eyes tried to persuade him to change his purpose, and to go with me in the evening to a place of worship. I pleaded in vain. He told me when we parted that I must not give him up as lost; for after he had attended the ball, he meant again to seek religion. The evening came: he went to the ball, and I to the house of God. Soon after the service began it pleased God to answer my prayer, and to make my soul rejoice in his love. Soon after the ball opened my young friend was standing at the top of the room with a young lady, preparing to lead down the dance, and, without a moment's warning, he fell dead on the floor."

Ah! little did that young man think, when he refused the invitation of his friend to attend the house of God, that it was the last invitation he would ever have, and that he was slighting his *last offer of mercy!*

4. You should attend to this duty *believingly*, or *with faith.*

When you come up to God's house and sing his praises, *try to believe* that God will hear and accept your thanksgiving. When you engage in prayer, try to believe that God will hear and answer your prayers. When you listen to the word of truth, and are told that "God so loved the world, that he gave his only-begotten Son, that whosoever believeth in him should not perish but have everlasting life;" try fully to believe—to *trust* in Christ. Look upon him as having died for *you*, as much for you as though you were the only sinners in the world: remember that he is as willing to save you as though you were the only sinners that ever lived. O pleasing, glorious truth! Did Christ die for *me!* as much for me as though I were the only sinner that ever lived! O then I OUGHT to *trust* in him; I *will trust* in him. Try thus to trust: God will give you the power, and Christ will receive you.

I have just read an account which may give you some light in reference to this trust. The account is given by a minister of the Gospel, and it took place in his own family.

He had gone into a cellar, which in winter time was quite dark, and entered by a trap-door. A little daughter, only three years old, was trying to find him, and she came to the trap-door; but on looking down all was dark, and she called, "Are you down cellar, papa?"

"Yes; would you like to come, Mary?"

"It is dark; I can't come, papa."

"Well, my dear, I am right below you, and I can see you, though you cannot see me; and if you will drop down I will catch you."

"O, I should fall! I can't see you, papa."

"I know it," he answered, "but I am *really here*, and you shall not fall or hurt yourself. If you will jump I will catch you safely."

Little Mary strained her eyes to the utmost, but could not see her father: she hesitated, then advanced a little further, and summoning all her resolution, she threw herself forward and was received safely in her father's arms.

A few days after she again found the cellar door open. Supposing her father was there, she called, "Shall I come again, papa?"

"Yes, my dear, in a minute," he replied; and had just time to reach his arms toward her, when, in her childish glee, she fell shouting into his arms, and, clasping his neck, said, "I *knew*, dear papa, I should not fall."

Now that was trust in her father, and she was not deceived. Try, my dear children, thus to trust in Christ, and you will never be deceived.

Be encouraged by the kind invitations and precious promises with which you so often meet in the word of God. It is full of them. Listen to one: "Come unto me, all ye that labor and are heavy laden, (saith Christ,) and I will give you rest. Take my yoke upon you, and learn of me: for I am meek and lowly in heart; and ye shall find rest unto your souls. For my yoke is easy, and my burden is light."

" He now stands knocking at the door
 Of every sinner's heart ;
The worst need keep him out no more,
 Or force him to depart."

5. You should attend to this duty with *self-application*, hearing the word of God for yourself, applying it to your own heart, and resolving to reduce it to practice. This is not so easy as at first sight you may think. Many persons hear the word for others, instead of hearing it for themselves ; many apply it to others, instead of applying it to themselves; and alas! how many there are who neglect to practice it. St. James says, " Be ye doers of the word, and not hearers only, deceiving your own selves, (i, 22;) and our Saviour says, "That servant which knew his lord's will, and prepared not himself, neither did according to his will, shall be beaten with many stripes." Luke xii, 47.

GO TO JESUS.

He shall feed his flock like a shepherd: he shall gather
the lambs with his arm, and carry them in his bosom.—
ISAIAH xl, 11.

MANY of you, my young friends, have
spent your pleasantest hours amid the
beauties of the garden, and the flowers of
the field; and have you not, in your summer rambles, seen the skipping lambs
looking innocently gay, and sporting by
the side of their dams? It delighted you
to see them thus happy, and enjoying
themselves in the cheerful sunshine; but,
perhaps, at other times, you have seen
the tender creatures exposed to stormy
winds, or pinching frost; your little hearts
have pitied them, and been ready to fear
that the severity of the winter would
destroy them. In this distressed situation,
how delightful to see the kind shepherd
come to their relief, gather them together,
and lead them to a place of shelter and
safety!

Delightful, indeed, to see him take up the tender and feeble in his arms, and carry them in his bosom, till the little creatures are revived and cherished! But, children, I can tell you what is still more pleasing and wonderful. You have heard of Jesus Christ, the Son of God, who came down from heaven to save sinners. You have heard how great and glorious a person he was before he came into our world. And will it not surprise you to hear that this Jesus calls himself a shepherd? His people, those who love and serve him, he calls his sheep; and the young and tender, such as you are, he calls his lambs.

He calls you lambs, because, like them, you are young, ignorant, and helpless; and, like them, you flee to others for safety and protection.

You are but of yesterday, and know but little; little indeed of the God that made you, and of the Saviour that came to redeem you. You know little of the world in which you live, or of that world in which you are to live forever. You stand in need of daily instruction, in the concerns both of your soul and of your body; but your compassionate Shepherd has promised that he will feed his flock; he will feed you with the sincere milk of his word, that you may grow thereby.

He has said, "Ask, and it shall be given you; seek, and ye shall find." Matt. vii, 7.

Are you at a loss what to ask? Ask, above all things, his favor, which is life; and his loving-kindness, which is better than life. Ask him to teach you more of himself, of his greatness and goodness, that you may love him more and serve him better.

You are not only ignorant, but, like the feeble lamb, you are helpless, and can do but little for your own safety and protection. You are exposed to many dangers which you know nothing of: there are many disorders to which your infant years are liable, and a thousand accidents to which your tender frames are exposed.

How happy, amid all this weakness

and danger, to reflect that your kind Shepherd has promised to gather you in his arms, and carry you in his bosom!

Your parents do much for you, and you have reason to thank God for them. But Jesus, your kind shepherd, can do much more; he can supply all your need; in sickness he can save you, and in death deliver you; he can make you happy in this world, and happy forever.

Often think, children, how much love and compassion are contained in those delightful words: " He shall gather them with his arm, and carry them in his bosom." You know what it is to be folded in the fond arms of a compassionate father, and to hang on the breasts of a tender mother.

How often have they wiped away your tears, and eased the little sorrows of your hearts! While you are enjoying their love and affection, think, "Thus has my kind Shepherd promised to fold me in his arms. How condescending in him to notice such an ignorant and helpless creature as I am! What an honor to be called one of his lambs! How safe I am under his protection! He is almighty, and none can pluck me out of his hands. The Lord is my shepherd; I shall not want anything that is good for me."

"Blessed Jesus! I desire to be one of the lambs that thou wilt gather in thy arms and carry in thy bosom. I am ignorant; but I come to thee that I may be taught. I am weak and helpless; but I flee to thy arms for safety and protection. Make me one of thy lambs, in love, meekness, and humility; let me never wander from thee, or provoke thee to cast me out of thy fold. Keep me from every danger in this world, and fit me to dwell with thee forever in thy heavenly kingdom. Amen."

PRAYER.

When thou prayest, enter into thy closet, and when thou hast shut thy door, pray to thy Father which is in secret; and thy Father which seeth in secret shall reward thee openly.—MATT. vi, 6.

Do you, children, love God above all things? Is he your Father, your heavenly Father? Then, surely, it must be your highest pleasure to pray to him; you have much to say to him, much to ask of him, and much to thank him for.

Go, children, if possible, where none can see you but God, your heavenly Father, and there pour out your hearts before him, with all the duty and affection of a child; remembering how much you are bound to love him for all his goodness to you, and how much more valuable is his favor, the light of his countenance, than all the good things that this world can give you.

You may there confess that your giddy hearts are apt to forget him amid the follies and vanities of childhood and youth; that you often pray to him without the reverence and affection which you ought ever to feel for him; that you often read his holy word with carelessness and indifference, as if it were the word of man, and not the word of God; and that you are not made holier and better by it.

You may lament over the pride, obstinacy, and perverseness that you sometimes feel in your hearts; and that you strive so little against these sins, that you may conquer and overcome them.

Thus may you humble yourselves before God for all your sins and follies, and beg that, for Christ's sake, he would forgive them all, and grant you the assistance of his good Spirit to help you to love him more and serve him better.

It is good, children, to draw near to God, to show forth his loving-kindness in the morning, and his faithfulness every night. Begin every day with this delightful service. You cannot surely awake in the morning to health, to friends, to every blessing of life, without thanking the God of your mercies, who giveth you all things richly to enjoy.

Dare not venture into the dangers and temptations of the day without praying that God would be with you, to keep you from sin and deliver you from evil. Nor can you surely lie down in peace at night without thanking the kind hand that has kept you from evil, and crowned the day with loving-kindness and tender mercies, and without asking forgiveness of your heavenly Father for all that you have done amiss. Thus may you commit yourselves to his care through the dangers of the night, for it is God only who can make you to dwell in safety.

Thus, children, you may converse in secret with your heavenly Father; and be assured, he who hears the young ravens when they cry will hear you when you pray unto him; he sees, in secret, the feeblest wish of your heart to love and serve him; he will remember the kindness of your youth, and will reward you openly. Fear not, children, though you should have only a dark corner to pray in; your heavenly Father sees you there. Fear not, though your companions should laugh at you for being so precise about your prayers; remember whom you are to fear; fear him who can kill both soul and body in hell.

Your heavenly Father sees when you are ashamed or afraid to pray to him. Jesus has said, "Whosoever shall be ashamed of me and of my words, of him also shall the Son of man be ashamed when he cometh in the glory of his Father with the holy angels." "Whosoever shall confess me before men, him shall the Son of man also confess before the angels of God." Mark viii, 38; Luke xii, 8.

Believe it, children, you will never pray to him in vain; he will reward you in this world with everything that he sees best for you; and, at the last day, he will reward you openly, and far more abundantly, before men and angels.

THE ONE THING NEEDFUL.

One thing is needful.—LUKE x, 42.

UPON hearing these words, I doubt not, my young friends, you are all eager to know what this one thing needful is. They are the words of Jesus Christ; and I will tell you upon what occasion they were spoken.

"Now it came to pass, as they went, that he entered into a certain village: and a certain woman, named Martha, received him into her house. And she had a sister called Mary, which also sat at Jesus' feet, and heard his word. But Martha was cumbered about much serving, and came to him, and said, Lord, dost thou not care that my sister hath left me to serve alone? Bid her therefore that she help me. And Jesus answered, and said unto her, Martha, Martha, thou art careful, and troubled about many things: but one thing is needful; and Mary hath chosen that good part, which shall not be taken away from her." Luke x, 38–42.

And now, children, from this story you may learn what the one thing needful is. It is to hear the words of eternal life, and inquire what you must do to be saved. And though you cannot now sit at Christ's feet, as Mary did while he was here upon earth, yet you may go to him as an humble learner; like her you may hear his words, and attend to the concerns of your souls; and, like her, choose that good part which shall never be taken away from you.

Religion is the one thing needful; because without it you cannot be happy in this world, and must be forever miserable in the world to come.

It is needful for all: for the rich, and for the poor; for the old, and for the young. It is needful for you, children, to know God, and serve him here on earth, that you may dwell with him, and be happy forever in heaven. It is more needful for you than riches, or honors, or all that this world can give you; for what would it profit you if you should gain the whole world, and lose your own soul?

Jesus Christ not only calls religion the one thing needful, but he calls it the good part.

Yes, children, it is a good thing to love God and Christ: the ways of religion are ways of pleasantness, and all her paths are peace. "There is no peace, saith my God, to the wicked;" but great peace have they who love his law. To pray to God, and to praise him, is a delightful employment; to show forth his loving-kindness in the morning, and his faithfulness every night.

Religion is a good thing; for it teaches us to be good ourselves, and to do good to all around us.

The pious child will be a good child: he will obey his parents, not only because he loves them, but because God has said, "Honor thy father and thy mother;" and has said, "Children, obey your parents in all things;" he will be merciful and kind, because his heavenly Father is merciful and kind to all: he will be diligent and industrious, because his Bible tells him he must not be slothful in business, but fervent in spirit, serving the Lord: he will be a good child, that he may be the child of God, and have God for his father and his friend forever. And now, my young friends, must not that be a good thing that will make you thus good and happy?

Jesus has said this good part shall never be taken away from you. Your parents and friends may be taken from you by death, but if you are good God will continue to bless you. Your riches may be taken away from you, but if you are good you have better treasures in heaven. Death itself cannot take away this good part from you; for you know that the righteous shall dwell with God and Christ forever in heaven.

And now, children, what shall I say more, to persuade you to choose this good part? Your parents tell you it is the good part; they have found it so themselves, and they wish, above all things, to see you make the choice. Jesus says it is the good part; go to him, sit at his feet, and say to him, " Blessed Jesus, to whom should we go but unto thee! Thou hast the words of eternal life: teach us what we must do to be saved; teach us the one thing needful; teach us, like Mary, to choose that good part that shall never be taken away from us."

GOOD TIDINGS.

And there were in the same country shepherds abiding in the field, keeping watch over their flock by night. And lo, the angel of the Lord came upon them, and the glory of the Lord shone round about them; and they were sore afraid. And the angel said unto them, Fear not: for behold, I bring you good tidings of great joy, which shall be to all people. For unto you is born this day, in the city of David, a Saviour, which is Christ the Lord. And this shall be a sign unto you: Ye shall find the babe wrapped in swaddling-clothes, lying in a manger. And suddenly there was with the angel a multitude of the heavenly host praising God, and saying, Glory to God in the highest, and on earth peace, good-will toward men.—LUKE ii, 8-14.

To you, children, as well as to the shepherds, are these glad tidings sent; for unto you was born a Saviour, which is Christ the Lord. His name was called

Jesus, because he should save his people from their sins.

And is not this joyful news, indeed, that Jesus, the beloved Son of God, should come down from heaven, and be born into the world a feeble infant, like one of us, that he might save us from our sins, that we might not perish, but have everlasting life?

And you see there is joy not only on earth, but in heaven too; the holy angels, those kind and friendly beings, rejoiced to bring these good news to man.

No sooner had the angel told the news to the shepherds, than suddenly there was with him a multitude of the heavenly host, praising God, and saying, "Glory to God in the highest!"

They sang glory to God, because he so loved the world as to give his only-begotten Son, that whosoever believeth on him should not perish, but have everlasting life.

They sang peace on earth. Jesus, the Prince of Peace, was now come to bring peace on earth; to reconcile guilty man to the blessed God, whom they had offended; and to teach them to love God and one another, that they might be fit to dwell with God, and with his holy angels, forever in heaven.

These holy and blessed spirits rejoiced to see, not sin and wickedness, hatred and strife, but righteousness, and peace, and joy among men.

They sang good-will to men. When man was first made, the holy angels, those morning stars, sang and rejoiced together; when man rebelled against his Maker, and was condemned to die, this joy departed from them. But they rejoiced again to see him restored to the favor and love of God, to holiness and happiness: to see the works of Satan, the great enemy of God and man, destroyed, and peace restored on earth.

They rejoiced to think that good men should come from the east, and from the west, and from all parts of the world, and dwell with them forever in heaven. The friendly angels had often been sent down, to do service to good men here below;

but they never came with so much joy as upon this occasion. This was good news to the whole world; good tidings of great joy to all people—to the rich and to the poor, to the old and to the young; for all stand in need of this Saviour.

Yes, children, to you is this salvation sent. And will you not receive it with joy? With the children in the temple, will you not cry "Hosanna! Blessed is he that cometh in the name of the Lord!" Will you not join with the holy angels in saying, "Glory to God in the highest, on earth peace, and good-will to men?" Do they glorify God for his love to you, and can you be silent? Do they rejoice in the hope of your salvation; and will you not wish to be saved from sin and hell, and to dwell with the holy angels forever in heaven?

It is pleasant to think of the holy angels being employed for our service here on earth; but it is still more delightful to think of joining with them in the praises of our God and Saviour in heaven.

Then shall we sing glory to God in higher strains than we can praise him in here on earth. There we shall join with those blessed spirits, who cease not day and night, saying, "Holy, holy, holy, Lord God Almighty, which was, and is, and is to come!" Then shall we join with thousands of angels, saying, "Worthy is the Lamb that was slain to receive power, and riches, and wisdom, and strength, and honor, and glory, and blessing. Blessing, and honor, and glory, and power, be unto him that sitteth upon the throne, and unto the Lamb, forever and ever. Amen." Rev. v, 12, 13.

THE GOOD PREACHER.

And the common people heard him gladly.—MARK xii, 37.

It seems, from the words of our text, that although some people who enjoyed the opportunity of listening to the blessed Jesus loved to hear him preach, there were some who did *not* hear him gladly. I suppose, in fact, there were some who did not take pains to hear him at all. They heard strange things *about* him; but they either had no time, or no inclination to hear him for themselves. And then there were others who heard him only to find fault with what he said. Now is not this very strange?

If the Saviour should come again to earth to preach his Gospel, would not you, my young friends, go a great distance rather than lose an opportunity of hearing him? and would not you hear him *gladly?* I trust you would, for he was the best preacher in the world. There had never

THE APOSTLES PREACHING THE GOSPEL.

But Peter . . . said unto them . . . This is that which was spoken by the prophet
Joel . . . your young men shall see visions, and your old men shall dream dreams.
(Acts 2: 14, 16, 17)

been so good a preacher before him, and there has never been his equal since.

Do you ask wherein he was the best preacher? In the first place, *He knew the most.* You, no doubt, have heard preachers who were very learned; but they did not know everything. They talked about God, but they knew but little about God; they attempted to describe heaven, but they admitted that they knew very little about heaven. But Jesus knew everything. He was not only well acquainted with the Almighty, having always been with him; but he thought it not robbery to be called equal with God. He not only knew all about heaven, for he had lived there, but he was acquainted with the very thoughts of his hearers' hearts. Yes, while he was preaching,—and sometimes he addressed a vast multitude of people at once,—he knew what every one of his hearers was thinking about.

Again, *He was a very humble preacher;* and you know meek and lowly ministers are always the best. He was so humble that he was willing to preach in any place. Some clergymen dislike to preach except in fine churches; but Christ not only preached in the temple, but in the street, the private house, on the mountain, or in the boat—wherever the people were disposed quietly to listen. Some preachers do not like to preach unless they can have a large congregation; but Jesus has been known to preach excellent discourses to very small audiences. What a blessed sermon that must have been which he preached along the road, as he was walking to Emmaus with two disciples, which made their hearts burn within them! And what a powerful sermon he preached to one person, the woman at Jacob's well, which not only converted her, but made her such a preacher of salvation to her neighbors that she set all Samaria in commotion!

In a word, Christ was the best preacher because *he was the holiest preacher that ever lived.* Unlike all other ministers, he had never sinned. In all his life he had never committed one sin; never had done a naughty deed; never had spoken an unkind word; never had indulged one impure thought. From a child he had been closely watched by enemies, but no one could detect anything wrong in him; and yet, strange to say, though he spent his whole time in doing good,—healing the sick, opening the eyes of the blind, raising the dead, and preaching the Gospel without asking any money for his services,—there were many who did not like him. Some would interrupt him while preaching, and others would go away offended; and I fear if he should come again on earth he would be treated .in the same manner, for the very classes of persons who did not like the Saviour's preaching are yet to be found among us.

I will now mention a few kinds of people who did not hear the Saviour gladly. *Hypocrites*, or those who concealed their real character, did not hear him gladly, because he could look right into their wicked hearts as easily as you can look out of the window. Nor did he fail to expose such deceivers, and faithfully warn them to escape the ruin they were bringing upon themselves.

Proud persons, who were vain of their learning, their persons, their dress, or their associates, did not hear him gladly. There were several things about him that vain persons did not like. They did not like his simple language; for though he knew all things, he did not appear learned. They did not like his origin,—for they knew not that God was his Father,—but despised him because he was called a Nazarene, and was brought up a mechanic. They did not like his appearance; for although he had a noble, heavenly countenance, his apparel was very plain, and his associates were poor fishermen. But more than all, they disliked his doctrines, in which he plainly told them that he that exalteth himself shall be abased; and that unless great men, and rich men, and learned men should be converted, and become like little children, they could never enter heaven.

Rich men, who trusted in their wealth, did not hear him gladly; for they were inclined to think, because they had more money, they were better than their neighbors; but when Jesus told them it was easier for a camel to go through the eye of a needle than for a rich (that is, a covetous) man to enter into the kingdom of heaven, and that in order to be saved they were to forsake all, as well as the poor man, and strive to enter into the strait gate,—the same little gate of repentance that the poor publican or any other sinner must pass through,—they were offended, and said hard things about him.

Now our Saviour did not wish to displease these persons. He never used harsh or vulgar language to irritate them: nothing of the kind. He was sorry to see them go away from him angry. He loved them, and wept over them, as a tender mother weeps when her children do wrong, for they were sinners on their way to hell; and he saw there was no hope for them until at least they were informed of their true condition.

Was not their opposition then, children, very unreasonable? As unreasonable as it would be for you to get angry at a person who earnestly cries out to you to get off the railway track when the locomotive is coming, or grasps you by your garments as you are about to stumble headlong over a frightful precipice. And yet, my young friends, I am afraid that some of you would treat our Saviour just as the pharisaical, the proud and aristocratic Jews did, if he should come again, and travel about preaching everywhere, as he did eighteen hundred years ago. I will tell you why I have such fears. In the first place, there are very many young as well as old people in these days, whose disposition is almost exactly like that of those who formerly did not hear the Saviour gladly; and, secondly, they are inclined to neglect, if they do not openly despise, those ministers of the Gospel whom Jesus has sent to take his place, and who try to preach as he did, and spend all their time in going about from place to place doing good. Tell me, children, have you always listened gladly to ministers while they were preaching, especially to those preachers who, like Jesus, mingled among the poor, wore plain clothes, and preached plain sermons?

But the text informs us there were some that did hear him gladly, namely, the *common* people. By the common people, I suppose is meant what is called the middle or laboring class; not, perhaps, the most poor and degraded, nor the most wealthy and noble. I doubt whether all the common people even heard him gladly. If they did, they were better than the common people are in these days. Many common people seem to have hearts as proud, deceitful, and covetous, as those who move in a higher circle; and there are others who have not the independence to be pleased with a good Christ-like sermon, unless they find out that their neighbors are pleased. I suppose the meaning of the text is, that more of the common people heard Jesus gladly than of other classes; and this is true of those who hear preaching in these days.

But why did the common people hear him gladly? What was there about

Christ that particularly arrested the attention of this class?

1. Common people could *understand* him; and this is one reason, no doubt, why some very wicked men did not like him. He preached so plainly that they, and their neighbors, and servants, could understand him too well. There was a holy minister who lived more than a hundred years ago, by the name of Richard Baxter. He preached very much as Christ did. One Sabbath he came out very plainly against profanity, and offended a wealthy man who was much addicted to swearing. The rich man called upon the minister the next day, and told him that if he must preach against such vices as the nobility were guilty of he wished he would preach in Latin, so that their servants and common folks would not understand the matter, and despise their superiors. But Mr. Baxter replied: "Sir, if you will sin in Latin, I will reprove you in Latin; but if you sin in English, I must, by the help of God, reprove you in English."

Now, in this respect, Baxter was like his divine Master. When Jesus preached he used language that the common people could understand. Some think he was too simple. They think it would be lowering the *dignity* of the pulpit if ministers in these days should imitate Christ, who when he preached told stories about common things, and talked about hair and sparrows, tares and wheat, lilies and thistles, hens and chickens, sheep and goats, making bread and heating ovens. He used these little things in nature and art which common people and children *did* understand, to explain the great things of God and religion which they *did not* understand. Yes, I have no doubt he had his eye upon children as well as others while he was preaching. He never would have taken pains to tell Peter not to forget to *feed his* LAMBS, if he was in the habit of forgetting them himself. He was unwilling they should go away, as a large congregation of children did a few years ago from a Sunday-school anniversary that I attended, complaining, as I happened to hear one boy say, " O dear, I wish some of the preachers had talked to *us*." The fact was, *all* the speakers *professed* to address the children; but there were so many doctors, lawyers, and other great men present, the orators shot high over the heads of the little ones to reach *their* nice ears. Not so did Jesus. He loved children, and was always pleased to see them in his meetings. He did not wish to have them kept at home. Some thought it was improper for parents to bring their children; but Jesus said, "Suffer little children to come unto me, and forbid them not." No doubt he took special pains to preach so plainly that they could understand most, if not all that he said. And I have always observed that preaching which is so simple that children are interested in it, is listened to with delight by common people generally.

2. The common people heard him gladly, because *he always had good news for them.* We always listen with gladness to those who bring us good tidings. Now, the word GOSPEL means good news; and

the gospel Christ preached was good news, especially for the common people. I cannot tell you a thousandth part of what he said; but the substance of his preaching was, that "God so loved the world that he gave his only-begotten Son, that whosoever believeth in him should not perish, but have everlasting life."

Children, can you wonder that when the poor heard from the lips of Jesus that God is love—that he loves everybody, the poor as well as the rich, the young as well as old; that his love is so great that he gave his only Son to die for sinners; and that pardon, peace, and heaven can be obtained without money and without price, by just asking for it in faith—do you wonder, I say, that they were delighted with such a sweet message, especially when they saw he was *sincere* in what he said?

3. And here is another reason why the common people heard Jesus gladly. *He was in earnest.* Though he told such great and glorious things, he told nothing but the truth. Every candid person was

convinced on hearing him that he meant
every word he said. His looks showed it.
The tones of his voice showed it. Every
glance of his piercing, yet mild eyes, ex-
hibited a degree of zeal which had never
been seen before. And who does not love
to see men in earnest? Who does not
like especially to hear earnest preachers—
preachers who mean just what they say?
Now Jesus showed so much seriousness
and energy in what he said, that even
those who did not like his doctrine were
astonished; and it was remarked that he
not only spoke as one having authority,
but as no preacher had ever spoken before.

4. And then he manifested such a *kind,
affectionate spirit* while he preached, and
at all times. Sometimes, it is true, he
said severe things; but when he did, his
tears of compassion showed that he felt
very sorry for the wicked—that he did not
wish to grieve them, but to make them
good. If he told the wicked it was a
dreadful thing to sin against God and go
to hell, it was that he might induce them

to come to him and find pardon, and learn the way to heaven.

5. And it ought also to be mentioned as a reason why the common people heard Jesus gladly, that he *practiced* what he preached. Adam Clarke says some ministers are just like stationary guide-boards, or "finger-posts;" they are always pointing in the right direction, but never stirring. Common people generally do not like to hear men who would bind heavy burdens upon others, as the Pharisees did, and yet not touch these duties with one of their own fingers; who would say, *you* ought to do this, and *you* ought to do that, and yet not follow their own teaching. Not so did Jesus. He not only told the people that they should pray, but he showed them how to pray. Did you ever learn the beautiful prayer he taught his disciples, called the "Lord's Prayer?" He prayed a great deal. Sometimes he would get up before daylight, and go away into some solitary place and pray; and on one occasion especially he spent a whole night in prayer. He not only told

the people they should be humble, but he showed them by example *how* to be humble, by washing his disciples' feet, and many other acts of condescension. He not only preached to the poor, and told them he had special regard for the afflicted, distressed, and forsaken, but he carried out his preaching in his life. Indeed, he was much oftener seen in the cottage of the poor than the palace of the rich; and he spent most of his time, when not alone, with common people. This he did, not because he did not love the souls of the rich and great, but because the poor had been sadly neglected he thought he could be more useful among them; and he knew also that ministers are in danger of neglecting this class, and hence he set them a good example to follow until the end of time.

I could say many, very many other things about the blessed Jesus and his preaching, but have not time now. I have already said more than was necessary to convince all my young friends, I trust, that Christ was an excellent preacher.

And now, children, before I close, I wish to mention three or four things which, it seems to me, this subject should make us think of.

1. *It is no small matter to be a preacher.* Some seem to think preaching the Gospel is small business. They would rather be anything than a preacher. But the truth is, preaching the Gospel is the noblest work a person can be engaged in, when God has called and fitted him for the work. Remember, God had only one Son, and he made not a merchant, nor a lawyer, nor a physician, nor a farmer of him, but a minister; yes, a *traveling* preacher. And would God, do you suppose, employ his beloved Son in *small* business? O, I hope some of my young readers will yet be ministers!—ministers like Jesus, imitating him in simplicity, earnestness, love, and a holy life ; and especially, like him, be willing, if necessary, to lay down their lives to please God, and save precious souls. I trust some of you have already given your hearts to God; and if his Spirit should teach you that you ought to

prepare for the ministry, do not quench the Spirit, or try to get rid of such thoughts. Do not indulge the idea that preaching is not a great business. An excellent missionary, now I believe in India, has seven sons. When they were quite young he prayed that God would make ministers of all of them. And why? (1.) He wished them to be very useful in the world. (2.) He wished them to go to heaven, and shine there. He remembered that the Bible says, "He that winneth souls is wise; and he that turneth many to righteousness shall shine as the stars forever and ever."

Well, the last I heard of that minister and his family was that his prayer is likely to be granted. Several of his sons have already entered the ministry, and the others are on the way. So he is indeed a happy man. Who would not be willing to suffer some reproach and hardship to be the means of teaching the ignorant, comforting the sick and afflicted, and saving sinners from endless ruin, and thus to please God, and enjoy forever a seat near the Saviour in heaven?

2. Even *good* preachers do not please *everybody*. Though Christ was the best preacher that ever lived, there were many who despised and rejected him, and finally crucified him. O what wickedness and cruelty! Children, learn from this not to take it for granted that a man who preaches is unfit to preach merely because some do not like him, and make sport of him. The best preachers in the world have been ridiculed and persecuted by wicked men. Those great and good men, John Wesley and George Whitefield, frequently tried to preach when stones and putrid eggs were thrown at them. At one time a large stone hit Mr. Whitefield on his forehead, and although it made a deep gash, and the blood flowed down his cheek, mingling with his tears of pity for his persecutors, he kept on preaching, and God greatly blessed his labors.

Be careful, children, how you indulge in a fault-finding spirit toward preachers of the Gospel. I have known some children come home from meeting and speak lightly of the preacher, as though *they* were wiser and better than their teacher. This does not look well, and besides such conduct is very wicked; for although he may not be a splendid preacher, (God does not send out many splendid preachers,) if God has sent him, by despising the humble minister you are trifling with your Maker, who sent him. The safest way is to "speak evil of no man," and then you will be sure not to condemn whom the great God approves.

3. We should be very thankful for the privilege of hearing the Gospel preached. Although it is not our privilege to hear it from the lips of the Saviour himself, we can hear the same precious truths which he preached. They are as applicable to us as they were to those to whom Jesus preached. Besides, *Christ is always present*, though we cannot see him when his servants preach. He promised to be with his ministers "always, even unto the end of the world," to help them preach the Gospel. O, if Jesus takes so much pains to have the Gospel preached to us, how

thankful should we be that we are permitted to hear it! And if he is always present in the congregation, he sees just how we hear, and knows how we feel. Let us, then, try to listen as attentively and thankfully as we would if we could see the Saviour in the Church as plainly as he sees us.

4. *Hearing* the truth gladly will do us but little good unless we also *obey* the truth. I fear when Christ preached in person, there were many who heard him gladly that did not follow his instructions. They were glad to hear that he came from heaven to die for them, but were unwilling to live for him. So there are many now who are glad to hear that Jesus came to save them from their sins, who are unwilling to give up their sins. They are glad to hear that Christ died for them, but are unwilling that he should reign over them. Let us remember that we should not only hear the Gospel, and hear it gladly, but believe it with all our heart; and we do not believe it with all the heart unless we do just what it re-

quires us to do. And let us also remember that Christ is coming again to earth ; not, however, as a poor traveling preacher, but as a mighty Judge, and all mankind will stand before him to answer how they have listened to and observed his messages of love.

O, then, let us take heed how we hear the Gospel preached. Let us hear it gladly, attentively, and obediently. Then, when he comes in the clouds of heaven, with power and great glory, with all his holy angels with him, and, with a voice louder than seven thunders, shall rouse the dead from their graves, and summon all that are living and have ever lived to his bar, we shall hear him gladly as he says to the righteous: "Well done, thou good and faithful servant; thou hast been faithful over a few things, I will make thee a ruler over many things : enter thou into the joy of thy Lord."

HEARING CHRIST.

Now therefore hearken unto me, O ye children!—
PROV. viii, 32.

THERE are many lovely sights, but none so lovely as a religious youth. What a lovely object is a large ship riding majestically upon the waves of the sea, with all her sails spread out to receive the winds, which waft her onward to distant shores! What a lovely sight is an orchard filled with fruit-trees of rich variety, beautified with blossoms which scent the very air with their fragrant perfume! What a lovely sight is a flock of lambs in the month of May, sporting together on a green meadow beside a flowing stream clear as crystal! There is something lovelier still, lovelier than them all. And what is that? Little children who love Jesus, who serve God, and who have begun the journey to the heavenly paradise. This is, indeed, a lovely sight. It is one which is worthy to be looked upon by cherubim; it is one which angels admire.

My dear little ones, I pray God that you may afford this lovely sight! This you can never afford unless you *hear* Christ's voice, *believe* Christ's Gospel, and *obey* Christ's law. Does any one say, "This is all true, but I cannot, I cannot; I have tried, and I find I have no strength; I am like the blind man who cannot see, and the lame man who cannot walk?" If you really feel and think what you say, I am well pleased. It is a promising mark, for there is always great hope of that child who sees his weakness and his sins. Remember this, dear children— Christ has grace and strength; he is willing to give you grace and strength, to enable you to hear his voice, to believe his Gospel, and to obey his law. He waits to be asked, and promises that, when he is asked, he will give, and you shall receive. And O how sweetly he says to you in the text, "Now, therefore, hearken unto me, O ye children!"

May the Holy Spirit give me grace, that

I may tell you what it is to HEARKEN unto Christ!

1. To hearken unto Christ is to *hear* his voice. Christ has a voice in heaven, but we cannot hear it. Your pious friends, whose bodies are sleeping in the grave, and whose souls are in glory, they now hear Christ's voice in heaven. It is a voice which is sweeter than the music of angels. You and I shall never hear that voice till we arrive at heaven. O that we may arrive at that holy, happy place!

Christ has a voice on earth as well as in heaven. That voice is the *Gospel*. When the Gospel is preached that voice is uttered. When the Gospel is preached Christ speaks. We sometimes say, when we hear the thunder roar, Jehovah speaks. Assuredly, my dear children, when the Gospel is preached Jesus speaks. Surely, when Jesus speaks you should hear. What will a dear young acquaintance or companion think of you, if you refuse to hear him when he speaks to you? And O! what will Jesus think if you refuse to hear him when he speaks?

Christ's voice deserves well to be heard. It is a *wise* voice, and they who hearken to it get wisdom. They who do not hearken to it can get no wisdom. They live fools, and, if grace do not change their hearts, they die fools.

Christ's voice is a *kind* voice. The little child thinks the voice of his mother kind, and so it is; he will know it among a hundred. Have you not often observed how kindly a mother speaks to her children? No mother's voice is so kindly as the voice of Christ. O how kindly he speaks in the Gospel of little children! He says, Matt. xix, 14, "Suffer little children to come unto me, and forbid them not." Now, is not that a kindly voice?

Christ's voice is an *entreating* voice. He says, Prov. iv, 10, "Hear, O my son, and receive my sayings; and the years of thy life shall be many." He says in another place, chap. viii, 4, "Unto you, O men, I call, and my voice is to the sons of men." Verse 17: "I love them that love me, and they that seek me early shall find me."

His voice is a *pardoning* voice. My dear children, though you are young, you are sinners. Though you are young, you have offended God. Though you are young, you deserve punishment. Though you are young, you must perish if your sins are not forgiven. In the preaching of the Gospel the blessed, lovely Jesus declares he is willing to pardon poor sinners who come to him. O yes! and he pardons all who come. He rejects none, he refuses none. To those who come he thus speaks: "I, even I, am he who blotteth out all your transgressions for my name's sake." Isaiah xliii, 25.

His voice is a *comforting* voice. When you are confined by sickness to your bed, is it not delightful to your heart to hear the comforting, affectionate voice of a loving, tender-hearted mother? Christ's voice is a most comforting voice; it can comfort all who are afflicted. It can comfort little children who have lost their fathers and mothers, who are helpless orphans. His voice has comforted thousands, and his voice can comfort you. It has comforted children as young, and younger than you. It has comforted them so much, that they have sometimes forgot their pains and sufferings. It has comforted them so much, that they have sometimes smiled at death with his pale countenance, and have sung sweet praises with their dying breath. What I have now told you was remarkably displayed in a dear little girl who died, aged only seven years. She loved prayer, and had learned many hymns, which she often repeated on her dying bed. When her little mouth was scarcely able to speak, and a very short while before her lips were silent in death, she uttered the following lines:—

"With thoughts of Christ, and things divine,
Fill up this foolish heart of mine,
That, hoping pardon through his blood,
I may lie down and wake with God."

Before her spirit fled to heaven she repeated distinctly the Lord's Prayer. A little after she said, "I see angels," then laid down her head and died.

O what a comforting voice is the voice of Christ, that could comfort a child so

young, and a child so afflicted! Surely
such a voice deserves to be heard:—

> " Now therefore hearken to my word,
> Ye children, and be wise:—
> Happy the man that keeps my ways;
> The man that shuns them dies."

2. Suffer me to inform you further, that
to hearken unto Christ is to *believe his
Gospel*. Do you know the meaning of
the word *Gospel?* It signifies *good tidings*.
If there be a man lying in a dungeon,
condemned to die, will not the news of
pardon from the governor be good tidings?
O yes! it will make the poor man to sing
and dance for joy! The Gospel brings
such good tidings. It brings the kind and
merciful news that God is willing to pardon the poor wretched sinner. Is there a
child weeping on account of his sins, and
saying, "I am afraid there is no mercy
for *me*, I am afraid that I am lost forever?" O what joy will pass through the
mind of the afflicted child to inform him
that, though he is a great sinner, there is
a great Saviour,—that, though his sins are
many, they may be forgiven,—that, though

he deserves hell, yet he may obtain heaven!
What is it which tells this? It is the Gospel. If it had not been for the Gospel
this had never been known. Surely such
a gospel deserves the name of *glad
tidings.*

This is all very true; but, if you do not
believe the Gospel, it will do you no good.
Dear children, you can never be made
better by the Gospel unless you believe it;
but, the moment you believe it, the Gospel will become your light, your life, your
joy. O may the Gospel become your
light, your life, your joy!

What is it to believe the Gospel? In
answering this question, I will endeavor
to make it as plain as I can to little
children.

To believe the Gospel is to believe that
Christ *speaks* in the Gospel. When a
son reads his father's letter he says, "I
know my father speaks in that letter."
When a believing child hears the Gospel
he says, "I know my dear Saviour speaks
in the Gospel."

This is not all. To believe the Gospel

is to believe that Christ speaks *to you*—
yes, to you, as really as if your name were
mentioned aloud. Dear children, when
Christ's ministers are preaching, it is truly
delightful if you can say within yourselves, "Christ is speaking to me!"

To believe the Gospel is to believe that
Christ *died* for you. To believe he died
will do you no good, if you do not believe
he died for you. O! that child is blessed
who can say from the heart, "When
Christ hung on the cross he thought on
me—he died for me!" May God enable
you, my young friends, to say the same,
and you shall be blessed too!

To believe the Gospel is to *receive* all
the blessings the Gospel makes known.
The Gospel makes known Christ as the
greatest and best of gifts. To believe the
Gospel is to receive Christ, and all good
things with him. And what do they receive who receive Christ? They receive
pardon, peace, hope, joy, and heaven.

Never forget this, that you have no
strength of your own to believe the Gospel. If you forget this you may be ruined

forever. There is only one who can instruct you in the lesson of believing. Do you know who he is? He is the Holy Spirit.

3. To hearken unto Christ is to *obey his laws*. It is not enough to hear Christ's laws. It is not enough to know them. They must be obeyed as well as known. Christ is a master; he is a kind master. You are all his creatures, and you should be all his servants. He made you, therefore you should obey him. He preserves you, therefore you should obey him. But, above all, he died to redeem you, to keep you from a miserable hell, and to convey you to a happy, happy heaven; therefore you ought to obey him.

O what blessed children will you be if you obey him! He pronounces all such persons blessed; and whom he blesses, they must be blessed. Rev. xxii, 14: "Blessed are they who do his commandments, for they shall have a right to the tree of life."

THE TRANSGRESSOR.

The way of transgressors is hard.—Prov. xiii, 15.

THERE was once a very great and good man who had an unusually promising son, possessed not only of a fine form and features, but blest with a mind of uncommon strength. The father, who was a powerful king, knew that the success of his son in life depended not on his beauty, nor his mental ability, but upon goodness of heart; so one day he called his son to him, and gave him in substance the following advice:—"Solomon, my son, if you would be truly wise and prosperous, acquaint yourself with God, by reading his word and praying to him every day. Serve him with a sincere heart and willing mind, for the Lord searches all hearts, and knows who serve him truly, and who do so only in form. If thou seek him, he will surely be found of thee; but if thou forsake him, he will cast thee off forever."

Now, these good counsels for a while seemed to have a favorable effect upon Solomon. He did seek the Lord, and he was so prospered that he became the greatest, wisest, and richest king in the world. But after a while he began to be vain, proud, and disobedient to God, until he became very wicked and very unhappy. Before he died he confessed that there was no peace to the wicked, and wrote the words of my text, "the way of transgressors is hard," that others might learn from his sufferings to shun the course he had taken. Surely, if Solomon, with all his knowledge, wealth, and power, found the way of transgressors hard, it cannot be less so to any of my young readers.

Now, children, if you will give me your close attention, I will try to explain to you more particularly *what it is to be a transgressor*, and then in my next discourse will show some of the hardships he has to endure.

What would you think of a school where there was no order kept, no rules to be observed? Would you like to attend a school where all the children, bad as well as good, had liberty to do as they pleased? I think not. You know all good schools have good teachers and good regulations. I have been in some schools where the teacher, every week, if not every day, reads his rules, that the scholars may not forget them. Sometimes I have seen them printed and pasted up on the wall, where the children may see and read them for themselves. A transgressor in a school or academy is one who breaks the laws of the school.

Now, if your teacher should keep his rules in his pocket and never let you know what they were, though you might act contrary to some of them, you would not feel that you were a transgressor, especially if you were desirous of knowing what the rules were, but could not get the desired information. But if the laws were read, and you should put your fingers in your ears, because you did not wish to know what they were, or they were nailed up and you would not look at them, your guilt would be increased by such willful ignorance.

The world, children, is like a great school-house. God is the teacher, and we are all scholars. The Bible is the principal book for us to study, and contains the rules of the school; and one great object of the blessed Sabbath school is to furnish children the means of learning what these Bible rules of the great God are, and how to keep them.

But suppose, in the day-school that you attend, your teacher had a rule which it was impossible for you to obey; for instance, to read a chapter from the Hebrew Bible every day, when you had never learned even the alphabet of that language, would you feel guilty if you did not observe it? But again, suppose that he required you to take your slate to perform a difficult example in the arithmetic, (which you had tried in vain to work out,) with the promise that he would look over with you and furnish such assistance as you might need, and that you should refuse to do anything because unable to do it all alone, would you not be a transgressor?

You see, then, from what I have said, that God is our great master, and because he is a good master he has a good law, which he has written down in a book called the Bible, or THE BOOK. He has caused it to be written so plainly, and in our own language, that even children may understand what is required of them to do, and to avoid doing. You are all able to keep his commandments, for his "yoke is easy," especially to those who are willing to receive the aid of his Spirit, promised to all who ask such aid. So you see if it is wicked to break the laws of your school teacher, or the rules of your parents, it is far more wicked to break the laws of God; for you have much greater reason to love and obey your great Creator than to obey any creature he has made; and yet it is a sad truth that many children sin every day against God.

I am going now to mention several classes of transgressors, that you may know whether you are a sinner, and exposed to the hardships of the wicked.

In the first place, all those children are transgressors *who do what God has plainly forbidden.* Thus, as God in his word has forbidden the use of profane language, and has declared he "will not hold him guiltless who takes his name in vain," if you indulge in swearing or irreverence, even if your words are not so awfully blasphemous as pirates and drunkards use, but which sound very much like their language, you are a transgressor. As God has said, "All liars shall have their part in the lake that burns with fire and brimstone," though you may never commit the crime of perjury, if you are guilty of what are sometimes called "white lies," that is, concealing part of the truth, or in any way, by act, or word, or look, endeavoring to deceive or make a wrong impression, it is plain you are a transgressor. Again, as God has said, "Thou shalt not steal;" if you should without liberty take the least thing that did not belong to you, or find a penknife and say nothing about

it, for fear the owner might apply for it if
you should make your discovery known,
why you are a thief. And as God has said,
"Thou shalt not kill," though you may
never dare even to think of the dreadful
crime of murdering any human being, yet
if you love to torture dumb animals, and
delight in teasing your brothers and sisters,
and indulge a feeling of hatred to any one,
and wish him evil, you are a transgressor
of the sixth commandment in God's law.

I have mentioned only these few things
which God has forbidden, to show you
how "exceeding broad" his law is; and I
trust you will remember that whosoever
does what God has plainly forbidden is a
transgressor, and he will sooner or later
find that his way is hard.

In the second place, those children are
transgressors who *refuse to do what God
has required*. There are many who seem
to think they are very good because they
do not commit shameful sins, such as
swearing, lying, stealing, and uncleanness,
and yet, if they reflect a moment, they
must be convinced that they neglect to

do many things that God has plainly enjoined.

Children, you are placed in this world not only to do no harm, but to do all the good you can; to serve God, and be useful to all around you. Suppose, for illustration, that you were a poor orphan boy, without either parents or home, and almost starved and naked, and you should go to the door of a good man who is very rich, and should ask him to take you into his family. The kind man consents, on condition that you try to be as *useful* to him as you can. But instead of being as useful as possible, though you should not steal, or swear, or set fire to his barn, you should neglect to do more than half of the reasonable service required, would you not feel that the master of the house would serve you right if he should turn you into the street for your willful disobedience, although you might avoid doing positive mischief? The truth is, however, if you are not doing good, you are almost certain to be doing evil; for

"Satan finds some mischief still
For idle hands to do."

Now, if you carefully study God's rules, you will find that he wants you to honor your parents, to remember the Sabbath-day and keep it holy, to believe in the Lord Jesus Christ who died for you, and like him to go about doing good to every-body; and to live a prayerful, grateful, contented, and industrious life; and hence, if you neglect these, or other duties, you are in danger of suffering the hardships of the transgressor.

In the third place, those children are transgressors who do what they are re-quired to do *in a wrong spirit*. To explain this, I will tell you a short story. There was a woman in feeble health, whose husband died and left her in charge of three boys and one girl. The names of the three boys, we will suppose, were Henry, Edgar, and John; and the name of the little girl was Mary. One day, the mother being more unwell than usual, sent Mary to the barn where her brothers were playing, and called them into the house. The sick widow desired Henry to go and call in the family physician. She told Edgar to go to the grocery and get some rice, and John to fill the wood-box, which was empty, and kindle the fire, which was entirely out. Now, as the boys were, when called, very much interested in their play, two of them showed no little impatience at the interruption. Indeed, the oldest had so little regard for his poor, sick mother, that he would not even start for the doctor until he was threatened with punishment, when he went moping off, grumbling as he went. Edgar, more fearless, did not seem to dread the blows which his feeble mother could inflict, but was induced to go after being promised that when he should return he might take a ride on old Dobbin. But John, as soon as he learned the wishes of his mother, not only with promptitude and cheerfulness did what she expressly desired, but several other little things which he thought would add to her comfort.

Now, do you not see a great difference in the disposition of these three boys? And yet they all did what their mother required of them. Two of them obeyed in an improper spirit, and in the sight of God and their mother were transgressors. Henry obeyed, not because he loved his mother, but dreaded the rod; Edgar, not from love of a tender parent, but the love of a ride on old Dobbin; while John obeyed, because, so ardently did he love his mother, that he took far more pleasure in trying to help and comfort her in her affliction, than to engage in any amusement, however agreeable, with his playmates.

So, my young friends, you see that, although God wants you to serve him, unless you pray to him, read his word, keep the Sabbath, and do all he requires with a willing mind and a loving heart, after all you are transgressors. Therefore, if you would not be numbered among those whose way is hard, you must not only cease to do evil and learn to do well, but see that your feelings are right toward God, that you may be able to do what God desires in a right spirit.

In closing this discourse, children, I wish to impress three things on your minds.

1. All children who are capable of

reading this book, are transgressors of God's law, until their hearts are changed by the Holy Spirit. You, no doubt, while reading this sermon, have been convinced that you are a sinner; and unless forgiven, and your naughty heart made to love and obey God, you must suffer his awful displeasure. Go at once, then, to the Saviour, and ask him to forgive your transgressions and give you a new heart, that hereafter you may not only serve God and keep all his commandments, but *love* to serve him all your days.

2. A person is not obliged to commit *many* sins to be a great sinner. One sin is enough to make you a transgressor, and unless repented of will ruin you forever. Adam and Eve, you know, just picked fruit *once*, and ate it contrary to the command of God, and O how guilty and wretched it made them feel! How awfully it displeased their Maker, and what dreadful misery this one act brought upon millions and millions, even of children as well as others! So Moses *once* spoke unadvisedly with his lips, and God

did not permit him to put his foot upon the promised land; and Ananias and Sapphira were punished with instant death just for telling *one* falsehood. Beware, then, of what seems *one little sin*.

Finally, some persons who seem very good are, in the sight of God, more wicked than others whose outward appearance and conduct are very vicious. And the reason is, some show their worst side, while others conceal their crimes; some have been trained up to do wrong by ignorant and wicked parents; while others have awfully wicked, deceitful, and rebellious hearts, in opposition to the prayers, instruction, and tears of pious parents and faithful Sunday-school teachers. God forbid that any of my beloved readers shall ever be numbered with this class! Then, while we examine our own hearts, let us be charitable in our judgment of the hearts of others. Let the prayer of each of us be: "Search me, O God, and know my heart: try me, and know my thoughts: and see if there be any wicked way in me, and lead me in the way everlasting."

A HARD WAY.

The way of transgressors is hard.—Prov. xiii, 15.

My Young Friends, you have often seen the little bird which had been caught and confined in a cage. You have observed how sadly it looked, and how mournful was its song, if indeed it could sing at all, in its wire cell. And when the cage hung outside of the veranda on a bright morning, as its brother or sister birdlings flitted by its prison, and as it tried in vain to escape and enjoy its wonted freedom with them, how often have you thought it was hard for that little creature to be thus confined, which was made to soar aloft on its nimble wings, warble in the pure, free air of heaven, and drink the dew from the sweet flowers.

Some of you remember, not long since, while passing down street, how your heart ached as you saw a man unmercifully whipping a poor horse, because he could not draw so heavy a load as had been placed upon his cart. You cannot forget how the poor creature, with expanded nostrils, panted, and sweat, and tugged; and how, as he looked around upon his brutal master, who had already raised huge ridges upon his side with the cart-whip, seemed to say, as well as a dumb animal could say, "O do not whip me so, for I am pulling as hard as I possibly can." As the tears streamed from your eyes to see this cruelty, and hear the oaths of the wretch who was flogging his faithful beast for a fault of his own, you could not help thinking of the dreadful hardships which many of God's creatures are compelled to suffer.

But, children, there is one creature that endures far greater hardships than the en-caged bird and the cart-horse. It is the character I tried to describe in the pre-ceding discourse, namely, the *transgressor of God's law.* A wicked human being is compelled to bear more humiliating and painful sufferings than animals can endure, with the additional reflection that his hardships are the result of wrongdoing, and that he brings them all on himself.

Hoping you will keep in mind what it is to be a transgressor of God's law, I wish now to show you some of the hardships he has to bear, unless he gets out of the way of transgression.

It is true that before a person commits a sin, it does not seem to him that the consequences will be very serious. A few years since a small boy thought it would do no harm to have a little sport with some live coals, although his mother strictly charged him when she left home not to play with the fire. For a while it did no injury; but at length the wind arose, and a spark caught among the leaves of a large forest near by, and in a few moments, as the weather was very dry, the whole woods were on fire. The fire raged dreadfully for several days before it could be extinguished; and, what is worse than all, a house and barn in the middle of the forest were consumed, and a woman with a sweet little babe were burned up.

Achan, who stole the wedge of gold,

THE SIN OF ACHAN.

and other things, as you will see by reading the seventh chapter of the Book of Joshua, thought, by converting these spoils to his own use, nobody would know it; but he had a different view of the matter when he saw what a terrible calamity his crime had brought upon the whole army of Israel, and especially when not only himself, but all his family, were suffering the horrible punishment of being stoned to death for this sin.

Now I will mention a few particular reasons why the way of transgressors is hard. This way is hard, because,

1. *One sin is almost certain to lead to many others.* Perhaps I cannot show this more clearly than by relating to you the confession of Achan. He said, " I have sinned against the Lord God of Israel, and thus and thus have I done. When I saw among the spoils a goodly Babylonish garment, and two hundred shekels of silver, and a wedge of gold of fifty shekels weight, then I coveted them, and took them; and behold, they are hid in the earth in the midst of my tent, and the

silver under it." I suppose that Achan did not mean to steal when he first commenced peeping and prying around, to see what he could discover among the goods which God had commanded the Israelites to let alone. His first sin, then, was vain curiosity—he looked; curiosity excited his covetousness, he lusted after the gold and silver; his covetousness set his fingers at work, he took them; and then his guilt and shame made him conceal his crime, which was soon detected, and he punished as before stated.

When I was at Auburn, a few months since, a young man was liberated from the great stone prison there. He had been locked up for breaking into a house one night. After being confined several dreary months, his mother, who had been to the governor of the state with a great many petitions, obtained a pardon on the ground that his former character had been good. It was stated that his crime of burglary, or house-breaking, was the result of his not having the courage to say No when some rude young men invited him to go to a tavern for amusement. His first sin was in going with bad company; the next was in drinking intoxicating liquor; and then, becoming insane, he scarcely knew or cared what he did, broke into a house, and was shut up in a felon's cell, and compelled to wear striped clothes as an outlaw, to his lasting disgrace and the great grief of his friends, who were very respectable. He seemed to feel very bad for what he had done; and the day he left the prison took the pledge of total abstinence, and declared he would in future be more careful how he associated with wicked young men.

You see, then, that the way of transgressors is hard, because one sin, however small, is almost certain to be followed by several others which are far greater.

2. *When sin has became a habit, it is almost impossible so stop sinning.* A certain boy, on a winter morning, thought he would have fine fun. There was a high, steep hill, not far from his father's house; and though its side was covered with ice, like crystal, almost to the top, he man-

aged, in disobedience to his parents' wishes, to get to the summit with his iron-shod sled. He thought of riding part of the way down, but intended to stop before he came to the steepest place near the base. So, seating himself, after some little effort to get under way, he rode very agreeably until he reached the most slippery part of the hill, when the sled had acquired such force that he could not check its speed. With frightful rapidity it dashed down the steep, until, coming in contact with a huge stone at the foot of the hill, the sled was broken into pieces, and the disobedient boy had his hip dislocated, and became a poor suffering invalid for life. Thus it is, children, when you allow yourselves to commit one sin, you are almost certain to keep on sinning. This sinning on becomes what is called a habit; and when a habit of sinning is formed, it is almost impossible to stop. Let me explain this still more clearly.

A few years since, an eminent physician unfortunately formed the habit of drinking rum. The habit increased upon him, so that it soon made fearful havoc with his health. Everybody but the rumseller seemed to be very sorry; for he was, in other respects, a most amiable man and excellent physician. A friend of his, one day, ventured to tell him how much anxiety was felt in his behalf, and expressed the fear that liquor would sooner or later destroy him, unless he abandoned the habit. The doctor seemed neither angry nor alarmed at this reproof, but replied: "I know my condition as well as any man can tell me. I know I cannot live six months unless I stop drinking;" but with emotion added, "I cannot stop drinking!" And, sad to say, he did not stop until death stopped him, which event occurred a short time before the time he predicted had expired. Surely the way of transgressors is hard.

3. Again, sinning is hard business, because *you cannot undo a wrong action when once committed.* It is true, God is so merciful, that for Christ's sake you may be forgiven the guilt, and saved from the punishment of sin, if you truly repent.

but you cannot undo the sin itself; that is, you cannot place things back as they were before. You may burn a frightful wound upon your cheek; and though the wound may be healed, there will always be a scar left, so that you will never be as comely as before the accident. So sin leaves a scar upon the soul that will never be entirely effaced. But this is not all; the consequences upon others you can never undo.

A boy was once playing with a piece of iron in the window of the fourth story of a house. Seeing one of his schoolmates pass along the walk below, he thought he would surprise him by throwing the piece of iron just before him on the walk. Without a moment's reflection down it went. As soon, however, as the weight was dropped he was very sorry, for fear it might hit his friend, and perhaps kill him. He would have given the world to arrest its progress, and get it back again into his own hand. But, alas! vain wish: his fears were realized. The iron fell directly upon the head of the unsuspecting boy, penetrated his skull, and he almost instantly died. Among the mourners at the funeral, and a long time afterward, no one wept so bitterly as the thoughtless boy, who in a moment had, by one careless act, killed a beloved child and playmate.

An old man, who had spent a long life in poisoning the minds of others with wicked books and pamphlets which he had written, became convinced at last that the Bible he had ridiculed was true, and that the sentiments he had published were false, and calculated to do great mischief. He earnestly begged, and, it is hoped, obtained forgiveness of God for what he had done, but he could not forgive himself; for, thought he, "I have set the ball of infidelity rolling, and I cannot stop it. It will keep rolling and rolling long after I am dead, producing untold and irreparable mischief wherever it goes." Now, children, think of this; you can set a ball of sin rolling in a moment, but when you have put it in motion it is out of your power to stop it, and its dreadful effects in this world and the world to come it is impossible to foresee. O what a bitter thing sin is! what terrible results have followed from one sinful act, one sinful word, one sinful thought!

4. The way of the transgressor is hard, because *he is sure to be detected in his iniquity.* Little boys and girls are sometimes tempted to do naughty things, which they could not be persuaded even to think of doing if Satan did not whisper, "Nobody will know it." What a liar the old serpent is! Children, remember that you cannot do a wicked thing, even in midnight darkness, nor speak a wicked word, nor think a wicked thought, but there are at least two that know all about it. One of these is the great God, who knows all things, and the other is yourself. And whatever opinion your parents or others may have of you before they find out your bad deeds, you will have a very mean opinion of yourself. Besides, in nine cases out of ten, he who commits secret sins which he hopes to conceal, is detected not only by God and his own

conscience, but by his fellow-men even in this world. The truth of the old saying, "Murder will out," has been verified to the sorrow of thousands, who did not believe it until too late. The Bible contains the same sentiment in the following words, which I wish you would find and commit to memory: "Be sure your sin will find you out."

5. Once more, *if you commit a sin you cannot forget it.* Now if a person who does a wicked thing could banish the thought of what he had done, and never think of it again, it would not be quite so hard; but here is the difficulty. God has made the memory so that it can never forget what you have done, whether good or evil. It is true, after a wicked action, you may get it out of the mind, and keep it out *for a while,* as Joseph's brethren did their iniquity in selling him to the Ishmaelites; but years afterward, when distress came upon them, and they were shut up in Egypt, how wretched they felt as they remembered how they had served their innocent brother, and deceived their

affectionate father. So it will be with you, if you transgress God's law. The memory is a scourge that never wears out, by which God punishes the wicked in this world and the world to come. A certain man, who had committed an awful crime, was shut up alone in a dark prison. He was the very picture of misery. And why? Not merely because he was confined in a little room in which the glorious sun never shone, nor because he had to work hard, for he had nothing to do; but because he could not *forget*. It was *think*, THINK, THINK, by day and by night. Thus he was continually tormented, and, what was worse than all, he saw no prospect of ever forgetting what mischief he had done to others, and what wretchedness he had brought upon himself.

6. But I have not time to mention all the hardships the transgressor of God's law will have to suffer, especially in the future, unless he repents and seeks forgiveness. I might speak of the horrors of a guilty conscience—of the terrors which get hold of the poor sinner when he

comes to die; and, by the way, those who are very wicked in their youth generally die young; they do "not live out half their days." But what are all the hardships that I have noticed compared to the everlasting punishment that God has prepared for the impenitent transgressor in the future world? O, children, if it is hard to be shut up in a solitary cell a few years, to live on bread and water, and have nothing to do but to think; can you bear the thought of being shut up in the prison of hell, to dwell in the blackness of darkness among devils and wicked spirits, where you will have nothing to do forever and ever but think what a fool you have been; what a good God you have disobeyed; what a blessed Saviour you have slighted; what kind parents you have grieved; how many hearts you have made to bleed, and what a blissful heaven you have lost, just by having your own way, instead of walking in the way of God's commandments.

Now let us learn from this subject at least these two things:—

1. *Sin is no trifle.* None but fools will make a mock of sin; and yet there are many fools in the world. Some years since a young man caught a very small rattlesnake alive, and thought he would tame it, and show his heroism in handling and caressing it. In vain was he warned that it was not safe to meddle with venomous reptiles. He thought it was so young that it could do him no harm, and that it was so tame that it had no inclination to bite. But one day while he was playing with the snake it suddenly snapped at his finger, and although the bite was so slight it was difficult to perceive that the skin was at all fractured, it was not long before the bitten finger began to swell, then his hand, then his arm, and finally his whole body became awfully inflamed by the deadly poison which had been diffused all through his system, and he died in dreadful agony. So, my young friends, it is with sin. Its beginnings may be small; but O, who can estimate the consequences? "It bites like a serpent, and stingeth like an adder." Surely, my young friends, sin

is no trifle. Beware, then, how you meddle with it.

2. *There is only one remedy for sin.* It is a disease like the bite of a rattlesnake, that will not work its own cure. No human skill can cure it. But there is a Physician who can. He was sent from heaven on purpose. His name was called Jesus, for he came to save his people from their sins. "He was wounded for our transgressions, he was bruised for our iniquities; the chastisement of our peace was upon him, and by his stripes we are healed." Yes, he tasted the bitterness of death for us, that we might drink of the cup of salvation. And there is no other remedy—no other name given under heaven by which guilt may be pardoned, and the terrible consequences of trangression of God's holy law avoided. O then, my young friends, look to him and be saved! As the Israelites, who had been bitten by fiery serpents, by the command of Moses looked to the uplifted brazen serpent and were healed, let me entreat all who have done those things you ought

not to have done, or left undone things which you ought to have done, to look right to Jesus by faith, and behold him extended, bleeding, and dying upon the cross for your offenses. If you look elsewhere for relief you will look in vain; but if you look to Jesus, believe in Jesus, love Jesus, and follow Jesus, you shall live: for the wages of sin is death, but the gift of God is eternal life through Jesus Christ our Lord.

THE BAD HEART.

The heart of the wicked is little worth.—Prov. x, 20.

A HEART that is little worth always meets with its punishment. Sometimes it meets its punishment in this world. If it is not changed before death, it never fails to meet with its punishment in the world to come. It is very dangerous for people to live in a house that is ready to fall; the sooner they get out of it the better. If they do not make haste to escape, the house may tumble down when they are fast asleep, and bury them in its ruins. It is as dangerous to live with a bad heart. If children whose hearts are little worth do not make haste to get them changed, they may be taken away by death, when all opportunities of getting their hearts made better will be forever lost!

I have read an affecting story of a large and beautiful town that was destroyed in a most shocking manner, and none were able to escape. Those who were the swiftest of foot were not able to flee; the richest noblemen and merchants had not time to get their horses out of the stable to avoid the calamity, so sudden was the destruction.

The name of the city was Herculaneum. It was a city of Naples, and stood near a mountain of which you may have heard— Mount Vesuvius. There is in the very top of that mountain a great opening, or mouth. Constantly the mouth sends forth smoke instead of breath, which ascends to the sky in black clouds. Very often this mouth utters the most awful murmuring sounds, as if it were the voices of evil spirits heard from afar! This dreadful mountain also at different times has sent out flames of fire, the brightness of which has been seen after the setting of the sun at an immense distance. This is not all; I have more to tell you; the very worst remains. The mountain at particular periods has sent from its horrid mouth streams of lava, red as fire itself, which have gushed down the sides of the mountain like a river of devouring flames.

As I told you a little while ago, the city of Herculaneum stood near that mountain. During the reign of Titus, the Roman emperor, this city was wholly ruined by the streams of burning lava! It poured down from the mount in such quantities as to cover the city, and in one day all the inhabitants were burned to death, and buried in a vast grave of living fire! O, it was a most affecting calamity! Magistrates on the bench of judgment, merchants in their counting-houses, shopkeepers while selling their goods, carpenters and masons while toiling at their ordinary employment, persons while attending the theater, the wicked while engaged in their haunts of iniquity, and little children in the streets and squares, while diverting themselves with their games and recreations—all of them were in a moment destroyed, and had no opportunity to run from the alarming visitation.

Do you not think, my beloved children, that it was a very dangerous thing to live in the neighborhood of such a mountain? Certainly it was. But mark what I have to say: it is as dangerous to live beside a bad heart. The poor inhabitants of Herculaneum perished because they dwelt so near the burning mount; and O! many, many thousands have perished, forever perished, because they lived and died with hearts which were *little worth!*

It is my design, through the aid of the Holy Spirit, to show you in what respects the heart of the wicked is *little worth.*

Were I, my young friends, to show you a garden full of weeds, would you consider such a garden valuable? You would look upon it as little worth. Were I to show you an old vessel filled with dust and ashes, and were I to ask you whether you considered it valuable, you would instantly reply, It is little worth. When I look into man's bad heart or soul, I see nothing valuable in it. I see that all which is in it is little worth—I see that all which comes from it is little worth. Surely, then, the heart must be *little worth* when all that is in it is little worth and when all that comes from it is little worth.

1. If you ask me, What do you see in the bad heart? in reply I say, I see the *hatred of God.* That is in every bad heart. It is this which makes bad hearts. If it were not for this there could be no bad hearts. The worst thing to be found in the heart of devils is this; the worst thing to be found in the heart of men is this. God is the best of beings, and is most worthy to be loved. They who hate the best of beings must be the worst of beings. God knows the heart well; and what does God say about the bad heart? He says, "The carnal mind is enmity against God." Rom. viii, 7.

2. Look with me into the bad heart, and you will see something else—you will see the *love of sin.* The heart must be little worth indeed if this is the case; for it hates that which deserves most to be loved, and loves that which deserves most to be hated. Such a heart must be thoroughly bad, and, more than everything we know, must be *little worth.* Sin is a murderer. Sin murders the happiness of the soul; and if a merciful God were not to prevent, sin would make it miserable through all eternity. Is not the heart little worth when it loves a murderer?

Many love sin because it gives them pleasures. All its pleasures are poison. There are several things very sweet and delicious in the mouth, but, when they go down into the belly they are bitter; they make the whole body shake, and they produce the most violent pains. This is exactly the case with the pleasures of sin: at first they are sweet, very sweet, but afterward they torment, they destroy. Surely the heart that loves sin must be *little worth!*

3. Look with me into the bad heart, and you will see something else: it is *indifference.* You know what it is to be indifferent about anything; it is, not to care whether you have it or not. The bad heart is indifferent; it has no care whether God be glorified or not. It must, then, be little worth. It is indifferent—it has no care whether the soul be saved or not; that is to say, it gives itself no concern at all about the soul. It must, then, be little worth.

What would you think of a sick man in great distress, who would take no cordial into his parched mouth if it were presented—who would take no medicine to lessen his agonizing pain—who would order a kind and skillful physician to go out of his house, and come near him no more;—what would you think of such a man? You must either think the man mad, or *indifferent* altogether to his interest. This is the case with bad children: they refuse the cordial of divine knowledge—they refuse the precious medicine of divine truth —they will have nothing to do with

Christ, the kind, the skillful Physician! And what must we think of such children? That they are indifferent about their souls. Alas! this is a sad case—a very sad case! To be indifferent whether their soul be lost or saved—to be indifferent whether it belong to Satan or Jesus—to be indifferent whether it be enslaved or free—to be indifferent whether it go to heaven or hell—is certainly a deplorable case indeed! Dear children, is it your case! If so, your heart is *little worth*, and you have great reason to be afraid.

If a jailer were to enter into one of the deepest and most wretched cells of a prison, and say to a poor criminal, "Friend, I have got good news to tell you!" perhaps the criminal would reply, "And what have you got to say to me?" The jailer might be commissioned to tell him, "I am sent to offer you your pardon—your liberty—your life! Rise up till I take from your hands those chains, and from your feet those iron fetters. Come along with me, and wash your body clean, and lay aside those rags which scarcely cover you, and

I will give you change of raiment, comely garments of beauty." If the poor criminal were to say, "Depart, depart; I prefer this dungeon to a palace, my iron fetters to golden chains and bracelets, my bread and water to a delicious feast of the most precious dainties: depart, depart; for I prefer bondage to liberty, my rags to robes, and death to life!"—if you heard the poor criminal speak in such language, would it not be ready to make you weep? yes, to break your heart? I know it would distress your feeling mind. You would be ready to say, "There never was so deluded a fool as this." My young friends, if you are indifferent about the salvation of your soul, you are such fools, and I cannot think of you without pitying you! May the Spirit of God fill your heart with grace, then you shall be delivered from spiritual bondage, you shall be clothed with the garments of salvation, you shall be made heirs of heaven!

May a spiritual change be produced on you similar to the change produced on the amiable child whom I am about to introduce to you. Her name was Mary. She lived and died in the county of Devon. She was by profession a lace-maker. Her endeavor to learn this business brought on the illness which terminated in death! God opened her eyes to see her heart: she was often heard to say, "I hope the dear, dear Saviour will pardon me—I am little and young, but I am a great sinner—I am but a child, but I am a great sinner. I have deserved the wrath of God, and the wrath of God is terrible indeed, for he can make sinners feel all the miseries of this life, the pains of death, and the torments of hell forever: but God is merciful, and he has sent Jesus Christ into the world to become the Saviour of sinful creatures. This I should not have known but for the Sunday school."

The following expressions, which she uttered on her dying bed, deserve to be recorded. They show that her heart, which was once little worth, filled with nothing but sin, was made unspeakably precious, filled with grace. She said, "God has afflicted my body, but I know it is for my good; blessed Lord, support me, and save me, a poor sinner! I can trust my body and soul in the hands of my dear Saviour; it is better for me to die *now ;* for if I were to live longer, I should commit more sin; and if I die now, I shall go to my dear Saviour."

The sayings of this child melted her father's heart, and before she died she had the pleasure of hearing him pray for the *first time.* This produced upon her face a most heavenly, joyful smile. It was her earnest wish that, before she died, God would give her some pleasing mark of the salvation of her father. God heard the prayer of the child for the parent, and the father was made the *spiritual son* of his own daughter. Since her death he has continued steadfast in the faith. A short time previous to her dissolution she said, "Lord, take me!—Jesus, take me!" and in a few hours her spirit fled to heaven, aged only thirteen years.

THE NEW HEART.

*A new heart also will I give you.—*EZEK. xxxvi, 26.

THERE was a good man, of whom you must have often heard, and of whom many of you must have often read—I mean Moses. He lived more than three thousand three hundred and ninety-four years ago. One day God appeared unto him in glorious flames of fire. The Lord told this good man, this great prophet, that he had appointed him to lead all the children of Israel out of the land of Egypt, and from the house of bondage. He further said to him that he must go without delay and inform King Pharaoh that he had orders from God to take the children of Israel out of Egypt. Moses said he was afraid to go, lest the king might think he was a wild impostor, and put him to death. He was also afraid the children of Israel would not believe him, and that they would perhaps say, "The Lord

hath not appeared unto thee." Exod. iv, 1.
"And the Lord said unto him, What is
that in thine hand? And he said, A rod.
And he said, Cast it on the ground. And
he cast it on the ground, and it became a
serpent: and Moses fled from before it.
And the Lord said unto Moses, Put forth
thy hand, and take it by the tail. And
he put forth his hand, and caught it, and
it became a rod in his hand." Exod. iv, 2–4.

Now, my young friends, what do you
think of all this? Is not this astonishing
—a rod changed into a serpent, a living
creature, moving on the ground, with
bright sparkling eyes? You will be ready
to say, "What a remarkable change is
this!—nothing but the power of God could
have done it!" If you think so you think
right. This same rod of Moses underwent
another great change. In one moment it
was changed into a most lovely branch
covered with leaves; on one part were
seen delightful blossoms, which perfumed
the very air with their fragrant odor,
and in another part were seen clusters of
almonds. You may read an account of

this in Numbers xvii. This was certainly another remarkable change. You will be ready to say, "Nothing but the power of God could have done this!"

I have now to speak to you of another change; and that is, the change which takes place upon the heart in the day of conversion. You know that the souls of children are very bad before God works upon them by his grace. The heart, before God changes it, is like a piece of hard flint. A flint can feel nothing; and the heart, before God changes it, can feel no love to God, and no hatred to sin. There is as little love to God in the bad heart as there is life in a dead man—and that is none.

In the day of conversion, namely, the day when God makes the bad heart good, there is as wonderful a change produced upon it as the change which took place on the rod of Moses when it was changed into a serpent, and from a serpent into a rod again, and from a dry stick into a fresh, green, fragrant almond branch, covered with blooming blossoms and ripe almonds.

If you saw a loathsome toad instantly changed into a turtle-dove, or a tottering cottage changed into a magnificent palace built of marble white as snow, adorned by rows of pillars, and its turrets gilded with gold, the change would be nothing compared with that which takes place upon the bad heart when God makes it good, compared with the change which takes place upon the old heart when God makes it new.

When I speak to you of the new heart, O may the Holy Spirit enable you earnestly to pray, " Lord, give me a new heart!"

1. The new heart has *new thoughts.* I cannot easily tell you what a thought is. You know it. You constantly feel thoughts in your minds. You know you are always thinking; you never stop thinking. You may stop walking or speaking, but you cannot stop thinking. Nay, if you try with all your might to give over thinking, you will find it is beyond your power. O what a mystery is this!

You know, my dear young friends, that

there is a resemblance in children to their parents. There is also a great resemblance between the thoughts and the heart. If the heart is bad, the thoughts will be bad; and if the heart is good, the thoughts will be good. If God give you a *new* heart, he will give you *new* thoughts. The old heart thinks on the world, the new heart thinks on God. The old heart thinks on sinful actions, the new heart thinks on holy duties.

Thoughts resemble bees. In their number they resemble them. What crowds of bees are there in a hive! and what crowds of thoughts are there in the heart! They resemble bees in their activity. Bees are remarkably active, and the thoughts of the mind are as active. Bees go in search of honey, and they light on lovely flowers, and suck the delicious treasure out of the honey-cups. Good thoughts are like bees; they suck honey out of the flowers which grow in the Bible. But bad thoughts are like wasps, which, I am told, never suck honey, but poison. There is a great difference between a wasp and a bee, but there is a greater difference between an old heart and a new, between old thoughts and new.

2. The new heart has *new desires*. My little children, you are always desiring something. You know, too, that you often desire what is not worth desiring, and wish to have what is not worth having. I will talk a little to you about desires. The old heart is filled with wicked desires, and the new heart is filled with holy desires. The old heart desires what does the soul harm, and the new heart desires what does it good. The old heart desires what God hates, the new heart desires what God loves.

Do you wish to know whether you have got new desires? I will tell you. Do you desire to know God, to fear God, to love God, to serve God, and to resemble God? Tell me, is this the case? If you can put your hand on your heart and say, Yes, then your desires are new, your heart is new.

3. The new heart has *new comforts*. My dear children, if a thing were to give

you comfort to-day which gave you pain yesterday, surely some change must have taken place upon you. Now, this is the case with children who have got new hearts: what once gave them pain, now gives them pleasure—what once gave them uneasiness, now gives them enjoyment.

Bad people try to make bad things their comforts; but they cannot do what they try to do. Bad things never have been comforts, and never shall be. It is a vain, a mad attempt. Never try to do this; for if you do, you shall most certainly be disappointed.

Good children are taught to make good things their comforts, and they are sure to find them comforts. Once the pleasures of sin were their false comforts, now the pleasures of religion are their real comforts. In what do pious children take comfort? This is a very important question, and I give to it the following answer: They take comfort in the love of God, they take comfort in the promises of God, they take comfort in the presence and fellowship of God, they take comfort in the salvation of their souls, by the obedience, sufferings, and death of the Son of God; they take comfort in their Bible, they take comfort in the house of God, in the preaching of the word, in the company of pious children, and in their hopes of a glorious heaven. Tell the truth: can you take comfort in any or in all of these? If so, I have no doubt whatever that your old heart is taken away, and that a new heart is given you.

4. The new heart has *new sorrows*. Be not alarmed when I tell you this. Good children need sorrows as long as they are in the world. The bitter sorrows of life prepare them for the sweet joys of heaven. When I say they have new sorrows, I mean this: that the things which gave them sorrow when they had the old heart, give them joy since they have got the new heart; and things which gave them delight when they had the old heart, give them grief since they received the new heart. Let me explain this a little more. Once they were grieved they had so little sinful pleasure: now they are grieved

they have so little grace. Once they were grieved when called to serve God; they would rather have gone six miles over a hard road, than have been obliged to sit one hour to hear a sermon. Now, what a change! They are grieved if anything arises to prevent them from entering God's house to hearken to the soft, mild, sweet strains of the trumpet—the silver trumpet of gospel love.

Once the company of the righteous gave them sorrow, now the company of the wicked gives them sorrow. Once the thoughts of religion gave them grief, now the thoughts of sin give them grief. My dear children, is this the case with you? If so, God has given you new hearts.

5. The new heart has *new hopes*. Perhaps there is scarcely a bad child to be found but will tell you he hopes, when death takes him, he shall go to heaven. The hopes of bad children are bad hopes. They are deceiving—they are destroying! Is there not something awful in hearing a bad boy on his death-bed saying he hopes to go to heaven?

The child who has the new heart has new hopes. His hopes are all laid on Jesus, and are, therefore, good hopes and sure hopes. May God graciously give you new hearts and new hopes!

It is with much pleasure I present before you a lovely instance of a little child, whose heart evidently appeared changed by divine grace. Long life was not given him, but a new heart was given him, and that was far better.

His disposition was lively, yet thoughtful. Most children are lively, but how few are thoughtful! He was both. He asked leave from his father, when a very little child, to go with him into his chamber. His father admitted him, and inquired if there was anything he wished his father to pray for, for his dear boy. The child replied with great sweetness, "That he might have a new heart, and a new spirit." For this the father prayed, and his prayer was heard.

God laid affliction upon the child! One day he was seen crying. His father asked the reason. The child answered, "He

was afraid he had not got a new heart!"
On this, he prayed with many tears that
God would prepare him for death. The
following conversation between the father
and him will most delightfully show what
grace did to the heart of this sweet
child :—

"Have you any righteousness, James?"

"I hope I have."

"What! of your own?"

"O no!—there is no righteousness but
Christ's."

"Do you love Christ?"

"I hope I do."

"Why do you love Christ?"

"Because he loves me."

"How do you know he loves you?"

"Because he has said, 'Suffer little
children to come unto me.'"

"Did you ever feel your need of the
grace of God, and long for it?"

"I hope I have."

"Why do you want it?"

"That I may go to heaven."

"Do you wish to go to heaven only
that you may escape hell?"

"No; that I may be with God."

"But God is a holy God, and you are an unholy creature."

"I must pray to Jesus Christ to make me holy, and fit for heaven."

My dear children, this young saint died when he was but eight years old. You may rejoice with wonder to think what God has done for little children, and what he is willing to do for you!

GIVING GOD THE HEART.

My son, give me thy heart.—Prov. xxiii, 26.

Do you hear these words, dear child? Here is some one asking for your heart; that is, for your love, your highest and best love. Is, then, the love of a little boy or girl, such as you are, worth seeking and asking for? I should suppose that it is not the voice of a stranger; for a stranger will not care about your heart, with a wish to possess it. No great man will condescend to ask for your love. A benefactor, who has done good to you, expects to have it without asking; and a fond parent has such a natural claim upon the affections of his family, that he looks for it, as a matter of course, that they should love him.

Who then can it be that stoops to say to you, "My son, or my daughter, give me thy heart?" In the words of the Prophet Isaiah we may say, when we think who it is that addresses us, "Hear, O heavens, and be astonished, O earth; for the Lord hath spoken." It is he who looks down from his throne of glory, and sees your thoughts wandering hither and thither, and your desires and affections fixing now upon one thing, then upon another; not gathering honey as the busy bee does, but flitting about, just as the little butterfly roves from flower to flower, as if in quest of amusement and happiness. God sees all this; and, because he knows that nothing can make you happy till your heart is fixed on him, therefore he says, "Give me thy heart."

See, then, what a *condescending request*

this is on the part of the great God. He
is adored by angels, he is loved by saints
in heaven, he is served by saints on earth;
and he might listen to the praises of these,
and delight himself with their grateful
homage, not at all concerning himself
about children such as you. But no: it
appears as though he passed by angels
and saints, that he might single you out,
to speak to you in particular, saying,
"Little boy, or little girl, give me thy
heart." What now will you answer?
Shall the God who made you stoop to
earth to ask your love, and will you refuse
him? Will you say to him, "I will not
have thee to reign over me: I will love
thy gifts, but I will not love thee?"
O what a hard heart that child must
have, who can think of God's condescension in this matter and not be touched
by it!

Notice, further, that this is a very *kind
request;* for remember that you cannot
make God more happy by giving what
he asks, neither can you make him less
happy by withholding it. He is always

perfectly blessed in himself; and you can never add to, or disturb his blessedness. It is not for his own sake that he says to you, " My son, give me thy heart:" it is entirely for your sake; because he loves you, and wishes to make you blessed in and with himself. When an earthly friend is kind to you, how do you feel toward that person? Why, you say, "I love my father; he is so kind to me:" or, "I love my mother; she is so kind to me:" or, "I love my playfellows; they are so kind to me." Just so; and ought you not, much more, to feel love toward God, who has done great things for you, and whose kindness prompts him to ask for your love in return. Think how he gave his only-begotten Son to suffer and to die for you. Think what the Lord Jesus Christ is doing for you, now that he is in heaven: how he pleads for you, watches over you, and invites you to his arms and to his bosom; and then say if it is not little enough for you to give him your heart, which is all that he requires.

You may also perceive that this is an

earnest request. " My son, give it me :" here is the affectionate entreaty of a father, as if he were anxious not to be denied; here is advice to do it now, immediately, without delay; here is persuasion, as if it were a thing of great importance. And so it is; for your life, your everlasting life, depends upon it. Your love will fix upon some object, and it is not a matter of indifference what you prefer as your chief good. Whatever you love best, that has your heart; and if you love anybody, or anything very much, you will come under their power, and become in a great degree like that person or thing. If, in early life, you give your heart to the world, the world will hold you fast, and try to make you its slave as long as you live. If you give your heart to sin, then evil will have dominion over you, and the devil will be your father. What a dreadful thought! Do you not fear lest you should become as wicked and miserable as he would seek to make you? Come, then, and give heed to the request of your kind and condescending Father in heaven, who is willing to save you from sin, and to make you happy in his love. Do not hesitate, but comply instantly with the sweet invitation, " My son, give me thy heart."

Again, look at this as a *serious request.* God is not to be trifled with. If a young friend or playfellow were to ask you to give him anything, you would do well to consider about it; and if you do not like to let him have it, you might refuse as kindly as possible, telling him that you cannot spare the thing which he asks for. But if your father or mother says to you, " Give me this, or that," you must recollect that, as a dutiful child, it becomes you to consent; and, if you are well-disposed, you will do it cheerfully. If, then, you owe such obedience to your earthly parents, much more should you attend to the voice of God. He speaks condescendingly, he speaks kindly, and he speaks earnestly; but he also speaks seriously, and expects that you will obey. He says, " Give me thy heart:" and will you be so wicked as to answer, " I cannot give my heart to thee, Lord; I will not give it to thee." You would not dare to say this, in so many words; but if you do not love God, if you offend him, if you do not take pleasure in reading the Bible if you feel no delight in his holy day, and would rather play in the fields on that day than worship God in his house of prayer; then it is all one as if you were to say, that though God invites, you will not hear, and though he asks for your love, you do not choose to give it to him. Now, if such is your spirit and behavior, what do you think God will say? how will he notice it? When some naughty children once mocked a prophet of the Lord, there came two she bears out of the wood and tare them to pieces. God would not suffer his servant to be made light of; and will he now permit children to make light of himself, to despise his word, and reject his mercy? Certainly not. Therefore think seriously, I beseech you, of what he says to you, and give him your whole heart, that he may cleanse it, and dwell in it, and make it happy forever.

There is nothing else that you can give to God in the stead of your heart. If you were to offer him all your time, and all your money, and everything else that you possess, he would not accept these things at your hand, unless you first gave him your heart. Bodily service is nothing without love; lip service is nothing without love; the heart is what God requires. God is love; and to love him because he hath first loved us, is at once our duty and our bliss.

SEEKING CHRIST EARLY.

They that seek me early shall find me.—Prov. viii, 17.

Supposing that a mother were to take her little boy to a large wood for the purpose of a walk, and they were to lose one another in the middle of the wood, O with what earnestness they would seek each other! Every person the mother would meet she would ask, Have you seen my little son wandering among the trees? And the boy would ask every person he might meet, Have you seen my mother? Perhaps when the child lost sight of his mother he was gathering some nuts or wild berries, or was entertaining himself by collecting a nosegay of beautiful fragrant flowers for his little sister. When he looked round he saw no mother—she was gone! He cried out, Mother! mother! but there was no answer. He still cries out, My mother! my mother! but, instead of a mother's voice, he hears nothing but the sound of the singing of birds. He runs from place to place, seeking his lost parent. He continues running till he is overcome with anguish and fatigue, and is ready to faint and die. He sits down and weeps; his little heart is ready to burst within him: at last he lays down his head on the green sod, and, quite exhausted, falls asleep.

While the boy was seeking the mother, the mother was seeking the child. At last she finds her son fast asleep under the shadow of a wide-spreading tree. She sees the big tears still resting on his rosy cheeks—she clasps him in her arms, she presses him to her breast, and exclaims, in raptures of gratitude and joy, "I have found my son! I have found my son!" The child awakes, and, to his astonishment, finds himself in the bosom of his mother.

As the mother sought her child, and as the child sought his mother, so should you, my dear young friends, seek Christ. A mother who loses her son may seek him, and not find him; but all who seek Christ early shall find him. He says so himself, and what he says is true.

When the child lost his mother in the wood, I need not tell you he was willing to seek her. He sought her with all his heart. But I must tell you that you are naturally unwilling to seek Christ. O, may the Holy Spirit make you willing! Then shall you begin in earnest to seek Christ, and you shall most assuredly find him.

1. Where are you to seek Christ? Seek Christ in the *Bible.* There he is to be found; and if he is not sought there he can never be found. My little children, you need never expect to see Christ in heaven if you do not seek Christ in the

Bible. Jesus says to all children, and he says to you, "Search the Scriptures." And why does he say so? He adds as a reason, "These are they which testify of me." John v, 39.

Seek Christ in the *closet*. In the evening, before you retire to rest, and in the morning, after you rise from rest, go into the closet, and on your bended knees seek Christ. I think I am not mistaken when I tell you, that if there is one place more than another that angels with their golden wings delight to visit, it is the closet where little children are on their knees seeking Christ in earnest prayer.

Seek Christ in the *school of affliction*. Does Christ visit that school? O yes, he does! He is there often—he is there every day. Some in the school of affliction do not see him; but I know he is there, whether they see him or not. Why do they not see him? It is because they do not seek him. That is the reason; for, be assured, if they sought him there they would find him there.

Ere long *you* may be in the school of

affliction. Think not that your youth will keep you out of it. At this moment, while I address you, there are many thousands of little children in that school! Who knows but that in a very few days you may be there likewise? Remember I tell you, if ever you are in that school, Christ is there; and if you seek him, you shall see him, and find him.

Seek Christ in the *sanctuary*. What is the meaning of the word sanctuary? Do you not know? It means a holy place. The sanctuary is the house of God. As the king is to be found in his palace, so God is to be found in his sanctuary. The sanctuary is one of God's royal palaces; and all who seek God in this his royal palace are sure to find him.

Once, on a visit to France, in the year 1822, I went to the magnificent palace of Versailles. I found no difficulty in gaining admittance. And why? Because the king was not there. On my return to Paris I passed by the palace of St. Cloud, the favorite residence of French monarchs. I could gain no admittance. And why?

Because the king was there. My dear children, because God is in his sanctuary you are not prevented from entering—because he is in his sanctuary you are encouraged to enter. Enter then his courts, and you shall see the King of kings—you shall see him arrayed in garments of beauty—you shall see him smiling upon you with loving-kindness and tender mercy.

2. When are you to seek Christ? You are to seek him *early*. To seek Christ early is to seek him in early life. Human life resembles a day. Youth resembles the morning, middle age resembles noon, old age resembles evening. We say youth resembles the morning. If a man has a very long journey which he intends to take that would require the whole of his day, do you think it were wise in him not to begin his journey till twelve or two o'clock? If he delays so long as that, he will not be able during the afternoon to accomplish his journey, which would have required the whole of the day. And, besides, night may come upon him; and robbers, or wild beasts, may fall upon him

and destroy him. How foolish it is to begin a journey in the middle of the day, when it is hot and sultry, or in the evening when the sun is setting, and the darkness of night is fast approaching!

My dear young friends, there is a journey before you—it is to eternity. There are two roads—the one leads to heaven, and the other to hell. You should begin in the morning of your life to seek the first, and avoid the second.

At what time of the year is it that the farmer sows the seed? It is in the spring —not in winter. Youth is the springtime of life, when Christ should be sought. It does not do to sow seeds in winter; neither does it answer to delay seeking Christ till the winter of human life.

When the children of Israel traveled through the wilderness on their way to Canaan, they lived on manna. It fell on the grass every morning. The first thing they were required to do in the morning was to go out and gather the manna. If they delayed, what was the consequence? Why, the manna was all melted by the heat of the sun, and there was no more to be found till next day. As the Israelites gathered manna in the morning, so Christ should be sought in the morning of life. If you delay, Christ may not be found.

Follow the example of young Samuel; he sought Christ as soon as he could speak. Follow the example of the young King Josiah; he sought Christ when he was a child. The lovely royal child had Judah's crown upon his head; he had something far better—he had the grace of God in his heart. Follow the example of John the Baptist; he sought Christ in early life. When a little child, his lips were perfumed with the oil of piety, and his holy words flowed like a honey stream. Follow the example of Timothy; he sought Christ in his boyish days. O, how often little Timothy read the Scriptures to his aged grandmother! It is said, to his honor, that, from a child, he knew the Scriptures.

Samuel, Josiah, John the Baptist, and Timothy, were once children like you; they sought Christ when young—they

never repented it. O no! it was their
joy, their glory, their triumph; and they
are now in heaven, beholding, admiring,
and praising that Saviour whom they
sought and found on earth! Be persuaded, little children, to seek Christ
early,—you will never repent it,—for
you shall find him, and be happy forever beside him, in his palace and on his
throne.

I am in earnest in entreating you to
seek Christ early. God is in earnest, angels are in earnest! are you in earnest?

Suffer me to place before you an example, that by the blessing of God you
may be stirred up to imitate it. Ruth
M—— died when about twelve years old.
From her very infancy she was given to
prayer, and expressed a concern for her
soul. God sent the child to the school of
affliction, where she often met with Christ,
and was filled with heavenly joy. Her
parents took her to the sea-side to Sheer-
ness, in hopes of her recovery; but her
increasing weakness obliged them soon to
return.

For some time she was in great darkness and fear about her soul, her safety, and her salvation; but in answer to her parents' prayers and her own supplications, the black clouds of fear vanished away, and her sky shone with the very brightness of heaven! While she lay on the bed of approaching death, she was like the glory of a morning-star. Her chamber was more like an ante-chamber to the celestial palace above than the chamber of the king of terrors. When death was at a distance she was afraid of his approach, but as he drew nearer and nearer her fears were destroyed; then she declared openly what God had done for her soul, and that she had found Jesus.

She said to her father, "If ever I go to heaven, you have taught me the way." Her father said, "Well, my dear, what is the way to God?" She answered, "Jesus Christ is the way, the truth, and the life." He further asked her, "Are you willing that Jesus should have all the glory of your salvation?" She replied, "O yes!"

With her dying, quivering lips, she repeated with great animation the following lines :—

> "Let the sweet hope that thou art mine
> My life and death attend;
> Thy presence through my journey shine,
> And crown my journey's end."

A friend asked her, "Ruth, is Jesus with you?"

"Yes."

"Do you love Jesus?"

"O yes."

"Why do you love him?"

"Because he loved me."

"How do you know that he loves you?"

"Because I feel it, and think it."

In a short time she was covered with the cold sweats of death; her body was thrown into violent convulsions; now and then she cried out, "Come, Lord Jesus!" and in a little time after fell asleep; and then awoke, surrounded with the glory of heaven, and in the presence of God and the Lamb!

CHILDREN WALKING IN TRUTH.

I rejoiced greatly, that I found of thy children walking in
truth.—2 JOHN 4.

BELOVED CHILDREN,—The book from which
my text is taken is the shortest in the
Bible. Look at it when you go home,
and you will find it so. It has only thirteen verses; but, short as it is, it is full of
important things, and I think the verse
I have just heard is one of them.

This book is an epistle, or letter, written
by the Apostle John. He wrote it to a
good Christian lady, whom he knew. This
lady had children, and some of them were
the children spoken of in the text.

It seems that John found some of this
good lady's children at a place where he
happened to go; and you see how well he
found them behaving. He was able to
write a good report of them to their
mother, and that is the report of our text:
"I rejoiced greatly, that I found of thy
children walking in truth."

Now, dear children, there are only two things I want to tell you about out of this text. Some of you, perhaps, are thinking this very minute, "What does walking in truth mean?" Others, perhaps, are thinking, "Why did John rejoice so greatly?" I shall try to answer these two questions.

I. Firstly, I shall try to show you "*when it can be said that children walk in truth.*"

II. Secondly, I shall try to show you "*what were the reasons that made the Apostle John rejoice so greatly.*"

Dear children, let me ask you all one favor,—let me ask you all to try to *attend.* I shall not keep you long. Come, then, and listen to what I have to tell you. May the Holy Spirit open all your hearts, and bless what I say!

I. I told you I would first try to show you this: "*When it can be said that children walk in truth.*" Let me set about it at once.

What does "*walking*" mean here? You must not think it means walking on your feet, as you have walked here to-

night. It means rather our way of behaving ourselves, our way of living and
going on. And shall I tell you why the
Bible calls this "*walking?*" It calls it so,
because a man's life is just like a journey.
From the time of our birth to the time of
our death, we are always traveling and
moving on. Life is a journey from the
cradle to the grave, and a person's manner of living is, on that account, often
called his "*walk.*"

But what does "*walking in truth*"
mean? It means walking in the ways of
true Bible religion, and not in the bad
ways of this evil world. The world, I am
sorry to tell you, is full of false notions
and untruths, and specially full of untruths
about religion. They all come from our
great enemy the devil. The devil deceived Adam and Eve in Eden, and made
them sin by telling them an untruth.
He told them they should not die if they
ate the forbidden fruit, and that was un-
true. And the devil is always at the same
work now. He is always trying to make
men and women and children have false

notions about God and about religion. He persuades them to believe that what is really evil is good, and what is really good is evil; that God's service is not pleasant, and that sin will do them no great harm. And, I grieve to say, vast numbers of people are deceived by him, and believe these untruths.

But those persons who walk in truth are very different. They pay no attention to the false notions there are in the world about religion. They follow the true way which God shows us in the Bible. Whatever others may do, their chief desire is to please God, and be his true servants. Now, this was the character of the children spoken of in the text. John writes home to their mother, and says, "I found them walking in truth."

Dear children, would you not like to know whether you are walking in truth yourselves? Would you not like to know the *marks* by which you may find it out? Listen, every one of you, while I try to set these marks before you in order. Let every boy and girl hear what I am going to say.

1. I tell you, then, for one thing, that children who walk in truth *know the truth about sin.*

What is sin? To break any command of God is sin; to do anything that God says ought not to be done is sin. And God is very holy and very pure, and every sin that is sinned displeases him exceedingly. But, in spite of all this, most people in the world, both old and young, think very little about sin. Some try to make out they are not great sinners, and do not often break God's commandments. Others say that sin is not so terrible a thing after all, and that God is not so particular and strict as ministers say he is. These are two great and dangerous mistakes.

Children who walk in truth think very differently. They have no such proud and high feelings. They feel themselves full of sin, and it grieves and humbles them. They believe that sin is the abominable thing which God hates. They look upon sin as their greatest enemy and plague; they hate it more than anything on earth.

There is nothing they so heartily desire to be free from as sin.

Dear children, there is the first mark of walking in truth. Look at it; think of it. *Do you hate sin?*

2. I tell you, for another thing, that children who walk in truth *love the true Saviour of sinners, and follow him.*

There are few men and women who do not feel they need in some way to be saved. They feel that after death comes the judgment, and from that awful judgment they would like to be saved.

But, alas! few of them will see that the Bible says there is only one Saviour, even Jesus Christ; and few go to Jesus Christ and ask him to save them. They trust rather to their own prayers, or their own repentance, or their own church-going, or their own regular attendance at sacrament, or their own goodness, or something of the kind. But these things, although useful in their place, cannot save any one soul from hell. These are false ways of salvation; they cannot put away sin; they are not Christ.

Nothing can save you or me but Jesus Christ, who died for sinners on the cross. Those only who trust entirely to him have their sins forgiven, and will go to heaven. These alone will find they have an Almighty friend in the day of judgment. This is the true way to be saved.

Children who walk in truth have learned all this, and if you ask them what they put their trust in, they will answer, "*Nothing but Christ.*" They remember his gracious words: "Suffer the little children to come unto me, and forbid them not." They try to follow Jesus as the lambs follow the good shepherd. And they love him, because they read in the Bible that he loved them, and gave himself for them.

Little children, there is the second mark of walking in truth. Look at it; think of it. *Do you love Christ?*

3. I tell you, for a third thing, that children who walk in truth *serve God with a true heart.*

I dare say you know it is very possible to serve God with outward service only.

Many do so. They will put on a grave face and pretend to be serious, while they do not feel it ; they will say beautiful prayers with their lips, and yet not mean what they say ; they will sit in their places at church every Sunday, and yet be thinking of other things all the time—and such service is outward service, and very wrong.

Bad children, I am sorry to say, are often guilty of this sin. They will say their prayers regularly when their parents make them, but not otherwise. They will seem to attend in church when the master's eye is upon them, but not at other times. Their *hearts* are far away.

Children who walk in truth are not so. They have another spirit in them. Their desire is to be honest in all they do with God, and to worship him in spirit and in truth. When they pray they try to be in earnest, and to mean all the words they say. When they go to church they try to be really serious, and to give their minds to what they hear. And it is one of their chief troubles that they cannot serve God more heartily than they do.

Little children, there is the third mark of walking in truth. Look at it; think of it. *Is your heart false or true?*

4. I tell you, for a last thing, that children who walk in truth *really try to do things right and true in the sight of God.*

God has told us very plainly what he thinks right. Nobody can mistake this who reads the Bible with an honest heart. But it is sad to see how few men and women care for pleasing God. Many break his commandments continually, and seem to think nothing of it. Some will tell lies, and swear, and quarrel, and cheat, and steal. Others use bad words, break the Sabbath, never pray to God at all, never read their Bibles. Others are unkind to their relations, or idle, or gluttonous, or bad-tempered, or selfish. And all these things, whatever people may choose to think, are very wicked and displeasing to the holy God.

Children who walk in truth are always trying to keep clear of bad ways. They take no pleasure in sinful things of any kind, and they dislike the company of those who do them. Their great wish is to be like Jesus, holy, harmless, and separate from sinners. They endeavor to be kind, gentle, obliging, obedient, honest, truthful, and good in all their ways. It grieves them they are not more holy than they are.

Little children, there is the last mark I shall give you of walking in truth. Look at it; think of it. *Are your doings right or wrong?*

Children, you have now heard some marks of walking in truth. I have tried to set them plainly before you. I hope you have understood them. *Knowing the truth about sin, loving the true Saviour, Jesus Christ, serving God with a true heart, doing the things true and right in the sight of God,*—there they are, all four together. Think about them I entreat you, and each ask yourself this question: "What am I doing at this very time?—am I walking in truth?"

I dare be sure that many boys and girls here know well what answer they ought to give; and God knows too, for he sees

your hearts as plainly as I see your faces
this minute. Children, the all-seeing God
sends you a question this moment by my
mouth. He says, *Are you walking in
truth?*

Why should you not? Thousands of
dear children have walked in truth
already, and found it pleasant. The way
is trodden by many little feet before your
own. Thousands of boys and girls are
walking in truth at this moment, and
there is yet room. Dear children, think
this night, "*why should not you?*"

II. And now I will go on to the second
thing I promised to speak of.

I said I would try to show you some of
the *reasons why John rejoiced to find this
lady's children walking in truth.* Let
me set about it. The text says, "I rejoiced greatly." Now, why did he
rejoice? There must have been some
good reasons. John was not a man to
rejoice without cause. Listen, dear children, and you shall hear what those
reasons were.

1. For one thing, John rejoiced *because he was a good man himself.*

All good people like to see others walking in truth as well as themselves. I dare say you have heard how the angels in heaven rejoice when they see one sinner repenting. Some of you, no doubt, have read it in the fifteenth chapter of Luke. Well, good people are like the angels in this,—they are full of love and compassion,—and when they see any one turning away from sin, it makes them feel happy.

Good people find walking in truth so pleasant, that they would like everybody else to walk in truth too. They do not wish to keep all this pleasantness to themselves, and to go to heaven alone. They want to see all about them loving Jesus Christ, and obeying him—all their relations, all their neighbors, all their old friends, all their young ones, indeed, all the world. The more they see walking in truth, the better they are pleased.

Children, John was a good man, and full of love to souls, and this was one reason why he rejoiced.

2. For another thing John rejoiced, *because it is very uncommon to see children walking in truth.*

Dear children, I am very sorry to tell you there are many bad boys and girls in the world. Too many are careless, thoughtless, self-willed, and disobedient. Nobody can rejoice over them.

I hear many fathers and mothers complaining about this. I hear many schoolmasters and schoolmistresses speak of it. I am afraid it is quite true.

There are many children who will not give their minds to anything that is good; they will not do what they are bid; they like to be idle, and to have their own way; they love playing better than learning; they do things which God says are wicked and wrong, and are not ashamed. And all this is very sad to see.

John, you may be sure, had found this out, for he was an aged man as well as an apostle, and had seen many things. He knew that even the children of good people sometimes turn out very badly. I dare say he remembered Jacob and David, and all the sorrow their families caused them. And, no doubt, he knew what Solomon says in the book of Proverbs: "Foolishness is bound in the heart of a child."

When, therefore, John saw this lady's children not turning out ill, like others, but walking in the way they should go, he might well feel it was a special mercy. I do not at all wonder that he greatly rejoiced.

3. For another thing John rejoiced, *because he knew that walking in truth would make these children really happy in this life.*

John was not one of those foolish persons who do not like much religion, and fancy it makes people unhappy. John knew that the more true religion people have, the more happy they are.

John knew that life is always full of care and trouble, and that the only way to get through life comfortably is to be a real follower and servant of Jesus Christ.

Dear children, remember what I say. If ever you would be happy in this evil world, you must give your hearts to Jesus

Christ and follow him. Give him the entire charge of your souls, and ask him to be your Saviour and your God, and *then* you will be happy. Have no will of your own, and only try to please him, and *then* your life will be pleasant.

Trust all to Christ, and he will undertake to manage all that concerns your soul. Trust in him at all times. Trust in him in every condition, in sickness and in health, in youth and in age, in poverty and in plenty, in sorrow and in joy. Trust in him, and he will be a shepherd to watch over you, a guide to lead you, a king to protect you, a friend to help you in time of need. Trust in him, and he says himself, "I will never leave thee nor forsake thee." He will put his Spirit into you, and give you a new heart; he will give you power to become a true child of God; he will give you grace to keep down bad tempers, to be no longer selfish, to love others as yourself; he will make your cares more light, and your work more easy; he will comfort you in time of trouble. Christ can make those happy who trust in him; Christ died to save them, and Christ ever lives to give them peace.

Dear children, John was well aware of these things. He had learned them by experience. He saw this lady's children likely to be happy in this world, and no wonder he rejoiced.

4. Lastly, John rejoiced *because he knew that walking in truth in the life that now is, would lead to glory and honor in the life to come.*

The life to come is the life we should all think most of. Many people seem only to care for what happens to them in this life; but they are sadly mistaken. This life is very short, it will soon be over. The oldest man will tell you, it seems only a few years since he was a child. The life to come is the life of real importance; it will have no end; it will be never-ending happiness, or never-ending pain. O, what a serious thought that is!

Children, I doubt not John was thinking of the life to come when he rejoiced. Our Lord Jesus Christ had often told him of the glorious rewards prepared for those who walk in truth. John thought of the rewards laid up in heaven for these children, and was glad.

I doubt not John looked forward in his heart to that day when Jesus shall come again. I dare say he saw in his mind's eye these dear children clothed in robes white as snow, having golden crowns on their heads, standing at Jesus Christ's right hand, enjoying pleasures for evermore. He saw them and their beloved mother meeting again in heaven—meeting in that blessed place where parting and sorrow shall be known no more.

Dear children, these must have been sweet and pleasant thoughts. I do not wonder that John rejoiced.

And now I have finished what I have to say about our text. I have done what I promised. I have told you *what it is to walk in truth.* That is one thing. I have told you *why John rejoiced so much* to find this lady's children walking in truth. That is another. Let me now wind up all by saying something which, by God's help, may fasten this sermon in your minds. Alas! how many sermons are forgotten! I want this sermon to abide in your hearts and do good.

Ask yourselves, then, every one, "Would John, if he knew me at this time, rejoice over me? Would John be pleased if he saw my ways and my behavior, or would he look sorrowful and grave?"

O children, children, do not neglect this question. This is no light matter. It may be your life. No wise man will ever rejoice over bad children. They may be clean and pretty, and have fine clothes, and look well *outwardly;* but a wise man will only feel sad when he sees them; he will feel they are wrong *inwardly.* They have not new hearts—they are not going to heaven. Believe me, it is far better to be good than to be pretty. It is far better to have grace in your hearts than to have much money in your pockets, or fine clothes on your backs. None but children who love Christ are the children who rejoice a wise man's heart.

Beloved children, hear the last words

I have to say to you. I give you all an invitation from Christ, my Master. I say to you, in his name, *Come and walk in truth.*

This is the way to gladden the hearts of your parents and relations. This is the one thing above all others which will please your ministers and teachers. You little know how happy you make us when you try to walk in truth. Then we feel that all is well, though we die and leave you behind us in this evil world. Then we feel that your souls are safe, though we are called away, and can help you and teach you no more. Then we feel that you are in the right way to be happy, and that you are prepared for troubles, however many may come upon you; for we know that walking in truth gives peace now, and we are sure that it leads to glory hereafter.

Come, then, this night, and begin to walk in truth. The devil will try to make you think it is too hard—you cannot do it. Believe him not; he is a liar. He wants to do you harm. Only trust in Christ, and follow him; you will soon say

his way is a way of pleasantness and a
path of peace. Only pray for the Holy
Spirit to come into your heart, and you will
soon feel strong. He can guide you into
all truth. Only read the Bible regularly,
and you will soon be made wise unto salvation. The Bible is the word of truth. Read
and pray; pray and read. Begin these habits, and keep them up. Do these things, and
before long you will not say it is impossible
to walk in truth. But *come—come at once.*

Children, I find Jesus Christ saying, in
the third chapter of Revelation, " Behold
I stand at the door and knock." Who
knows but this may have been going on
to-night? Who knows but Jesus may
have been knocking at some of your
hearts all through this sermon? If it be
so, do not keep him waiting any longer.
If it be so, go to him this night on your
knees in prayer,—go to him, and ask him
at once to come in. Ask Jesus to come
and dwell in your heart, and take care of
it as his own,—ask him to put your name
in his book of life,—ask him to enable
you to walk in truth.

O, think how many children in the world have never been invited as you are; how many boys and girls have never had the chance of being saved that you enjoy; how many, perhaps, would leap for joy, and walk in truth at once, if they were invited! Beloved children, *take care.* You, at least, cannot say you were not invited. Jesus invites you,—the Bible invites you, —I, the servant of Christ, invite you all. O, come to Christ! Come, and be happy! Come, and WALK IN TRUTH!

------◆------

GIVING AND RECEIVING.

It is more blessed to give than to receive.—ACTS xx, 35.

LET us inquire into the meaning of these important words.

It is not stated that it is not blessed to *receive.* The little starving girl of Ireland, of whom you have read, would have thought it blessed to receive when she piteously cried out, "Only three grains of corn, mother; can't you spare me three grains of corn?" A certain sick boy, far away from home, when he sighed for a gentle mother's care, a mother's sympathy, and a mother's hand to smooth his feverish brow, found it blessed to receive the same attention from a good woman who tried to supply the place of a mother as well as she could. You who are permitted to attend Sabbath school, no doubt find it very pleasant and refreshing to receive instruction from your teachers, who take much pains not only to meet you every Sabbath, but to furnish you a good lesson of religious truth to suit your wants.

But while it is blessed to receive, observe, our Saviour does not say, it is more blessed to *receive* than to give. I am sorry to say most people seem to understand it so. They seem to take more pleasure in *getting* money than in *giving* it to the needy. And I know some little children who are always receiving presents, and whose wealthy uncles and aunts are always giving them everything they desire, such as jewelry, toys, and gay clothes, and yet they are quite unhappy. Not long since, in a beautiful village in the state of New-York, a little girl of this description, who had been greatly petted and indulged by fond but unwise parents, was heard to exclaim at a party, "O dear! I wish there was a house on fire!" And when asked the reason of so strange a desire, she said, "I would like to see the excitement!" That is, she desired to have some building consumed, and of course to have whole families cast out in the streets without shelter, and perhaps without clothes, and lose all their property, if not their lives, that she might see the blaze, and the crowds of people running, and hear all the village bells furiously ringing together! What a cruel girl! Why, it made me think of the tyrant Nero in olden time, who set the splendid city of Rome on fire, to enjoy the sport of seeing magnificent buildings fall, and hearing the sad wails of suffering women and children.

A very distinguished poet of England, who had been favored with an attractive person and an excellent education, was nevertheless so unhappy because he was selfish and wicked, that he was heard to say, "I wish I had never been born!" He had many admirers, but still he was very wretched. It is said that Mr. Stephen Girard, who died in Philadelphia a few years ago, worth millions of dollars, acknowledged that before he had any property he could call his own he was more happy than when possessed of his millions. So you see it is possible to receive great gifts, and possess a great deal of money, and honor, and learning, and after all not be very happy; and yet too many young people, and some old people, seem to think that happiness is obtained not by *giving*, but by *getting*.

I suppose it was because our blessed Saviour observed that mankind are naturally selfish that he so often cautioned the people against covetousness, and encouraged the practice of liberality.

But are all who *appear* to be generous, happy? The Lord Jesus does not say so. A miserable rumseller, seeing a number of boys passing his grocery one day, called them in and gave them some intoxicating liquor, sweetened nicely with sugar, which, after much coaxing, they drank; and thus of course they not only soon began to act very foolishly, but became very sick. But do you suppose that mean act made him happy?

A certain boy gave another boy a bunch of fire-crackers, which somehow took fire in his pocket, and burned him dreadfully, so that he never entirely recovered from the effect. Do you suppose the remembrance of that gift was a source of pleasure to him who made the present? No, you reply; neither the boy who gave away his fire-crackers, nor the man who gave away his rum, found it blessed to give; for they gave what was not only worthless, but mischievous, and calculated to make their fellow-creatures miserable rather than happy. So with a foolish woman who bought a large quantity of glittering jewelry, and put it upon the ears and wrists and fingers of a very vain little girl; for it made her more haughty

than ever. She became so consequen-
tial that she looked with disdain upon
her plainly-attired yet amiable playmates, who really pitied her weakness;
and, worse than all, she even *despised her
own mother*, and made her a great deal of
trouble.

Again, children sometimes give away
good things, and yet are not happy in so
doing. The little boy who had received
a fine large orange from his grandpapa,
gave part of it to his sister, but he looked
very unhappy when he did it. The truth
is, he gave it *grudgingly*. He did not
intend to give any of it to her, but being
reproved not only by his mother, but by
the wishful looks of his sister, he cut it,
but not in the middle. One part was
nearly a third larger than the other, and
he evinced his selfishness by giving the
smaller part to her, reserving nearly two-
thirds of the orange for himself. How
different was his feeling from that of the
same little sister, when, not long after, her
aunt brought her a nice, large pine-apple!
She was inclined to give the whole of it

to her brother, at his request, and when her mother would not allow her to do that, she cut it in two parts, but not in the middle, giving the best half by far to her brother, who was so ill-deserving. You see, then, it is not the child that gives what is worthless, or gives grudgingly, that is happy. Nor is it the boy or girl who gives *boastingly*—who gives only to tell of his wonderful deed of charity, that finds the bliss of which our Saviour speaks; but the person who gives because he *loves* to give, and loves to give because his heart is moved with pity toward those who are needy, and desires above all things to please God—who is always giving liber ally, even to the unthankful and wicked.

We have, then, at last arrived at the true meaning of the words of the Lord Jesus under examination. It is this: *Those persons are most happy who are most useful.*

THE LITTLE FOXES THAT SPOIL THE VINES.

LITTLE THINGS.

Take us the foxes, the little foxes, that spoil the vines.—
SOLOMON'S SONG ii, 15.

IT is well known that foxes are very fond of grapes, but it seems these thievish animals are not satisfied with stealing the *fruit;* the *little* foxes especially are inclined to spoil the *vines.* I might tell you many very curious stories about foxes and their cunning tricks; but as little foxes sometimes, as the text shows, do great mischief,—the grape in some countries being the chief article of commerce and food,—I wish to impress upon your minds the important truth that *little causes often produce great effects,* or that great good and great mischief often grow out of very small things.

You remember the lines—

> "Large streams from little fountains flow,
> Tall oaks from little acorns grow."

But did you ever realize, when you have gazed upon the mighty oak, monarch of the hills, that had resisted the winds and storms of a hundred winters, that that oak was once a little pliant twig, almost as tender as the grass you tread upon, and sprung from an acorn not as large perhaps as your mother's thimble, and which it may be a little Indian boy covered up with leaves in his childish sports? And have you reflected that some of the greatest and noblest rivers in the world, which pour their mighty waters into the ocean, and which bear upon their bosom hundreds of sloops and steam-palaces, may be traced up to little rivulets no larger than the road-side brooks you used to dam up near the district school-house, where you set your tiny water-wheel running?

Once a certain farmer sowed some wheat, and although he was not sure it was perfectly clean, he did not stop to examine it carefully, thinking that a *little* bad seed would do no harm; but now his farm is all covered over with Canada thistles, which have greatly diminished its beauty and value, and he finds to his sorrow that, although a *little* negligence overspread his lands with noxious weeds, *great* effort will be required to extirpate them.

You have read in the Bible how a little arrow, which a certain man let fly from his bow at a venture, killed a great king, and decided an important battle; an event which neither the man who made the arrow, nor the man who shot it, had any idea would be produced by it. You remember also how David, the shepherd-boy, with nothing but a simple sling, and a little smooth stone which he picked from a brook, slew the wicked giant Goliath of Gath, who was armed with a mighty spear and sword, and had defied the armies of Israel. The Bible, indeed, is full of illustrations of the truth that *small* things are often very *important* things.

Our blessed Saviour while upon earth was very observing of small things. He not only took special notice of little children, and invited them to come to him, and then took them in his arms and blessed them; but he observed the gorgeous lily, the luxuriant vine, the tiny sparrow, and the smallest token of kindness which he saw manifested either toward himself or others. No tear-drop of penitence or pain fell from sorrow's cheek but he saw and felt it; no syllable of prayer or profanity was ever uttered, but it entered into his ear and affected his heart. No opportunity of doing good, however small, which is omitted or improved, but he takes a note of it. For instance, when the poor widow, spoken of in the twenty-first chapter of Luke, cast two mites (which make only a farthing, or about a quarter of a penny) into the Lord's treasury, she did not think that her act would have attracted the particular attention of the Saviour. No doubt as she had so little to give, compared with the rich around her, she made very little show about it—she crept up very quietly to the contribution-box, and perhaps she was not generally observed by the congregation; but the evangelist Luke tells us "Jesus saw her," and he knew exactly how much she gave when he said, "Of a truth this poor widow hath cast in more than they all. For all these have of their abundance cast in unto the offerings of God: but she of her penury hath cast in all the living that she had." And thus, by that seemingly little act of duty, this obscure woman's example has been recorded, and her character, if not her name, is, and will be, embalmed in the memory of the good of all generations.

Now as a little act of virtue often produces a great result of goodness, so little sinful acts often produce dreadful results of mischief. There is much truth in the saying of Dr. Franklin, that by neglecting a nail, a shoe is lost; by losing a shoe, the horse is lost; and by the loss of the horse, the rider, if not lost himself, suffers in person, in property, or in family, perhaps, a loss which is irreparable. Thus a little carelessness in losing a few minutes of time, and the engineer of the railroad comes into collision with another train of cars, and then what awful havoc is instantly made of human life! How many children are in a moment bereaved of parents, wives of husbands, and husbands of wives! And though it is all done in an instant, as the result of a little carelessness perhaps of only one man, the woes it occasions are innumerable and incurable. Tears begin to flow which are never dried up, and groans are heaved that echo through eternity.

Our first parents, Adam and Eve, when they ate of the forbidden tree by the suggestion of that old liar, Satan, were no doubt told by him that although God had forbidden it, the sin was so trifling, so small a matter, that he would not take pains to bring them to an account for it; and besides, if he should, the *wisdom* and enjoyment which would result from the eating of it might far overbalance the little displeasure God might manifest toward them. But, alas! how different was the result? They found to their sorrow, and the whole world ever since has been taught by the fearful consequences of this transgression, that a *small* act of willful disobedience to God is a *great* sin, and unless forgiven, and the guilt washed away

by the blood of the atonement, will produce great suffering in this world and the
world to come.

A little boy by the name of Charles
was one morning enticed to go away from
home, instead of staying to keep his sick
mother company. He was quite sure his
mother would be unwilling to have him
leave, so he determined to go away slily,
and of course without permission; but she
saw him before he reached the gate, and
very kindly urged him to stay with her.
Instead of honoring his mother, as the fifth
commandment requires, he rudely replied,
"*I won't.*" A tear, it is said, stood in his
mother's eye as she then lifted up her heart
and asked God to make Charley a better
boy. Her prayer was answered, and
Charles became a good man; but he now
says he never can forget that word of un-
kindness, and that act of disobedience.
He was unhappy all that day. It was almost dark before he returned home. He
asked for his mother, but she was so ill
(the disease being, no doubt, aggravated
by his misconduct) that the nurse would

not permit him to see her. He never saw her again alive. "Even now," said he, "I would give all I am worth to be able to kneel at her feet, and hear words of forgiveness. Her look of sadness as I said, *I won't,* will haunt me to my dying day." So much for one little naughty word.

How different was the conduct of another boy, whose name was George, who was very anxious to take a long voyage at sea. He had got his trunks packed, for he did not know how much opposed his beloved mother was to his going until his baggage had been carried out of the house by a servant. Just then he happened to look into the face of his mother, which was pale with sadness, while her eyes were full of tears. He knew the cause; and though it cost him a severe inward struggle, he immediately called out to the servant, "Bring back my trunk; I am not going away to leave my kind mother when she feels so bad."

Now can you guess what George that was? Ah! you have often heard of

Washington; and no doubt all his subsequent prosperity and honor, as a good man, a great general, and the first President of the United States, and even the success of the Revolutionary War, by which liberty is secured to us such as is enjoyed by no other nation, is the result of that one little act of honor to his mother. For if he had gone to sea, even if he had not become a poor dissipated sailor, which is not unlikely, he would at least have felt the shame and misery of guilt and ingratitude, and thus have been incapable of noble achievements. Besides, he would thus have excited the displeasure of his Maker, without whose kindly guidance even a mind as strong and a spirit as brave as Washington's could have effected but little.

In December, 1811, a boy, who was living in Richmond, Virginia, had a dollar handed to him by a relative to go into the theater that evening. But he refused to take it, as his mother, who lived in the country, had charged him on leaving home not to go to the theater. This he told the

man, adding, *I can't disobey my mother.*
He was treated with contempt for paying
attention to parental advice about such
trifling matters ; but the sequel showed it
was not a small matter, as this act of obedience in all probability saved his life;
for the theater that very evening took
fire, and seventy-five persons perished.

Perhaps you have heard, children, of
another little boy, who being very poor,
and without a father to take care of him,
called one day upon a merchant, and begged to be taken into his employment as
a waiter, to do any service required of
him. As he had furnished testimonials
of his honesty, while the merchant was
attending to other matters and considering
the subject presented by the boy, the latter, who had been taught that " a pin a
day is a groat a year," busied himself in
searching for pins at the door of the store.
This little circumstance was not overlook-
ed by the shop-keeper, and it determined
him to employ the ragged boy, who was
soon promoted from an errand-boy to an
accountant; and from a prudent, honest,

active clerk, he became a successful, influential, and wealthy partner in the establishment. Thus it is; many a person's destiny has turned upon as small an event or thing as a *little pin*.

The truth that great results hang upon little things is so important, and so frequently forgotten by children, that although I have mentioned quite a number of incidents that illustrate it, I trust you will bear with me in just glancing at two or three facts more.

The first of these is that of a boy who was in the service of a wicked merchant, who desired him to do some business on the Sabbath day. The youth had been taught in the Sunday school to "Remember the Sabbath day to keep it holy;" and, therefore, with a sorrowful countenance and tearful eyes, as he feared his hesitation might deprive him of his place, he said that *he had rather not break the holy Sabbath, and offend God.* The man was surprised at this answer; but instead of becoming enraged, and dismissing the God-fearing youth from his service, esteemed him more highly than ever, as he said, "James, you are right, and I am wrong. I have more confidence in you than ever; for *he who is true to his Maker will be true to me.*"

A young man who had been wicked and careless about religion was taken suddenly sick. During the intervals of his agony he was told of his danger, and asked whether he was prepared to die. He assured his heart-broken parents that his peace was made with God. On his bed of death he declared what God had done for his soul, and by what means the great change in his heart had been effected. It seems that, a short time before he was taken sick, he was walking leisurely with cart and oxen along the public road, when his eye caught sight of a little piece of paper, which a breath of passing wind gently stirred up and set in motion. It was the fragment of a Bible-leaf. He read as he followed the team. That little leaf awakened him to a sense of his danger, and pointed him to the Lamb of God which taketh away the sins of the world.

O what a glorious result was this from a very small cause!

In fine, children, when you consider that the nerve of a tooth, not so large as a fine cambric needle, will sometimes become so painful as to drive a strong man to distraction; that a musquito can drive an elephant to madness; that the coral rock which causes a navy to founder is the work of tiny worms; and that the sting of the bee, the bite of a spider, or scratch of a pin, has more than once prostrated the tall, the wise, and the mighty man upon the bed of death, you must be convinced that little causes produce great effects.

In another discourse, I wish to explain why I have taken so much pains to impress upon your minds the importance of little things.

SMALL AND GREAT THINGS.

Is it not a little one?—GENESIS xix, 20.

IN my last discourse I told you several
stories about "little things," and promised
that in my next I would try to show some
reasons why the connection between small
and great things should be remembered
by children. To a few of these lessons we
will now give our attention.

In the first place, if so much depends
upon little things, *we should be careful
to neglect no duty because it seems to be
but a small matter.*

Indeed, is it proper to say *any* duty
which the Bible enjoins is a *small* duty?
Everything that the great and holy God
has seen fit to require must be a matter
of importance. Although some sins, of
course, are more heinous than others,
there can be no such thing as a *small* sin
against the *great* God.

A few days since I visited the state-prison at Auburn, in which were between seven and eight hundred persons of different ages shut up for serious crimes. I taught a class in the prison Sunday school, composed of convicts; and I never shall forget how sad it made me feel to see those poor, unhappy criminals, clad in striped jackets and trowsers, confined so closely, and watched over by armed men, who stood at the door and sat in each window of the prison chapel, even during the session of the Sunday school.

I had a serious talk with the members of my class, all of whom were young men between the ages of sixteen and thirty. Now I have no doubt, if I had asked every one of the seven hundred prisoners what brought them there, nine at least of every ten would have replied, if they had answered at all, "I never should have been here if I had not at first neglected *small* duties and committed *small* sins."

One of the convicts, a young man of intelligence, who had been well-educated by fond, but over-indulgent parents, and who had, by the influence of his pious

Sunday-school teacher, become apparently a sincere penitent, wrote with a pencil, in a beautiful hand, a letter which he greatly desired his teacher to copy and send to his parents. At my request a copy of the letter was placed in my hands, and as it strikingly illustrates my subject, I will here give it, with the exception of a few sentences, the publication of which would be of no special service:—

"MY DEAR FATHER,—Scarcely do I know how to address you in a manner suitably to express the mingled feelings I experience at this time and in this place. Language is certainly inadequate, with my feeble power, to perform the mournful task before me, how I have fallen by reason of crime, bringing dishonor upon myself, and inflicting disgrace upon my relatives and friends; yet of all, my sins against God have the most venomous sting and the deepest guilt. It is true I have fallen before temptation, forgetful of your ever kind but too-much-slighted instructions. Those counsels and instructions I now see and feel would have conducted me along the bright and peaceful path of life and honor. I feel my disgrace and deplorable condition. I could not have the heart to write these lines to any but you. I feel that I am justly, in the true sense of the term, *fatherless, motherless*, and *friendless;* my crimes having cut me off from the sympathy of all whose love I once shared. My cup of sorrow is constantly running over. I seem to be "out of humanity's reach; I must travel my dark journey alone." *All my ruin came from disobedience to my kind parents.* O pray for me, that I may have God's grace to bear me up in my afflictions, and that I may more constantly realize that in him only is my help. Words cannot express my feelings. I would give a kingdom, were it mine to give, to be placed back again where I once was; but I must now suffer, first, imprisonment, then the pangs of remorse till death. My sentence seems to me a life-time—NINE years yet! I see to my sorrow that the way of the transgressor is

truly hard. I have resolved to forsake
every known sin ; this is my only safe
way; any other will be dangerous for such
a one as me. I must cleave to God as my
only Saviour. O the thought of home!
My heart almost breaks when I think of
my once bright, happy, sweet home. I
can say no more, father; but if you cannot
without too much pains see me here, I
trust that, by God's help, I shall be prepared to meet you where sin, and disgrace,
and shame, and sorrow, will never come.

"Your erring son."

The point in this letter which I wish
my young friends particularly to notice is
this confession: "*All my ruin came from
disobedience to my kind parents.*" Had
he not considered that little commandment which says, "*Honor thy father and
thy mother*" a small matter, and trifled
with it, he would not have lost his character, forfeited his liberty, and been compelled to spend the best part of his life
in a gloomy prison. O, then, neglect no
duty, I pray you, children, because it

seems a small matter. To be more particular, if you would not neglect little things,—

1. *Rise early.* I never shall forget the earnest exclamation of that wonderful man, George Whitefield, in one of his printed sermons on the subject of Conversion: "Lord, convert us from lying in bed too late in the morning." Early rising, indeed, has more to do with a religious life than many young Christians, and some aged ones, are aware of. There is an old proverb which I came across the other day worth remembering, namely: "It is better to wear out shoes than sheets." You understand this maxim, children; it is not, of course, to encourage a needless waste of shoes, by sliding on the ice, or in any other improper manner, but it teaches that activity is much better than indolence.

There is a great deal of truth, depend upon it, in the old couplet with which doubtless you are all familiar:—

> " Early to bed, and early to rise,
> Makes the boy healthy, wealthy, and wise."

Show me a little boy or girl who loves to sit up late at night, and get up late in the morning, and I will in a few years show you a sickly and shiftless man or woman, that wonders how it happens that others are so healthy and so thrifty, while he or she is so feeble and so unsuccessful.

Especially let us avoid the sinful habit of lying in bed late on Sabbath mornings. Judging from the conduct of some people, we might suppose that the fourth commandment reads thus: Remember the Sabbath-day, and keep it in bed. But you know very well there is a mighty difference between keeping the Sabbath holy, like adoring and active angels, and wasting it in indolence, like the grunting swine.

2. *Waste no time.* Last week I called to see a very aged Christian lady. She is in her ninety-ninth year, and is very sprightly and happy, spending most of her wakeful hours in prayer and praise. Within a few weeks she has become so blind that she cannot read a word of her well-worn, but precious Bible. Her

granddaughter showed us her old hymn-book, which was published by John Dickens, in Philadelphia, about sixty years ago. I read the first line of several beautiful hymns, and then, to my surprise, she would repeat with perfect accuracy the whole hymn, having learned a large part of the contents of the book in early life. "O," said she, "how thankful I am now, in my old age and blindness, that when I had good eyesight I improved my precious time in committing to memory so many sweet promises in my Bible, and so many excellent prayers in my hymn-book; for the hymns in my hymn-book are nearly all blessed prayers!"

Now, children, while your eyes are good, and your memories are retentive, waste no time. Commit something valuable to memory every day. It is surprising how much can be learned every year by improving a few spare minutes each day. "Take care of minutes, and hours will take care of themselves." The great philosopher, Sir Isaac Newton, who in youth was not considered brighter than

ordinary boys, was one day asked how he
had acquired such a vast amount of scien-
tific knowledge. He replied, " By form-
ing the habit in early life of improving all
my time, and employing it to some useful
purpose."

Thus a certain mechanic, who had to
work very hard every day, learned several
difficult languages besides his own, just by
snatching up the spare moments in each
day that most young persons were in the
habit of idling away.

3. *Treat everybody with kindness.* It
may seem to be hardly worth while to take
pains to show kindness to everybody—the
rich, the poor, the aged, the young, friends
and enemies ; but let me tell you, if it is
a small matter, it may lead to great results.
Napoleon's writing-master found it so, for,
when he so patiently bore with the heed-
lessness of the young Corsican, he had no
idea that his pupil, who made such awk-
ward work at penmanship, would ever be
an emperor, or that he himself would ever
be in circumstances of necessity so great
as to ask favors at his hand. But it was

even so; and as soon as he made himself known as his old writing-master, Napoleon not only remembered him personally, but recollected his forbearance and kindness, and was pleased to show his gratitude by settling upon him a pension for life. A kind act, a kind word, a kind look, costs us little or nothing, my young friends, and yet it is inconceivable how much the happiness of others and our own happiness depends upon these little things. When I say, be kind to your parents, brothers, sisters, and everybody, I do not merely mean *appear* kind, but BE kind; that is, study to cultivate such a disposition of *heart*, and then it will be very easy to look kindly, speak kindly, and perform kind deeds. The face of a person is very much like the face of a watch. Unless the main-spring and wheels of a watch are in order, the dial and hands, you know, will indicate false time; so, children, if your heart be not right, not only your hands, but even your countenance, will sooner or later show the internal disorder.

Now, to get such an inward disposition,

such a good heart, you must go to the Saviour, who came to heal the broken-hearted, and pray him to "create in you a clean heart and renew in you a right spirit," that, like him, you may love not only your friends but your enemies, and do good to those who despitefully use you and persecute you. And thus, though wicked boys may occasionally make up faces at you, or try to provoke you with naughty words, or even strike you, you will find that you can conquer them much more easily by showing them a big *heart*, than by flourishing a big *fist*.

4. *Do not forget your little prayer.* That sweet evening prayer which, I trust, you learned when you were very small—

> " Now I lay me down to sleep,
> I pray the Lord my soul to keep;
> If I should die before I wake,
> I pray the Lord my soul to take."

It may seem to you, now you are older, to be too small for you; but let me assure you it is a very important prayer.

The great and good Bishop Hedding remarked, a short time before his death,

that this little prayer, which his sainted
mother taught him in infancy, he had
continued to repeat almost every night
since. And that distinguished statesman
and philanthropist, John Quincy Adams,
who had also been taught to use this
prayer when a child, never forgot it, but
repeated it every evening, even when he
lived in "the great white house" at
Washington as President of the United
States, and, no doubt, kept it up until the
day of his death. O, I pity any child
that has grown up to despise or forget the
prayers or pretty verses which his pious
parents or teachers taught him! Remember, children, a prayer may be very simple
in language, and very short, and yet,
when offered up in sincerity and faith,
may produce great results. The Bible
tells us of a certain good man, when there
was a great famine by reason of a terrible
drought, no rain having fallen for more
than three years, who went out and prayed
for rain; and it was not long before, in
answer to prayer, a little cloud, no larger
than a man's hand, was seen, which grew

larger and larger, blacker and blacker, until the refreshing rain came in torrents. Now, I do not suppose Elijah made what is generally called a great prayer, that produced such a great result. O no. You have, no doubt, read in your Testament of a blind man who had his eyesight restored by Jesus, as the result of a very short prayer: "Have mercy upon *me*." The wicked publican or tax-gatherer who did not dare go inside the temple, nor look up toward heaven, cried out, "God be merciful to me, a sinner;" and he went home a forgiven and happy man. A still more interesting case is that of the thief on the cross, who, just before he expired, exclaimed, "Lord, remember me when thou comest into thy kingdom." And although our blessed Saviour was himself at that time suffering dreadfully upon the cross, he listened to the little prayer of the dying thief, and answered, "This day shalt thou be with me in paradise." Learn, then, children, from these examples, that though your prayers may seem very small and feeble, if they are offered

up to God in the all-prevailing name of
Jesus, with earnestness and confidence, as
you ask your mother for food when very
hungry, you will find that great and glorious results will follow, sooner or later.

Another thing: be punctual and regular
in prayer. Do not let small things prevent your attendance on private devotion.
For instance, do not omit your morning
and evening prayer if an irreligious or
even scoffing person should happen to
sleep in the same room; for a little duty
improved under such circumstances often
produces incalculable good; and a little
duty neglected at such times often occasions irreparable loss, if not mischief. The
pious youth in England, who happened to
lodge one night with an ungodly boy, no
doubt had an inward struggle, as he knelt
as usual by his bedside, before retiring to
offer up his evening sacrifice; but he little
thought that his example would be the
means of the awakening and conversion
of that prayerless boy, and transforming
him into a flaming herald of the cross. Indeed, it is quite likely, had the conscien-

tious youth only restrained prayer that night, his own soul would have been stung with remorse, and the name of JOHN ANGELL JAMES, now everywhere known and honored as one of the most useful writers and successful preachers of the age, would never have been heard of out of his own neighborhood.

5. *Learn to say*, No. This is a little, but very important word. When quite young, and living away from home, one Sabbath, during the intermission of divine service at noon, I took a short walk to the wharf of the lake. It happened that a company of young men were just ready to put out in a small sail-boat, and they urged me to jump in, assuring me that they intended to take only one little tack, as they called it, and would be back again in a few minutes. There was a fine breeze; they were quite urgent, and I had not the courage to say No. Aboard I went, and bitterly did I rue it; for the wind immediately changed and blew us far from shore, and the gale became so severe that we were in imminent danger of drown-

ing. One flaw of wind struck our frail vessel, that would doubtless have capsized it had not the mast broken; as it was, we buffeted the storm nearly all day. My associates were rough and profane, and when I reached land some miles from the village, I was not only grateful for my deliverance from a shameful and wicked death, but determined to keep away from the wharf on the Sabbath, and to learn "the art of saying *No,*" when persuaded to do that which my conscience condemned. Alas! how many promising youth have disgraced and utterly ruined themselves, by not having the courage to say *No* when they were enticed into drinking saloons, gambling-rooms, and houses of ill-fame! Boys, when you are invited by any person to attend the horse-race, the circus, the theater, or to "try just one little glass" of intoxicating liquor, do not hesitate, but thunder out the word No, so suddenly and emphatically as to startle your seducer, and make his ears tingle. This is your only safety.

6. *Allow no opportunity of usefulness,*

however small, to pass unimproved. Those who are constantly omitting every-day opportunities of doing a little good, in the expectation that they are going to do great things when they get grown up, never accomplish much. A minister of great learning one Sabbath preached a *great* sermon to convert a *great* man who was an infidel. A few days afterward this man became a humble believer, not by the great sermon, however, but by one expression made the same day by an infirm old colored woman whom he had assisted down the steps of the church. The expression was this: "I thank you, massa; but O how I do wish you loved my Jesus!"

The woman that improved the opportunity to speak a few words to a very profane and wicked boy in Bedford, England, had no idea at the time that, by that little act, she was the honored instrument of the conversion of John Bunyan, the swearing tinker, into John Bunyan, the author of the Pilgrim's Progress, which everybody has read, or ought to read. So, boys and girls, be encouraged to do at least a little good every day.

Finally, *allow yourself to do nothing, however small, which you are not sure is right.* Beware of little *actions* that are wrong; touch not, taste not, handle not anything, however small, which you ought not to touch. Beware of little *words* that are wicked. One slanderous word, carelessly uttered, has often made hearts to bleed that time, nor money, nor tears could ever heal. Beware of little *thoughts* that are wicked. Never say, "No matter what I think, if I keep my thoughts to myself." O, *every* thing depends upon having good thoughts! Then, like the Psalmist, instead of cherishing, let us "hate vain thoughts," and pray God to "cleanse us from secret faults."

DOING AND RECEIVING HARM.

Do thyself no harm.—ACTS xvi, 28.

PAUL, the great apostle, said these words to a man who was about to kill himself. If you will look into the sixteenth chapter of Acts, you may read for yourself the particulars of this wonderful affair,—how Paul and Silas were cast into prison for preaching the truth,—how they were happy even in the dark, filthy dungeon, and sang and prayed in the night,—how God caused a great earthquake to break open the prison-doors, and the stocks and chains which confined these good men; and how the jailor was terribly frightened, and would have destroyed himself if Paul had not entreated him not to cut his own throat. O, it is impossible to tell the amount of harm the jailer would have brought upon himself if he had taken his own life! He would have been a self-murderer, and of course would have been miserable forever, for no murderer can enter into heaven: and what a terrible calamity that would have been! Is it not strange that men will be so unwise as to harm *themselves*, even if they are so wicked as to wish harm to others? Yet there are folks, especially little folks, who are so foolish as to do themselves great harm.

Now, children, while I urge you to attend to the caution, "Do thyself no harm," I wish you to bear in mind that I mean not the jailer, nor somebody else, but *you*. Children are very apt to say, "You need not give *me* such advice; there is no danger in *my* case. I will take care of myself." So many have said, and yet have utterly ruined themselves in a short time afterward.

I. I will now mention some ways in which children do themselves harm.

1. Some do themselves harm by doing *nothing*. Children, God made you to become working men and working women; and hence, if in early life you should form

indolent habits you would do yourselves much harm. Do you not know if you should now stop using your right hand, it would in a short time become so weak that you *could* not use it? Dr. Scudder, in his tales about the heathen in India, tells us he saw some devotees who had held up their arms above their heads so long, that they could not bring them down by their sides if they should try. And as it is with the arm, so with the whole body, and so also with the mind. Why is it that some boys and girls are often heard to say, " O! I forgot?" They are indolent; they do not try hard to remember. Why is it that some children, when called upon to do examples in school that require study, so often say, " I can't?" They are lazy—do not try hard to think; and thus they do themselves great harm, by becoming not only dunces and drones, but very unhappy creatures. Some of the most wretched creatures in the world are those who have nothing to do, or have no disposition to work. The poor colliers that work all the time under ground are much happier than lordly aristocrats, who spend the live-long day yawning on sofas, and knawing the ends of their delicate jeweled fingers in indolence.

2. Some do themselves harm by *eating too much*. A physician, some time since, remarked that the world is full of grave-diggers. On being asked to explain his meaning, he said thousands and tens of thousands of people dig their own graves *with their teeth*. In other words, they shorten their lives either by eating too much, or eating unwholesome food.

About two years since, a lady sitting at a table remarked, "I will eat this piece of mince-pie, although I know it will hurt me, as mince-pie always does; but I love it, and will eat it." I told her plainly she was a suicide, that is, a self-murderer. She seemed quite surprised, if not offended at my remark. She is now in her grave.

Solomon, you know, says, "Put a knife to thy throat if thou be a man given to appetite." A lady at a sewing society, being asked to mention a passage of

Scripture as a topic of conversation, repeated the just-quoted verse; but no one
appeared exactly prepared to explain its
meaning. Now, I do not suppose that
Solomon designed to encourage persons
actually to cut their throats, but to teach
us that it is as wicked to shorten our lives
by gluttony, as by using the knife or
halter. Children, do not think too much
about gratifying your appetite; do not
murder yourselves by eating candies,
sweetmeats, and other dainties, which you
have reason to believe will injure you, simply because you like them.

3. Many boys, if not girls, do themselves
immense harm by using that filthy weed
called tobacco; and I fear the rage for its use
is increasing in our country. O how sad it
has made me feel, quite lately, to see little
beardless boys puffing cigars along the
streets, and their mouths looking like the
foul chimneys of steam-tugs! My Uncle
Toby, or some other uncle, was not far out
of the way when he defined a cigar to be
" a dark roll of twisted leaves, with a fire
at one end and a fool at the other." In-

deed, it is not only a very foolish, but *wick-ed* habit. Boys, never chew nor smoke tobacco; girls, there is only one kind of snuff I would recommend you to take, and that is the early morning air. A person that uses tobacco is more filthy than the swine; for hogs, though not the most neat in their personal habits and dwellings, will not touch tobacco; and it is said nothing is regarded by the sagacious elephant as so great an insult as the offer of a quid of this nasty weed. I was in a menagerie, many years ago, when a man inclosed a plug in an apple and offered it to the elephant, which so enraged him that it was with great difficulty the man who had deceived him escaped with his life. Those who use tobacco do themselves great harm, for it is not only a filthy practice, but it often subjects those who use it to mortifying inconvenience, is very expensive, weakens the mind, produces numerous distressing diseases, and naturally excites an appetite for intoxicating liquors. Yes, children, if you learn to smoke, or chew, or take snuff, you are not only binding your body and soul with chains, that, sooner or later, will gall you worse than fetters of steel, but you will be more liable *to become degraded drunkards* than otherwise.

Tobacco, it is true, has its ·use, it is good to destroy vermin; but that is no reason why we should poison ourselves with it.

4. Children do themselves no small harm when they *tell wrong stories.* No wonder a certain good minister spent a sleepless night on learning that his little boy, not more than five or six years old, had told a falsehood. For he knew that *one* willful lie was sufficient to make his son a *liar;* and he thought of that fearful text, "All liars shall have their part in the lake that burneth with fire and brimstone." Children sometimes think they will gain more by telling a falsehood than by telling the truth; but it is a sad mistake. One *little* lie generally leads to many great ones; and when the habit of telling false stories is formed, then your character is ruined, (for who does not abhor a liar?) and then

your happiness and peace of mind are at an end. Remember, *every species of deception is lying.* A certain lady, who had learned politeness from some other book rather than the Bible, while visiting a friend, had sprats, which are small fish, set before her on the table. "I do not know whether you are fond of sprats?" said the lady of the house, inquiringly. "O yes," was the reply, "I am very fond of them indeed;" when in reality she detested them, and could scarcely swallow a mouthful. The good woman of the house, supposing her guest sincere, supplied her bountifully with sprats every day while at her house, which, though a merited retribution, was by no means the worst consequence of her fibbing propensity.

Never say at the door when a friend calls, "I am very glad to see you, and hope you will call again soon," unless you *feel* so. How many such falsehoods are practiced; and although they deceive and injure others, the worst harm at last falls upon those who indulge in such habits of hypocrisy.

5. Young persons who *read bad books* have no idea at the time how much harm they are thus doing themselves.

Now all books are bad which cause us to indulge in wicked, vain, or impure thoughts. Bad books are *poison*. They poison the mind; and it is far worse to have the mind, which is destined to live forever, poisoned, than the body, which at best must soon crumble into dust. A boy may read an impure book, and shut it up and hide it, or pass it to some one else to read, and may think he is not hurt at all; but he is mistaken. He has been taking poison. There are, you know, some kinds of poison taken into the stomach that produce no *immediate* effect. No pain is felt at first; but the poison is imperceptibly working and working all through the system, until the whole constitution is tainted, and horrid ulcers appear on the surface of the body, and the entire form, however beautiful once, becomes a loathsome mass of corruption. Such is the effect of bad books upon the mind. The first effect of them is the change produced by their perusal in the *thoughts* of the heart. The poison keeps working in the thoughts until it begins to affect the *tongue.* That is, the poisoned mind shows itself in filthy or blasphemous *words;* and finally, his heart has become so corrupt that all his wicked *actions* show that he is a poisoned, rotten-hearted, ruined wretch. A man of my acquaintance, who loves liquor, lodging one night away from home, discovered in a cupboard in his bedroom a bottle which he supposed to contain whisky. He hastily put it to his mouth, and had swallowed but a little before he found out his mistake. It was corrosive sublimate. In a few minutes the poison began to work. He hoped, as he had taken so little, that he would get over it without exposing himself; but his pain increasing, he was compelled to roar out for help. The family were aroused. A physician was immediately sent for, and with great difficulty his life was saved ; but the poor man never will get over the bad effect of that one small draft which he thought nobody would know he had taken.

O how true it is that a person's "sin will surely find him out!" Children, I advise you to adopt this rule: Never read any book that you are ashamed your parents or Sunday-school teacher should know that you are perusing.

6. Boys who use *profane language* do themselves much harm. It is certain no one can take the name of God in vain and get the slightest advantage from it. A person who curses and swears gets nothing but harm in return for his pains. He exposes himself to the wrath of God, and is despised even by profane wretches themselves. Have you ever read the little tract called the "Swearer's Prayer?" It tells us that many who have prayed for God to kill them and damn their souls have had their prayers instantly answered. God will not be mocked with impunity.

A certain woman had a boy who was beginning to contract the abominable habit of using profane and impure language, and to break him of the practice she made him wash out his mouth with strong soap suds every time she heard him use improper and wicked words. This perhaps did him some good; but the worst of it is, soap and water cannot wash away guilt from the conscience and pollution from the heart.

7. Persons who allow themselves to commit little acts of *dishonesty* do themselves much harm. That pilfering boy, when he takes the penknife from his schoolmate without liberty, or steals a sixpence from the till of his employer, knows that he is doing those he robs great injustice; but he little dreams that he is doing *himself* a thousand times as much harm as he is doing others.

But of all thieves, the boy that tries to cheat God is the worst. I knew a young man who for several weeks employed each returning Sabbath in hard labor on the shoemaker's bench, in order to accumulate a great deal of money. But he did himself immense harm. He not only deprived himself of the sweet rest, spiritual delights, and instructions of God's house, and defiled his own conscience, but ruined his health, so that he lost a thousand times more than he gained. His physician told him frankly that his sickness was, without doubt, solely the result of not observing the Sabbath as a day of rest from labor.

Remember, my young friends, you cannot commit even a *small* fraud upon God, or your fellows, without doing *enormous* injustice to yourselves.

8. The child that indulges a *peevish, fretful, discontented* disposition does himself great harm. Girls, if you wish to know how to become completely wretched, and make every body dread you as if you were a leper, learn when a child to fret and scold at every little thing that does not suit your notions.

I read not long since of a woman who, when young, had formed this habit, and after her marriage she seemed to try every method to make her husband unhappy. She was contented nowhere, nor satisfied with anything he purchased for her. At one time he tore to pieces a very comfortable house, and rebuilt it at great expense to gratify her whim; and after all she was not pleased, and he was obliged to dispose of it at a sacrifice and purchase another, with which she promised to be content. It was, however, not long before she was uneasy, and insisted upon his selling out and going elsewhere, for a trifling reason.

Do not forget, children, that a *fretful mind* makes a *scowling, homely face;* and when the lines of discontent frequently disfigure the countenance, the features become fixed, that is, permanently disagreeable and repulsive; which certainly is a sort of harm that no person in his senses ought to inflict upon himself.

9. The boy that *retaliates*, or strikes back, does himself no small harm. I know it is *natural* for one to say, if he is injured without just cause or provocation, " I'll come up with him some day for that; I will give him his pay;" but remember, my son, you cannot return injury for injury, railing for railing, without doing yourself at least as much harm as you can do him.

A foolish man once saw a large hen-hawk dart down in his barn-yard, and seize in his talons a fine fat chicken. The hawk, bearing off his prize, was followed by the enraged man, who with a huge club foamed and fretted as he ran from field to field in vain pursuit of the bird of prey, that proudly sailed above him. When asked by a neighbor whether he expected to overtake and kill the hawk, he answered, "No, but I mean to *worry* him most dreadfully!" He forgot that by far the greatest worriment was endured by himself.

Boys, I know of no better way to "come up with" those who injure you, than to heap coals of fire (that is, melted love) upon their heads, by showing them special kindness, and letting them know that if they have a hard fist, you have a tender heart.

10. I must not omit to say, that the child who *abandons the Sunday school* does himself harm. Some boys, as soon as they get into their teens, tease their parents to allow them to leave the school, on the ground that they are getting *too old* to attend. But those who do so commit

a great blunder. Those who quit the Sunday school when it is their privilege to attend, deprive themselves of blessings far more valuable than gold, and expose themselves to many temptations and perils.

Boys, do you wish to know at what age you ought to leave the Sunday school? When you are so old and infirm that you are unable to crawl to the hallowed school-room, then you are old enough to cease attending, and not before.

I like the spirit of a young man who was tauntingly asked if he attended the Sunday school yet. "To be sure I do," said he; "I am *married* to the Sabbath school. I have joined it for life. I mean to have a share in that concern as long as I live."

11. I can only add, those children do themselves irreparable harm who *neglect religion in early life.*

I need not tell you that religion will be the "one thing needful" when you shall be *old.* You know you *must* have it when you come to *die.* My young friends, if you neglect to give your hearts to God in the days of your youth, you will be very likely to neglect to do so when old, and thus you will die without it, and then what can compensate for the harm you would thus do yourself? What will it profit you if you gain the whole world and lose your own soul? But the truth is, you will not gain much, even of this world, without religion. Would you not think a mariner very foolish to go to sea without any compass or chart to guide him? Would you not think a traveler, about to pass through a dreary and dangerous desert, very unwise not to take a guide-book that is kindly offered him? But the mariner does not need the compass to navigate the tempestuous ocean, nor the traveler through the wilderness a guide-book half as much as you need religion to guide you safely through the dangers and snares of this unfriendly world.

There are some kinds of harm children may do themselves which can be repaired. Franklin did a foolish thing when, in childhood, he gave all his money for a whistle; but he earned more money afterward. The boy who jumped from the hay-mow and broke his leg did himself much harm, and caused himself much suffering; but the bone grew together again, and is now nearly as strong as the other. The careless school-boy who neglected his books when a child, may possibly recover his loss by studying very hard when he is grown up; but nothing, *nothing* can make up the injury a person does his soul by neglecting in early life to give his heart to God. O, children, remember, to be useful here and happy hereafter your hearts must be changed; you must love and serve God. Jesus invites you to come to him and be converted and saved. If you refuse to go to him, you are not only wronging your Maker, grieving the Spirit, and blasting the hopes of your best friends, but you are *cheating* your own soul.

II. In concluding this discourse, I wish to give you two or three special reasons why children should do themselves no harm.

1. A *little* harm done yourselves in childhood, often amounts to serious injury when you are grown up. See that gnarled, crooked, and half-dead tree. What is the matter? Why, perhaps when it was a small twig it was twisted a little, and the bark bruised on one side. It seemed *then* a small matter, but it is *now* a mutilated, ill-shapen, and short-lived tree. So with children who form bad habits of any kind while young. The twists and bruises which they make in their character become fixed, and grow more apparent and injurious as they grow older.

See those masons at work. They are about erecting a large building. Observe how deep they dig below the surface of the ground, and how careful they are to select and lay good stones at the bottom. Why do they not put those shelly, half-rotten stones where they will not be seen, and place those huge substantial blocks on the top? Ah! they know the building, however beautiful, will be useless without a good foundation: it will tumble down, and great will be the fall of it! Now, as the masons are building an edifice, so, children, you are building your own character. Every action is a stone in that building. You are now working on the most particular part of your house—the foundation. One wicked action, like a defective stone at the base, may greatly harm, if not destroy the whole building.

How foolish would a ship-builder be to put a poor worm-eaten plank at the bottom of the ship. A good ship-builder, though he begins at the keel, if he must use any poor timber reserves it for the last—the upper part of the vessel, where it can be employed with the least injury. So, boys, *if you must* do mischief, would it not be better to wait until you become old and gray-headed, when the effects of your misconduct will not be so serious to yourselves?

2. You cannot do *yourselves* harm without wronging *others*.

A young man once stepped up to the bar of a hotel and called for liquor. A brother, fearing he might one day become a drunkard, whispered kindly to him to "put down the bowl." But he was angry, and told his brother to mind his *own* business. Said he, "I know when to stop, and whatever becomes of *me* it is none of *your* concern." He became a miserable tippler, and not only disgraced his brother, but caused him and the whole family an amount of anxiety, trouble, and expense, in a thousand ways, which no language can describe, and finally brought not only himself to an untimely end, but brought down the gray hairs of his parents in sorrow to the grave.

A wicked boy can no more live in a community without doing mischief to other boys, than a person infected with the small-pox, or some other contagious disease, can mingle freely in society without spreading disorder and death wherever he goes. Remember, then, whenever you do *yourself* harm, you are also inflicting wrongs upon not only your brothers, sisters, parents, and associates, but committing a fearful offense against God.

3. Finally, if you do *yourselves* no harm, *nobody else can very seriously injure you.*

There is an old heathen saying that is worth remembering: "The gods take care of those who take care of themselves." The Bible, which, by the way, is much better authority, assures us that nothing can harm us if we be followers of that which is good. It is true, children, you may suffer sickness, disappointment, and occasional reproach even if you live a godly, blameless, and prayerful life; but God will suffer no evil to befall you, if you do his will and trust in him, that shall not, *in the long run*, be overruled to your good. All things work together for good to them that love God. If you aim to do right in all things, with humble reliance upon the blessed Saviour, so sure as God delivered Paul and Silas from prison, Daniel from the lions' den, and the three Hebrew children from the burning furnace, he will take care of you, even if to do so he has to make a world for your benefit; for a world he can make from nothing in a moment, but he *cannot lie.*

One word more. If you do *yourselves*

harm, you must suffer the consequences *yourselves.* Like the wounded stag that retires into some solitary place to bleed, you must suffer alone, with the stinging reflection added, that you are the authors of your own misery. O, what sad reflections are these: "I am reaping the fruit of my own doings! I knew my duty, but did it not!" I beseech you, then, do yourselves no harm. Do your bodies no harm; do your minds no harm; above all, do your precious immortal souls no harm.

And let me tell you that the only way to succeed in avoiding harm, is to be constantly engaged in doing good. Keep yourselves usefully employed, and you will be sure to keep out of harm's way.

MY FATHER'S BUSINESS.

I must be about my Father's business.—LUKE ii, 49.

WHEN Jesus was about twelve years of age, he accompanied his mother Mary and her husband Joseph up to Jerusalem from Nazareth. After staying there about a week, worshiping God, Mary and Joseph, with their neighbors, started for home. Before they arrived there, they were surprised to find out that Jesus was not with them. When they reached home they made diligent inquiry for him, but he had not been seen; so they returned to Jerusalem, and, after searching some time, they found him in the temple. It seems there were some wise men in Jerusalem who used to teach children about God and the Bible. Sometimes they would ask Jesus questions, which he promptly answered; and then he would modestly ask them questions. Never had the doctors conversed before with so lovely and wise a child. But his mother said to him, "Son, why hast thou thus dealt with us? Behold thy father and I have sought thee three days sorrowing." Then Jesus meekly answered, "Do you not know that I must be about my Father's business?" as if he had said, "It is time for me to engage in the work that my heavenly Father sent me into the world to accomplish."

Jesus was a model child; and although no boy ever was or ever will be as pure and perfect on earth as he was, it is the duty of every one to imitate him as closely as possible, especially by engaging while young in his heavenly Father's service.

From the words of the child Jesus, "I must be about my Father's business," we learn,—

I. *That we all have something to do in this world.* There are many boys, and girls too, who do not seem to realize that there is anything of importance for *them* to do, so they idle away their precious time, either in doing nothing or doing mischief. And as they do not try to be useful to others, when they die they are soon forgotten.

Children, I wish now to impress upon your minds the truth, that although you were not sent into this world to do the wonderful work that Jesus was sent from heaven to accomplish, namely, to *redeem* mankind, and open the door of mercy for all who choose to escape eternal death and obtain everlasting life, yet you were sent for *some* purpose. There is *something* for *you* to do. It is to me a very comfortable thought that the King of heaven, who made the sun, moon, and stars, and upholds the universe, is disposed to employ even unworthy *me*—that there is any place in his vineyard where I may be useful; for it is worse than death to live, and yet to live only as a burden upon others.

II. Another lesson taught by these words of Jesus is this: *It is our duty to inquire what the great business of life is.* There are many who seem to be always busy, yet they never accomplish much, for they have no important work laid out. They do not consult the great guide-book, the

Bible, to know what is the great business
of life, and how that business is to be done.
The Bible tells us that our business in this
world is to *serve God;* and there are two
ways of ascertaining just what kind of
work God is disposed to set us about.
One is by searching his *word,* and the other
is in going to God in *prayer,* and, in the
name of Christ, asking "what he would
have us to do." And, children, whether
you study God's will by prayer or by
reading his word, you will find that, to
serve God aright, in the first place *you
must* LOVE *him.* Depend upon it, you cannot do what God desires you to do, and
do it *right,* unless you love him, and love
him better than you love anybody else.
Would you wish any one to work for you
who hated you? By no means. So God
cannot accept of any service from those
who do not love him. Jesus was prepared when only twelve years of age to
do his Father's business, because he loved
God with all his heart. Hence it was a
pleasure to do and suffer everything God
required at his hands. Children, are you

thus prepared to serve God? Do you love him? Do you like to think of him, to talk of him, and read of him? Do you love to thank him for the multitude of blessings you are every day receiving from him? If you find that your heart is not right with God, you must pray earnestly for the Holy Spirit to make it right, that you may *know* you love him.

2. To serve God acceptably, you must try to realize that he is always *present* with you. It is said that a certain heathen king, in order that he might be restrained from wickedness, and incited to do right, required his servant every day to say to him, "Philip, remember thou art mortal!" No doubt the solemn thought that he was every day liable to die had a good effect; but it is still better to bear in mind that God's eye is continually upon us, and that we cannot for a single moment, by night or by day, get away from his presence, even if we should desire to do so. When little boys get angry and strike their sister; when they use bad language, run away from home without liberty, and commit

wrong deeds that they would be ashamed to have exposed to their most intimate associates, it is when they forget that God is looking directly at them.

A day or two since I saw a little boy and girl walking down street, and on a stand before a fruit-shop were some very fine apples displayed for sale, which certainly looked very inviting. As they approached the fruit the boy paused, looked wishfully at the apples, and then gazed around to see if any one saw him. Not seeing the shop-keeper, he stretched out his little fingers, and no doubt would have snatched one, had not his sister, who appeared to be younger than himself, caught his hand and pulled him away. Was not that kind in the little girl, for who can tell what might have been the consequence if he had actually stolen the apple? Do you suppose he would have dared even to think of such wickedness if he had realized that the great God was looking not only at his pilfering hand, but into his covetous heart, and knew all his wicked thoughts?

Another advantage of bearing in mind that God is always near us is, that if we are disposed to do his will he is ever ready to help us; for without him we can do nothing, but by his gracious aid we can do everything that he requires.

3. But again, children, if you would serve God you must *make it your aim in all things to please him.* It is a good thing to desire to please everybody, to please your young associates, to please your teacher, and especially to please your parents; but it is of far greater importance that you please God. Even if your *parents* should command you to do that which you know is wrong, you are not to please them by doing what they require, because you would thus displease God. A little boy not long since, in one of the Western states, an adopted child, was whipped to death because he would not tell a lie. His little hands were tied together, and fastened with a rope to the rafters, and he was whipped and whipped until the blood flowed down his legs and made quite a puddle on the floor. Al-

though he over and over again declared he had not told a lie, and that he did not *dare* to tell a lie, his father, at the instigation of his brutal mother, continued to apply the rod until he said most beseechingly, "Now, father, won't you stop? I feel so faint;" and in a few minutes his mangled body was a lifeless corpse, and his spirit, no doubt, was taken where the "wicked cease from troubling."

O, if that good boy had not been *very* anxious to please God, he would have told a falsehood to save his life! How thankful, children, should you feel that you have not such parents as this boy had. There are very few fathers or mothers who punish their children to make them do *wrong;* if they do so, it is to make them do *right*. A child, however, who serves God, and aims to please him in all things, will generally please his parents.

Now, if you desire to please God in all things, you must *think of God at all times;* and especially whenever you think of doing anything, or going anywhere, ask yourself, "Will it please God if I *do* this, or *go* there? for I must be far more anxious to please my heavenly Father than to please myself." I once read about an excellent lady who spends nearly all her time in visiting the sick, aiding the poor, and doing good to those in prison. Every morning the first thing she thinks of when she awakes is the goodness of God, and her first inquiry is, " Lord, what wilt thou have me to do *to-day?*" Thus in " all her ways she acknowledges God, and he directs her paths." Let me entreat you early in life to follow her example, and let not a single day pass without at least *trying* to do something for Him who has done so much for you.

I need not mention the particular items of business that children can do for God. For if you study his word; if you bear in mind that God sees you every moment; and if you really *wish* to please him all the time, I have no doubt you will find something useful to do every day. You will not be likely to spend all your time in indolence, reading novels, or foolish play; nor will you be inclined to associate with the wicked, attend the circus, theater, or dancing-school; or to drink intoxicating liquor, or smoke, or chew tobacco. No, it is not until boys forget God—lose sight of the truth that they belong to God—that he made them, preserves them, and redeemed them, and that at the great day of judgment they must stand before him to give an account of their conduct—it is not until they forget these things that boys and girls *dare* do those acts of wickedness which are plainly forbidden in God's word, and leave undone those duties which are plainly enjoined. But we must pass to consider another lesson taught by the words of the holy child Jesus.

III. Children must *be about* their Master's business very early in life.

And here I wish to warn my young friends to keep at a respectful distance from a certain lazy, mean, deceitful, smooth-tongued old thief named PROCRASTINATION. He is commonly called the "thief of *time;*" but he is worse than that, for he not only steals precious time, but precious *souls*, and ruins them forever. An ancient king lost not only his kingdom, but, I think, his head, by listening to the suggestion of this old thief. He had a great feast at his palace, and while he was regaling himself with wine, surrounded by hundreds of gay princes and ladies, a servant interrupted him by a letter, with the statement that it contained a message so important as to demand his immediate attention; but he flippantly pocketed the letter, exclaiming, "Business to-morrow!" To-morrow came; but it was too late to save either his throne or his life.

O how often does procrastination insinuate the idea into youthful minds, "You are too young to begin to serve God!" Beware of him; he is a *liar* as well as a thief. Remember, Jesus was only twelve years old when he said, "I must be about my Father's business." Perhaps the boy or girl who is now reading these lines is twelve years of age, and yet has not commenced the service of God. I have no doubt Jesus began to pray, read the Bible, and do good, before he was twelve years old; and I have known many little girls and boys who were very devoted and useful Christians before they reached that age.

Now, children, if you will give your attention, I will very briefly state a few reasons why you should at once be about your heavenly Father's business.

1. God created you on purpose that you should serve him, that you may enjoy him forever. For this purpose he gave you the Bible, the Sabbath, and all the good things you enjoy. He did not create you to be a butterfly, to show yourself off; to be a sensual swine, only to eat and drink; to be a selfish, stingy snail, to be crouched up in a cell; nor a moth, to consume the substance of others; but he made you to be useful, like the busy bee that

"Gathers honey all the day
From every opening flower,"

not merely for itself but for others. O when you think not only of God's kindness, in your creation, in protecting you during your helpless infancy, and providing for your numerous wants, but especially in giving his Son to live a while on earth with us, to show us how to live, and to *die* for us, that we might have everlasting life, can you refrain from saying, "What shall I render unto the Lord for all his benefits? *I must be about my Father's business.*"

2. The longer you put off the great business of serving God, the more difficult it will be to engage in it. Not long since I advised a little boy, not twelve years of age, to give his heart to the Saviour. But he said, "I cannot love Jesus; my heart is so naughty and wicked that I cannot make it *try* to serve God." This boy was inclined to wait until his heart grew better before he began the great business of life. I told him, however, that the heart gets no better, but worse, by staying away from Christ. And so I say to all. If your heart is so hard, vain, proud, and self-willed now, when you are only eight, ten, or twelve years old, O how hard it will

be by the time you are fifteen or twenty!

3. Remember, also, you cannot be truly happy until you are engaged in the service of God. A person who refuses to serve God is wicked, and the Bible says "there is no peace to the wicked." What are the wicked like? "I was thinking the other night," says Robert Newton, "when on the ocean, and when the raging billows dashed against the vessel, of the language of the prophet: 'The wicked is like the troubled sea,'—not the sea when it is calm, and serene, and placid, but the ocean when tempest-tossed,—all agitation, commotion, and disorder."

Alfred Edmonds has a very kind father and mother, who do all they can to make him pleasant and happy; and yet he is very restless and discontented. He wants this, and he wants that; and nothing will satisfy him. One day, after much teasing, his father bought him a gun, but he soon got dissatisfied with it, and wished to visit his Uncle Thomas; but after spending a week visiting, he came home more peevish and irritable than ever. Now what ails that boy? The fact is he has a bad *heart*— a heart that does not love and obey God. A person may have fine clothes, rich jewelry, nice horses, splendid houses, and a large number of rich relatives, and yet be extremely unhappy, if he is not employed in the service of God: so a person may be very poor, and yet very happy. Jesus was very happy while on earth, and yet he had no house to live in, and no carriage to ride in ; and when he was crucified, all the property he left was a seamless coat, and his body was laid in a borrowed tomb. But what made him happy? Not sumptuous dinners, for he did not have them. He tells us in one short sentence in what his comfort consisted : "My meat and drink is to do the will of my Father who sent me." That is, he took more pleasure in working for God than a very hungry person takes in eating delicious food. And although he was all the time engaged in his Father's business, he did not get tired of it. And so it is with all who engage with all their heart in his service.

4. Once more ; you have none too much time to do the work God has for you to do if you begin now. It is true there are some who, after neglecting religion until they are old, find forgiveness in the name of Christ, and will probably go to heaven when they die ; but they are very sorry, and always will be, even in heaven, that they did not devote the morning of life to the service of God. They are not as useful and happy, and *never will be*, as they would have been if they had not wasted so much precious time, and contracted so many bad habits while young.

Besides, it is by no means certain, if you refuse to obey God's call now, that he will accept of your service after you get old and comparatively useless. The Bible says, "Seek the Lord *while* he may be found." But when may he with certainty be found? God says, "They that seek me *early* shall find me." Now if you were extremely hungry, and ragged, and poor, and you should receive a letter from a very good and rich man, stating that he felt sorry for you, and promising that if you would come to his mansion to-morrow, and become his servant, he would provide for all your wants, and give you a deed of a fine house and lot for you to occupy in a few years, would you hesitate to go? But suppose further that the letter expressly says, "Come *early in the morning*, and then you will be *sure* to find me, and get employment." Would you say, "There is no great need of my being in haste; I will play all the forenoon, and in the afternoon I will comply with the invitation of the rich man; *perhaps* I shall find him, and I will tell him that it was not exactly *convenient for me* to come earlier." No, no; you would not dare to be so impudent, nor so foolish as to run so great a risk; but if your companions should entice you to loiter, and say, "Time enough yet," you would reply, "I must make sure of my place. My good master invited me to come early, and I intend to show him how punctual and faithful I can be." All this, and more, I am sure you would do if a man should offer you a comfortable home on earth; but how trifling are houses and lands, and food and clothing, compared to the mansions in heaven, which are promised those who faithfully serve God on earth! Remember this: the longer and more faithfully you serve God in *this* world, the richer and happier you will be in the *next*.

5. I have only time to add, that you should be about your heavenly Father's business, because you may die very young. When you visit the grave-yard next time, I wish you particularly to notice what a large number of short graves there are. When I visited the Greenwood Cemetery, I saw nothing there so affecting as the thousands and thousands of children's graves, all in beautiful rows. The rural glens, the little lakes, the solemn vaults, and the costly monuments, were interesting; but those acres of children's graves were doubly so. O, I thought, how few of those children whose graves have no mark, except perhaps a little box covered with grass containing their playthings, or a small plaster image of a guardian angel which was rapidly decaying—how few of these ex-

pected, when their tender minds began to think, and their bright eyes began to look out upon the world, that they were to sicken, and pine away, and die while young? I asked myself, how many of them were members of the Sunday school? How many had given their hearts to the Saviour? How many died while engaged in doing the will of God? I trust many of them died happy; but I fear some have neglected religion, expecting while well to live a great while, and when sick to get well, until it was too late to repent. O it is a solemn thing to die! It is a dreadful thing to die unprepared! The last words a certain young lady, who had neglected the great business of serving God, uttered in the ear of her agonized mother were these: "Mother, I did not think it was so hard to die a sinner and go to hell!" How different was the language of the good Sunday scholar who died singing, "There is a happy land." The truth is, the latter girl had been thinking a great deal of that happy land, had been getting ready to go there, and

when death came she was found ready.
She did not depend upon her good works,
however, to *earn* for her a home in that
happy land; for she knew that although
it was her duty to do all she could for
God, as a test of her love to him, after all
she felt that she was an unprofitable servant, dependent entirely upon the merit
of Christ, who had purchased and provided her a sweet home in heaven. My
young friend, would you live with God in
heaven? Then begin now, and serve him
on earth as faithfully as though everything
depended upon your good works, and at
the same time look to Jesus, and pray to
him to make you holy and fit you for
heaven, as though you had done nothing.
There is a beautiful hymn that expresses
the feelings of every heart that truly
desires to be made right, and to do right,
as the servant of the Most High. Here
are two stanzas of it:—

"Rock of Ages, cleft for me,
Let me hide myself in thee;
Let the water and the blood,
From thy wounded side which flow'd,

Be of sin the double cure.—
Save from wrath and make me pure.

" Could my tears forever flow,—
Could my zeal no languor know,—
These for sin could not atone ;
Thou must save, and thou alone :
In my hand no price I bring ;
Simply to the cross I cling."

———◆———

PATHS OF PEACE.

Her ways are ways of pleasantness, and all her paths are
peace.—Prov. iii, 17.

ALL paths are not alike, my dear children ; there are many crooked ways, and
many bad ways, as well as a good and
right way : and there are many guides
that take young people by the hand, inviting and leading them into these several
paths. Sin and folly point to a very broad
road, in which a great many persons are
going ; and they say, " Come and walk
here ; do as others do ; please yourself ;
and you will find many gay flowers along
this way." But they say nothing about

the end to which it leads, because they wish to hide the fact that it conducts to a deep pit, into which those who continue to walk in that way must fall at last, and so be lost forever.

On the other hand, wisdom invites you to try her ways; and the text assures you that "her ways are ways of pleasantness, and all her paths are peace." How, then, is a little boy, or girl, to know what is best to choose? I will tell you the only way of judging: ask what God says about the matter; for he is the God of truth, who cannot lie, and who never tempts any one into a false and dangerous way. It is God, in the person of his dear Son, who calls upon you to walk in the narrow path that will lead to heaven: it is he who tells you about wisdom's ways, how sweet and comfortable they are, that he may allure your footsteps into them, and bring you to the happy place which he has provided for you at the end of the journey of life. Listen, then, to the voice of God, and yield yourself to his voice and guidance: for as a tender father leads his young ones, and when they come to a rough place lifts them up and carries them over, lest they should dash their foot against a stone, and fall and hurt themselves, so your heavenly Father will guide you safely through life, and secure you from the dangers that may beset your path.

The ways of wisdom are the same as those of true religion. They begin in the fear of the Lord, and are marked throughout by hatred of sin, and a care to avoid it. People do not naturally enter upon this good way as soon as they are born into the world; they rather like to go in a path of their own choosing. Accordingly, one turns to the right hand, and another to the left; and all proceed some little distance, at least, till either they find their own way very hard and disagreeable, or they hear a voice behind them saying, "This is the way; walk ye in it:" and the heavenly sound engages their ears, attracts their hearts, and sweetly constrains them to pray, "Turn thou me, and I shall be turned; for thou art the Lord my God."

What way are you now in, my little boy or girl? Are your feet walking in the ways of the Lord, or in some thoughtless and wicked way? That you may be helped to find out where you are, and whither you are going, I will show you some of the way-marks that you must pass in the highway to the kingdom of heaven. The first of these that you come to is *Serious reflection.* When you get so far, you begin to think thus: "Who made me? For what end did God make me? Am I loving him, and doing his will?" Next comes *Repentance toward God.* You there begin to see, that though you are young in years, yet you have been a sinner against God in thought, word, and deed: then you are sorry for your sins, and mourn on account of the exceeding sinfulness of your heart. The next stage in this good way is, *Faith toward our Lord Jesus Christ;* by which you apply to him for pardon and acceptance with God. Faith will lead you on to *prayer* for the influences of the Holy Spirit to make your heart clean; and thus you will go on, by the way-mark of *holiness*, till you reach the heavenly city where God dwells, and where you will be forever with the Lord.

Consider, now, whether you know anything of the road that I have been pointing out. If you do, then be encouraged to go forward. Look to the Lord for grace and strength to persevere in his good ways and to be faithful unto death; that, at last, you may inherit the crown of life.

But, if you have never yet begun to tread the paths of holiness, be prevailed on *now*, without delay, to turn your face in a new direction, and to set out in wisdom's blessed ways. They are very inviting; for what says the text? "Her ways are ways of *pleasantness*, and all her paths are peace." You like things that are pleasant, and can anything be more pleasant than to have God for your father and friend, to have his dear Son for your Saviour, his holy word for your light and guide, his promises for your support, and his heaven for your everlasting home? O, it is pleasant to enjoy the favor of God, and to be assured that he will never, never, no, never forsake us! It is pleasant to love God; the feeling is more than pleasant—it is pleasantness itself. Much do little children lose of true pleasure by not beginning to seek the Lord betimes. There is something more than pleasantness to be found in the ways of religion; for it is said, "all her paths are *peace*." And what a good thing peace is—peace with God, and peace with all mankind! The Bible tells you that "there is no peace to the wicked;" and you, my dear children, are by nature enemies to God, and, therefore, not at peace with him. But your heavenly Father has pitied you, and sent his Son into the world, that, by his death upon the cross, he might make peace for you, and bring you back to him, whose you ought to be, and whom you are bound to serve. Would you, then, live in the enjoyment of that peace which flows from the favor of God? Seek it in wisdom's ways, where only it can be found; and, if you seek it there, you will not be disappointed.

Learn, from this subject, that religion is not a gloomy or melancholy thing, as some people think who know nothing about it. /What think you? Is pleasantness a gloomy thing? Is peace to be shunned as hurtful and disagreeable? No; be assured of this, that the children of God, who walk in wisdom's ways, are the only happy people in the world. The ungodly, who care nothing about heaven and hell, may laugh and look very gay; but their laughter soon comes to an end, and they have neither " pleasantness " nor " peace " in their hearts or in their ways. Ask yourself what will be the end of these things; and if the end is not pleasant, be sure that the way to it cannot be so, however it may appear. Choose you this day what way you will walk in; and may the God of peace dispose your young hearts to resolve, that whatever others may do, you will seek his Holy Spirit's help to enable you to walk in wisdom's ways, seeing " her ways are ways of pleasantness, and all her paths are peace." Amen.

LITTLE AND WISE.

There be four things which are little upon the earth, but
they are exceeding wise: The ants are a people not
strong, yet they prepare their meat in the summer; the
conies are but a feeble folk, yet make they their houses
in the rocks; the locusts have no king, yet go they forth
all of them by bands; the spider taketh hold with her
hands, and is in king's palaces.—PROVERBS xxx, 24–28.

DEAR CHILDREN,—I should like you all
to be very wise.   Wisdom is far better than
money, or fine clothes, or grand houses,
or horses and carriages.   People who are
not wise seldom get on well; they are
seldom happy.   My best wish for any
dear boys and girls that I love is, that
they may grow up very wise.

But how are we to be wise? some of
you will ask.   What are we to do in order
to get this wisdom, which you tell us is
such a good thing?

Dear children, if you would be wise,
you must pray to God to put his Holy
Spirit in your hearts, and give you wisdom.   This is one thing.

Besides this, you must read God's holy

LITTLE AND WISE.

book, the Bible. There you will find out what true wisdom is. There you will see what kind of things wise people do. This is another thing.

And now let me talk to you about the four verses in the Bible which I have looked out for you. They are verses which tell us about wisdom. I hope they will do you much good.

There you see that God tells you to learn a lesson of four little creatures,—the ant, the cony, the locust, and the spider. He seems to say that they are all patterns of wisdom. They are all poor little weak things. An ant is a little creeping insect, that everybody knows. A cony is a little creature very like a rabbit. A locust is like a large grasshopper. A spider is a thing that the least child need not be afraid of. But God tells you that the ant, the cony, the locust, and the spider, are very wise. Come then, dear children, and listen to me, while I tell you something about them. Some of you are but little now. But here you see it is possible to be little and yet wise.

I. First of all, what are you to learn of the ants? You must learn of the little ants to take thought about time to come.

"The ants," says the Bible, "prepare their meat in the summer." God has made the ants so wise and thoughtful that they go about gathering food in the harvest time. They are not idle in the fine long days, when the sun shines. They get all the grains of corn they can find, and lay them up in their nests; and so when frosts and snow come the ants are not starved. They lie snug in their nests, and have plenty to eat.

The butterflies are much prettier to look at than the ants. They have beautiful wings, and make a much finer show; but the butterflies, poor things, are not so wise as the ants. They fly about among the flowers, and enjoy themselves all the summer. They never think of gathering food for the winter. But what happens when the winter comes? The poor butterflies all die, while the ants keep alive.

And now, dear children, I want you each to learn wisdom of the ants. I want you, like them, to think of time to come.

You have each got within you a soul that will live forever. Your body will die some time. Your soul never will. And your soul needs thought and care as much as your body. It needs to have its sins pardoned. It needs grace to make it please God. It needs power to be good. It needs to have God for its best friend, in order to be happy.

And, dear children, the best time for seeking pardon, grace, and the friendship of God, is the time of youth. Youth and childhood are your summer. Now you are strong and well. Now you have plenty of time. Now you have few cares and troubles to distract you. Now is the best time for laying up food for your souls.

Ah! my beloved children, you must remember that winter is before you. Old age is your winter. Your frost, and snow, and rain, and storms, are all yet to come. Sorrow, pain, sickness, death, and judgment, will all come with old age.

Happy are those who get ready for it betimes! Happy are those who, like the ants, take thought for things to come!

Those are wise boys and girls who read their Bibles, and learn many texts by heart. Those are wise boys and girls who pray God every day to give them his Holy Spirit. Those are wise who mind what their parents and teachers tell them, and take pains to be good. Those are wise who dislike all bad ways, and bad words, and always tell the truth. Such boys and girls are like the little ants. They are laying up store against time to come.

Dear children, if you have not done so before, I hope you will begin to do so now. If you have done so, I hope you will keep on doing so, and do so more and more. Do not be like the foolish butterflies. Be like the ants. Think of time to come, and be wise.

II. But let us now go on and see what you are to learn of the conies. You must learn of the little conies to have a place of safety to flee to in time of danger.

"The conies," says the Bible, "make their houses in the rocks." The conies are afraid of foxes, and dogs, and cruel men, who hunt and kill them. They are poor weak things, and are not strong enough to fight and take care of themselves. So what do they do? They make their holes among stones and rocks whenever they can. They go where men cannot dig them out. They go where dogs and foxes cannot follow them. And then, when they see men, or dogs, or foxes coming, they run away into these holes, and are safe.

The hare can run much faster than the cony, for it has much longer legs. The stag is much bigger than the cony, and has got fine horns. But the hare and the stag have got no holes to run into. They lie out on the open fields. And so when men come to hunt them with dogs and guns, they are soon caught and killed. But the little cony has a hiding-place to run to, and in this way he often escapes.

Now, dear children, I want you to learn wisdom from the little conies. I want you to have a place of safety for your souls.

Your souls have many enemies. You are in danger from many things which may do them harm. You have each of you a wicked heart within you. Have you not often found how hard it is to be good? You have each a terrible enemy, seeking to ruin you forever, and take you to hell. That enemy is the devil. You cannot see him. But he is never far off. You are each living in a world where there are many bad people, and few good. Dear children, all these things are against you.

You need the help of One who can keep you safe. You need a hiding-place for your precious souls. You need a dear friend, who is able to save you from your evil hearts, from the devil, and from the bad example of wicked people. Listen to me, and I will tell you about him.

There is One who is able to keep your souls quite safe. His name is Jesus Christ. He is strong enough to save you, for he is God's own Son. He is willing to save you,

for he came down from heaven, and died
upon the cross for your sakes. And he
loves all children. He liked to have them
with him when he was upon earth. He
took them up in his arms and blessed
them.

Dear children, those boys and girls are
wise who put their trust in Jesus Christ,
and ask him to take care of their souls.
Such boys and girls will be kept safe.
Jesus Christ loves them. Jesus Christ
will not let them come to harm. He will
not allow the devil, or wicked people, to
ruin their souls. Jesus is the true Rock
for children to flee to. Boys and girls
who trust in him will be cared for while
they live, and go to heaven when they
die. Jesus is the true hiding-place. Boys
and girls who love him will be safe and
happy.

Dear children, I hope you will all try
to have your souls kept safe. Do not put
off asking the Lord Jesus Christ to take
care of them. Do not say to yourselves,
" O, we shall have plenty of time by-and-
by!" Who knows what my happen to

you before long? Perhaps you may be sick and ill. Perhaps you may lose all your kind friends, and be left alone. O, go and pray to Jesus now! Be like the wise little conies. Get a safe hiding-place for your souls.

III. Let us now see what you are to learn of the locusts. You must learn of the locusts to love one another, to keep together, and help one another.

"The locusts," says the Bible, "have no king, yet go they forth all of them in bands." They have nobody over them to tell them what to do. They are poor little weak insects by themselves. One locust alone can do very little. The least boy or girl would kill a locust if he were to tread on it. It would be dead at once.

But the little locusts are so wise that they always keep together. They fly about in such numbers that you could not count them; you would think they were a black cloud. They do not quarrel with one other. They help each other. And in this way the locusts are able to do a very great deal. They make the farmers and gardeners quite afraid when they are seen coming. They eat up the grass and corn. They strip all the leaves off the trees. And this is because they help one another.

Dear children, I want you to learn of the little locusts always to love one another, and never to quarrel. You should try to be kind and good-natured to other boys and girls. You should make it a rule never to be selfish—never to be spiteful—never to get into a passion—never to fight with one another. Boys and girls who do such things are not wise. They are more foolish than the locusts.

Dear children, quarreling is very wicked. It pleases the devil, for he is always trying to make people wicked like himself. It does not please God, for God is love. Selfishness and quarreling are most improper in Christian children. They should try to be like Christ. Christ was never selfish. He pleased not himself.

Think what a great deal of good boys

and girls might do, if they would be like the little locusts, and love one another. Think how useful they might be to their fathers and mothers. They might save them much trouble, and help them in many little ways. Think what a great deal of money they might collect to help the missionaries to the poor heathen. If every child in Christian lands would collect sixpence a year, by asking people for pennies to help the missionaries, it would amount to a very great sum. Think, above all, what good boys and girls might do, if they agreed to pray for one another. How happy they would soon be! Such prayers would be heard.

Dear children, as long as you live, love one another. Try to be of one mind. Have nothing to do with quarreling and fighting. Hate it, and think it a great sin. You ought to agree together far better than the little locusts. They have no king to teach them. You have a King who has promised his Spirit to teach you, and that king is Christ. O be wise like the locusts, and love one another!

IV. And now, last of all, let us see what you are to learn of the spider. You must learn of the spider not to give up trying to be good because of a little trouble.

"The spider," says the Bible, "taketh hold with her hands, and is in kings' palaces." The spider is a poor little feeble thing, you all know. But the spider takes great pains in making her web. The spider creeps into grand houses, and climbs to the top of the finest rooms; and there she spins her web. There seems no keeping her out. The servants come and brush the web away. The spider sets to work at once, and makes it again new. No insect is so persevering as the spider. She does her work over and over again. She will not give up.

I remember a story of a great king who got back his kingdom by taking example from a spider. Poor man! he had been driven away from his kingdom, like David, by wicked rebels. He had tried often to get his kingdom back. He had fought many battles, but had always been beaten. At last he began to think it was no use. He would give up, and fight no more. It happened at that time that he was lying awake in bed very early one summer's morning, when he saw a spider at work. The spider was trying to make a thread from one side of the room to the other. Twelve times she tried in vain. Twelve times the thread broke, and she fell to the ground. Twelve times she got up and tried again. But she did not give up. She persevered, and the thirteenth time she succeeded. Now when the king saw that, he said to himself, "Why should not I persevere too, in trying to get back my kingdom? Why should not I succeed at last, though I have so often failed?" He did try again. He succeeded. He conquered his cruel enemies, and got back his kingdom. Dear children, this king's name was Robert Bruce. He got back his kingdom, in Scotland, by copying the spider.

Now I want you to make the spider your pattern about your souls. I want you, like the spider, to persevere in stick-

ing to what is good. I should like you to
determine that you will never give up. I
want you to keep on trying not to do what
is evil, and trying always to do what is
good, and pleasing to God.

Ah! dear children, it is a wicked world,
I am sorry to say; and there are many
who will try hard to make you wicked,
as you grow up. The devil will try hard
to make you forget God. Bad men and
women will tell you there is no need for
you to be so good.

I beg you not to give way. I beseech
you to persevere. Keep on praying every
day. Keep on reading your Bibles regularly. Keep on regularly going to church
on Sunday. Alas! there are many boys
and girls who give up everything that
is good as soon as they leave school.
While they are at school they use their
Bibles, and hymn-books, and prayer-books.
When they leave off going to school, they
leave off using all their books too. They
often get into bad company. They often
take up bad ways. They often go idling
about all Sunday. They seem to forget

all that has been taught them. Alas! this is not persevering. This is being more foolish than the little spider. It is wicked and unwise.

Dear children, there is a glorious house in heaven, where I hope I shall see some of you. There is a palace there belonging to Jesus Christ far finer than any palace on earth, in which all Jesus Christ's people shall live and be happy forever and ever. Dear children, I hope I shall see many of you there.

But remember, if you and I are to meet in that glorious palace, you must persevere, and take pains about your souls. You must pray heartily. You must read your Bibles regularly. You must fight against sin daily. You must say when bad people entice you to do wrong, "I will not give up my religion, I will try to please Christ. O, let the little spider be your pattern all your lives! Persevere, and be wise.

And now, dear children, I will finish by asking you to think of what I have been telling you. I have told you of four little creatures which are very wise,—the ants, the conies, the locusts, and the spiders. I have shown you that the ants are a pattern of wisdom, because they think of time to come. The conies are a pattern of wisdom, because they make their houses in safe places. The locusts are a pattern of wisdom, because they help one another. The spiders are a pattern of wisdom, because they persevere. Dear children, I want you to be like them. Some of you may possibly never live to be men and women. But one thing you may be, even now. You may be wise.

Be wise, like the ants. Consider these two verses of the Bible, and learn them by heart. "Remember thy Creator in the days of thy youth." Eccles. xii, 1. "Prepare to meet thy God." Amos iv, 12.

Be wise, like the conies. Consider these two verses of the Bible, and learn them by heart: "Believe on the Lord Jesus Christ, and thou shalt be saved." Acts xvi, 31. "Thou art my hiding-place: thou shalt preserve me from trouble." Psalm xxxii, 7.

Be wise, like the locusts. Consider these two verses of the Bible, and learn them by heart: "By this shall all men know that ye are my disciples, if ye have love one toward another." John xiii, 35. "He that loveth not his brother, whom he hath seen, how can he love God, whom he hath not seen?" 1 John iv, 20.

Be wise, like the spiders. Consider these words of the Bible, and learn them by heart: "Ask, and it shall be given you: seek, and ye shall find." Matt. vii, 7. "Let us lay aside every weight, and the sin which doth so easily beset us: and let us run with patience the race that is set before us, looking unto Jesus." Hebrews xii, 1, 2.

Dear children, think on these things. This is the way to be both happy and wise. Never forget what God says in the Bible: "Better is a poor and wise child, than an old and foolish king." Eccles. iv, 13. "The wise shall inherit glory." Prov. iii, 35.

CUP OF SALVATION.

I will take the Cup of Salvation.—PSALM cxvi, 13.

MAY God the Holy Spirit bless this sermon on the Cup of Salvation! By his gracious influence may it be the means of persuading many young immortals to take and drink of the Cup of Salvation. While you are reading this sermon, send up your supplications to Heaven's throne, and pray that the God of Salvation may enable you to take and drink of the Cup of Salvation!

CUP in Scripture has different meanings. In the following passage it is taken in its literal sense. It contains a counsel which particularly applies to drinkers of wine; or, as they are commonly called, *wine-bibbers*. Prov. xxiii, 31, "Look not thou upon the wine when it is red, when it ·giveth his color in the cup, when it moveth itself aright. At the last it biteth like a serpent, and stingeth like an adder."

God, as a gracious God, and as the God

of Salvation, is called a CUP,—the believer's Cup. Psa. xvi, 5, "The Lord is the portion of mine inheritance and of MY CUP." Blessed is that child who can say, "Jesus is my Cup!"

The abundant blessings of Providence are called a cup. Psa. xxiii, 5, "Thou preparest a table before me in the presence of mine enemies: thou anointest my head with oil; my cup runneth over." Does the cup of our lot run over with the blessings of Providence? O, may our hearts overflow with feelings of thankfulness and love!

Erroneous doctrines are called a Cup. In speaking of these, the apostle uses very strong language. He says, (1 Cor. x, 21,) "Ye cannot drink the cup of the Lord, and the *cup of devils.*" Satan is the father of errors as well as the father of liars. He fills the cup with the deadly poison of error; and woe will be to those who drink the deadly cup!

A *wicked city* is called a cup. Such was Babylon, because she corrupted cities and nations. Jer. li, 7, "Babylon hath been a golden cup in the Lord's hand, and made all the earth drunken: the nations have drunken of her wine; therefore the nations are mad."

An afflicted city is called a cup, and a cup of trembling. Zech. xii, 2, "Behold, I will make Jerusalem a cup of trembling to all the people round about, when they shall be in the siege, both against Judah and against Jerusalem." This intimates the strong judgments which made them tremble with fear, and anguish, and horror. A short while ago the cities of Paris, Berlin, and Vienna, were cups of trembling. By some dreadful riots, it is not long since Glasgow was likely to have been a cup of trembling; but God most graciously heard his people's prayers, and disappointed their fears.

God's wrath is called a cup. Psalm lxxv, 8, "For in the hand of the Lord there is a cup, and the wine is red; it is full of mixture, and he poureth out of the same: but the dregs thereof, all the wicked of the earth shall wring them out, and drink them."

Christ's *sufferings* are called a cup. Matt. xxvi, 39, "He prayed, saying, If it be possible, let this cup pass from me: nevertheless, not as I will, but as thou wilt.

Salvation, with all its blessings, is called a cup. As we find in the words of our text, David says, with holy devotion, thankfulness, and joy, "I will take the cup of salvation, and call upon the name of the Lord."

By the assistance of the Holy Spirit, I shall endeavor to show,

I. *What* the Cup of Salvation is.

II. Mention some *properties* of this remarkable cup.

III. Point out some *strong reasons* why you should take and drink this cup, and introduce to your notice several persons mentioned in Scripture who took and drank of this Cup of Salvation.

And may God the Holy Spirit bless this sermon, for the conviction and conversion of many youthful immortals!

I. I SHALL SHOW WHAT THE CUP OF SALVATION IS.

There is, first, the *Cup;* and, secondly, *what* the Cup contains—*Salvation.*

1. There is the CUP.

After thinking seriously on this Cup, I conclude that it must mean the *Gospel.* There are some very remarkable cups. If I showed you one of them, and asked you the following question, "What is this cup made of?" you would answer, "It is made of silver, and gold, and precious stones." The chief part of the cup is formed of silver, the beautiful mouth, or edge of the cup, is made of gold, and on the sides of the cup there are precious stones, and jewels of sparkling beauty. Then you would say, "What a lovely, costly cup!" Come, now, and see what this Cup of Salvation is made of—this Gospel cup. As to the word *Gospel* itself, it means good news, or good tidings; as the angel said to the shepherds at Bethlehem, (Luke ii, 10,) "Behold I bring you *good tidings* of great joy." I have mentioned a literal cup, consisting of three things,—gold, silver, and precious stones. Now, this Gospel cup consists of *four* things more precious than gold, and silver, and rubies. Beloved young friends, particularly observe these *four*. This Gospel cup consists of precious doctrines, precious invitations of mercy, precious offers of grace, and precious promises of truth. O what a cup! what a wonderful cup!

This Gospel cup consists of precious *doctrines*. What is a *doctrine?* It is something taught, whether good or bad. A bad book, an infidel book, teaches bad infidel doctrines or opinions. But what the Gospel teaches are good doctrines— holy, divine truths. The following is a specimen. The Gospel teaches the doctrine of One Jehovah, the Father, Son, and Holy Ghost, One God. It teaches another doctrine, namely, God's plans and purposes of wisdom and of mercy. It teaches the doctrine of the covenant of grace, in which the Father and the Son agreed from all eternity on the great subject of the salvation of men. It teaches the doctrine of redemption through the person and righteousness of Christ alone;

and it teaches the doctrines of the immortality of the soul, the resurrection of the body, and the eternal blessedness of heaven. A minister who faithfully preaches these doctrines is called "a doctrinal preacher." Thus, I have told you that the first thing of which the Gospel cup consists is doctrines.

This cup consists, secondly, of "precious invitations of mercy." You know what an *invitation* is. If a friend ask you to come to his house and dine with him, that is an invitation. There are many invitations of mercy found in the Gospel, and these add very much to the richness and beauty of the cup. Take the following as a specimen. Jesus says in his kind, inviting voice, " Come unto me, all ye that are weary and heavy laden, and I will give you rest. Take my yoke upon you, and learn of me; for I am meek and lowly in heart; and ye shall find rest unto your souls. For my yoke is easy, and my burden is light." Matt. xi, 28–30. Young friends, seek grace, that you may hear and accept these merciful invitations!

This Gospel cup also consists of precious *offers of grace.* In the Gospel, Jesus comes to young sinners with all the blessings of salvation in his hand. He holds up these great blessings before their eyes, and he offers them most kindly for their acceptance. Jesus is called *Wisdom.* And what does Wisdom say? and what does Wisdom offer? Thus Wisdom speaks, and thus Wisdom offers, (Prov. viii, 10, 11,) " Receive my instruction, and not silver; and knowledge rather than choice gold. For wisdom is better than rubies, and all the things that may be desired are not to be compared unto it." May the Holy Spirit enable my young friends to accept the *offers of grace!*

This Gospel cup consists, fourthly, of *precious promises.* If we compare the Bible to the sky, the promises are the stars which sparkle and shine with great brightness in that sacred sky. Have you not been often astonished, when you have looked up to the sky after the sun had set, and beheld the vast multitude of beautiful stars in all their glory, shining in the firmament? But the promises which shine in such vast numbers in the firmament of the Bible are stars of far greater brightness and far greater loveliness. Come, and see, and admire, the two following promises. The first is especially the promise for the young: "I love them that love me: and those that seek me early shall find me." Proverbs viii, 17. May this promise rejoice your heart! The following precious promise has rejoiced the hearts of myriads, and may it gladden yours : "Incline your ear, and come unto me: hear, and your soul shall live: and I will make an everlasting covenant with you, even the sure mercies of David." Isa. lv, 3.

I have thus endeavored, with great plainness, to describe the Gospel cup as consisting of doctrines, invitations, offers, and promises. And no cup in the palaces of kings, though consisting of silver and gold, and precious stones, was ever worthy to be compared with this.

2. We are to show what this wonderful Cup contains. It contains SALVATION.

And because it contains salvation it is called the *Cup of Salvation.* One cup may contain honey and milk, another may contain refreshing water from the fountain, and another may contain wine; but what these cups contain is nothing compared with what this Cup contai. s. These cups contain what is useful for the body; this Cup that which is useful for the never-dying soul. What these cups contain must perish: what this Cup contains shall endure forever. What these cups contain is useful for the life that now is: what this Cup contains prepares for a life of glory, and immortality in heaven.

This Cup contains salvation. Some think that salvation only consists in deliverance from the miseries of hell, or in having their sins forgiven; but they are in a great mistake. Salvation certainly contains these two, but it contains *much more.*

Endeavor, young friends, seriously to attend, while I attempt to show you of what salvation consists, or what it contains. The loveliest jewels of the diadems of kings are despicable when compared with the precious blessings which salvation contains. The following are among the rich collection, namely,—conversion, the pardon of sin, acceptance with God, admission into the family of God, the graces of the Spirit, fellowship with God, a happy death, a glorious resurrection, and a blessed heaven. I think I hear a pious child exclaim, "O how lovely! O how precious these blessings of a great salvation are!"

Look at the *first*, namely, "Conversion." May this be yours! Then your hard heart will be softened, your black heart be made as white as snow, and your heart of enmity be changed into a heart of love. Then "old things shall pass away, and all things shall become new." 2 Cor. v, 17.

Look at the *second*, namely, "The Pardon of Sin." O seek pardon with penitent hearts, looking to Jesus, and God *will* forgive you! He will say, "I, even I, am he that blotteth out thy transgressions for mine own sake, and will not remember thy sins." Isa. xliii, 25.

Look at the *third* blessing, namely, "Acceptance with God." If a son greatly offends his father, he may for some time not allow him to come into his presence. Some days after the offending son is penitent, comes to his father, bathed in tears, and says, "Father, I have sinned against thee!" The kind father throws his arms around his son's neck, receives him into his favor, and changes his frowns into smiles. This is *acceptance.* Thus God accepts penitent children, who cry to him for mercy through a Saviour's death. And then they sing with joyful hearts "to the praise of the glory of his grace, wherein he hath made us accepted in the beloved." Eph. i, 6.

Look at the *fourth* blessing, namely, "Adoption." To be adopted, is to be made a child of God—to be made one of his family. A rich man takes pity upon the child of a poor beggar-woman, puts him among the number of his children, and makes him his son. You see him playing with the other children, on a bright summer's day on the soft green lawn, before the rich man's noble dwelling, attended by a kind maid-servant. O what a change in that child! He is adopted! It is this which God does to little children who seek his grace. He adopts them. He takes them from Satan's family and makes them his sons. He says then, "Wilt thou not from this time cry unto me, My Father, thou art the guide of my youth?" Jer. iii, 4.

Look at the *fifth* blessing, "The Graces of the Spirit." Do you wish me to name some of these graces? I will do it with pleasure. Repentance, faith, love, hope, joy, patience, zeal, meekness, gentleness, and heavenly-mindedness. These are the graces of the Spirit. Pray that they may be yours. Then you shall be "like the wings of a dove covered with silver, and her feathers with yellow gold." Psa. lxviii, 13.

Look at the *sixth* blessing, "Fellowship with God." To speak with God in prayer, and to converse with God in the ordinances of religion—what a privilege! what an enjoyment! Then the pious child can say, "I sat down under his shadow with great delight, and his fruit was sweet to my taste." Cant. ii, 3.

Look at the *seventh* blessing, "A Happy Death." O may that blessing be yours! When you die, may you fall asleep in the bosom of Jesus; for "blessed are the dead who die in the Lord." Revelations xiv, 13.

Look at the *eighth* blessing, "A Glorious Resurrection." May that blessing be yours! Then, though your bodies may slumber for many centuries in the tomb, you shall at last awake, come forth, and shine brighter than the stars forever and ever. Dan. xii, 3.

Look at the *last* blessing, "A Happy Heaven." O may this blessing be yours! At last may you land on the heavenly Canaan's blessed, peaceful shores! In the prospect may you and I sing, in holy expectation of that blessed land, "Far, far away."

Next I will speak of—

II. THE PROPERTIES AND EXCELLENCES OF THE CUP OF SALVATION.

May your young hearts be deeply, seriously, and delightfully impressed while I tell you some remarkable things about this Cup.

1. God made the Cup. No angel, with all his wisdom, could contrive this wonderful Cup; and no archangel, with all his power, could make this wonderful Cup. God alone is the Contriver of the Cup. God alone is the Maker of the Cup. Boundless love moved him to contrive the Cup; and boundless love to our ruined race, and to ruined children, moved him to make the Cup. As God our Saviour contrived and made the Cup of Salvation, O how well does he deserve to be called "The God of Salvation!" May every child who reads these lines be taught to say, " Behold, God is my Salvation!" Isa. xii, 2.

2. It is a very *precious* Cup. It is so precious that we cannot tell, we cannot conceive *how* precious, how valuable it is. A diamond as large as the world would

be nothing, yes, nothing, less than nothing, and vanity, compared with it. How rich are they who can say, "This Cup is mine!" And the poorest child among you is welcome to receive this Cup—yes, to call this Cup your own. And when you can call *this* Cup your own, you are more wealthy than if you could call the whole world your own. So precious is this Cup that it cost Jesus his *blood*, his *life!*

3. It is a very *ancient* Cup. There are some few golden cups, in the palaces of kings, several hundred years old; but this Cup is nearly six thousand years old. It is as ancient as the days of Adam. He, and Eve, and Abel, their pious son, were the first who put this Cup to their lips, and drank the refreshing water of salvation which it contains. This Cup suffers nothing by age; it looks as well as it did at the beginning. It is as bright, and beautiful, and glorious as ever. The sun loses nothing by age, neither does this Cup, this wonderful Cup.

4. It is very *large*. The bed of the great ocean may be called an immense

cup. It is filled with briny waters. But the bed of the Atlantic, or the bed of the Pacific Ocean, which is much larger, is nothing like this great Cup of Salvation, provided for all the kingdoms of the world, and for all the generations of men that shall ever live upon the face of the earth.

5. It is a *full* Cup. It is not only full, but overflowing, and ever flowing over. O what multitudes have drunk of this Cup from the days of Adam till the present day! and the Cup has never diminished. The blessings which it contains are as abundant as ever, and these blessings shall overflow forever and ever. Young friends, drink of this overflowing Cup!

6. It is a *free* Cup. Blessed, blessed truth! You are required to pay nothing to drink. And it is well; for you have nothing to pay. What *could* you pay? Come and drink, without money, and without price. This Cup is as free to the beggar as to the prince; as free to the poor as to the rich; as free to murderers as to saints; as free to the worst

of men as to the best of men. Wonderful truth!

7. It is a *very beautiful* Cup. It is beautified by the perfections of God. These are, his wisdom, his power, his holiness, his justice, his love, and his truth. These are glorious perfections, and they all add to the beauty of this beautiful Cup.

I see some beautiful figures or pictures on this Cup. There are many silver and gold cups with flowers and figures upon the outside, and around the mouth, which add greatly to their beauty. But what do I see on this beautiful Cup? I see the figure of a *Lamb*. That is the emblem of Jesus, the Lamb of God, who was slain for us. I see the figure of a *Dove*. That is the emblem of the Holy Spirit, who descended on the head of Jesus at his baptism in the form of a dove. I see a *lily*. That is the emblem of the Church, or people of Christ. I see the figure of the *rose of Sharon*, and of the *apple-tree*. These are emblems of Jesus. What a lovely cup is the Cup of Salvation! Beloved young friends, drink of this lovely Cup!

8. This Cup has remarkable *inscriptions*. Many costly silver cups are given in presents, and as marks of friendship and esteem. All these cups have inscriptions. These inscriptions show *to* whom, *by* whom, and for what *reason* these costly cups were given. Look at some of the inscriptions on the Cup of Salvation. I mention four. First: "God is love." 1 John iv, 8. Second inscription: "God so loved the world that he gave his only-begotten Son, that whosoever believeth in him should not perish, but have everlasting life." John iii, 16. Third inscription: "This is a faithful saying, and worthy of all acceptation, that Christ Jesus came into the world to save sinners." 1 Tim. i, 15. Fourth inscription: "The Spirit and the bride say, Come. And let him that heareth say, Come. And let him that is athirst come. And whosoever will, let him take the water of life freely." Rev. xxii, 17. Young friends, can you read these loving inscriptions, and refuse to drink of this precious Cup? May divine grace employ them in persuading you

now to drink of the Cup of Salvation!

9. This Cup will last forever. It is a Cup of everlasting Salvation. "But Israel shall be saved in the Lord with an *everlasting* salvation." Isa. xlv, 17. This Cup is filled with joy, which is "everlasting joy." Isa. xxxv, 10. It is filled with pleasures, but "pleasures for evermore." Psa. xvi, 11. The cup of carnal pleasure shall soon cease. The cup of the drunkard shall soon be no more. But the Cup of Salvation shall continue to fill the minds of the inhabitants of heaven with blessedness, felicity, and joy, forever and ever.

> " There everlasting spring abides,
>   And never-with'ring flowers ;
> Death, like a narrow sea, divides
>   This heavenly land from ours."

III. I now proceed to mention some persons spoken of in Scripture who drank of this precious Cup. O may you, my young friends, be taught to follow their good example! First, I shall mention some who were very *wicked;* and secondly, some who were very young.

First, I shall mention some who were very *wicked* who drank of this Cup.

1. *King Manasseh* was very wicked. He was a shocking idolater, and a most cruel murderer. He was taken prisoner, and cast into a dungeon in Babylon. 2 Chron. xxxiii, 11. God met with him in the dungeon. He cried to God for mercy. His prayer was heard. The Cup of Salvation was presented to him. He took it, and drank it. O what a trophy of regenerating and redeeming grace! 2 Chron. xxxiii, 12–16.

2. *Mary Magdalene* was very wicked. Uncleanness was her reigning sin. On one occasion she heard our Saviour preach. She was convinced; she was converted. Jesus by his power expelled from her heart seven unclean spirits. O what a change! The Cup of Salvation was presented; she put it to her lips. She drank with thankfulness, joy, and praise. Mark xvi, 9; Luke viii, 2.

3. The *thief on the cross* was very wicked. He was nailed to the cross because of his wickedness and crimes. In the agonies

of death he cried to Jesus for mercy. Jesus heard his penitential prayer. Jesus presented the Cup of Salvation to the dying penitent. He put it to his parched, quivering, thirsty lips. With ecstasies of joy he drank the Cup. He is now in the Paradise of the blessed.

4: *Christ's murderers*, who not only consented to the Saviour's death, but who nailed him to the cross, were very wicked. Some of them heard Peter preach on the day of Pentecost in the temple. They were cut to the heart! They cried out, in the midst of the faithful sermon, "Men and brethren, what shall we do?" Peter preached salvation to them through the very death of the Saviour they murdered. How astonishing! By grace they believed. The Cup of Salvation was presented; they received it; they drank of it, and were saved. O what grace, what wonderful grace!

5. *Saul of Tarsus* was very wicked. When the cruel Jews were stoning the holy Stephen to death, Saul was present watching the garments of the murderers.

Acts vii, 58. He assisted in dragging men and women to prison, and rejoiced when the followers of Jesus were put to death. He was sent to Damascus with a commission of death in his bosom against all who professed Christ; but under the walls of Damascus, and before he entered the city, Jesus spoke to him with a voice from heaven. Conviction reached his conscience; conversion reached his heart. The Cup of Salvation was put into his hand; he drank it. The persecutor became a preacher of Christ. The child of Satan became a son of God. Acts ix, 6. O what a prodigy of grace!

Secondly, some very young persons who drank of this Cup are mentioned in Scripture.

1. *Abel* was most probably of this number. After our first parents, he was the first convert. For his piety, he was the first martyr. He fell by the hand of his brother Cain, and he was the first saint that entered heaven.

2. *Joseph*, when he was a child, drank of this Cup. He was the most pious of

Jacob's sons. Jacob loved him more than all his sons; for, amid them all, his youthful piety shone forth with peculiar brightness.

3. *Samuel*, when a child, drank the Cup of Salvation. 1 Sam. iii, 1, &c. When he was yet a child he ministered unto the Lord before Eli the high priest. Great was the delight which Hannah the pious mother had in Samuel her pious child. Every year she made a little coat for him with her own hands, and brought it up to him every year, when she came up to the yearly sacrifice. 1 Sam. ii, 19.

4. *Obadiah*, when he was a youth, drank of the Cup of Salvation. 1 Kings xviii, 12. This good man said to Elijah, with much humility and thankfulness, "But I thy servant fear the Lord from my youth up." When he became a man his piety shone like a sun. He saved the lives of a hundred prophets from the murdering hands of Queen Jezebel.

5. *King Josiah*, when he was a child, drank of the Cup of Salvation. What an interesting account is given of the early

piety of this lovely, holy prince, in 2 Kings xxii.

6. *Timothy*, when he was a child, drank of this Cup of Salvation. My young friends, how blessed, how honored you would be, if we could say of you what was said of Timothy, (2 Tim. iii, 15,) "From a child thou hast known the Holy Scriptures, which are able to make thee wise unto salvation, through faith which is in Christ Jesus." What a comfort Timothy was to his grandmother Lois and his mother Eunice!

CONCLUSION.

Allow me, in the name of Christ, earnestly and affectionately to call upon you to *take* and *drink* the Cup of Salvation. But what is it "to *take* and *drink* the Cup of Salvation?" It is to receive Christ as your Saviour. Beloved young friends, when you can say with the heart and in faith, "Blessed Jesus, I receive thee as my Saviour;—as my Prophet I receive thee, to give me wisdom;—as my Priest I receive thee, to take away my guilt and intercede for me;—I receive thee as my King, to reign over and to deliver me from all my enemies;"—when you can say this with the heart, you *have* taken the Cup of Salvation, and have drank its refreshing waters.

Believe it, and may the Holy Spirit enable you to believe it! Jesus, who died on Calvary to prepare the Cup of Salvation, calls upon you, earnestly invites you, to drink of the Cup of Salvation. He says to you, in language the most affectionate—O hear his voice!—he says, "Drink abundantly, O beloved!" He is the Fountain from which the cup is filled, and he says to every little child—

> "Ho! ye that thirst, approach the Spring
>   Where living waters flow;
> Free to that sacred Fountain all
>   Without a price may go.
>
> "Seek ye the Lord, while yet his ear
>   Is open to your call;
> While offer'd mercy still is near,
>   Before his footstool fall."

Amen.

RESURRECTION AND JUDGMENT-DAY.

And I saw the dead, small and great, stand before God.
—Rev. xx, 12.

My Little Children, I call your attention
to a most wonderful day. It is the Day
of Judgment. A great poet, in speaking
of this solemn day, makes use of the following language, which I can never read
without being solemnly impressed:—

> "The day of wrath, that dreadful day
> When heaven and earth shall pass away,
> What power shall be the sinner's stay?
> How shall he meet that dreadful day?

> "When, shriveling like a parched scroll,
> The flaming heavens together roll;
> When louder yet, and yet more dread,
> Swells the high trump that wakes the dead:

> "O on that day, that wrathful day,
> When man to judgment wakes from clay,
> Be thou the trembling sinner's stay,
> Though heaven and earth shall pass away."

That was a memorable day when God
created the world. It was a wonderful

day when Christ came to save the world. It was a wonderful day when Christ died to redeem the world. And that will be a wonderful, a solemn day, a day never to be forgotten, when Christ shall come to judge the world. He came to *make* the world, he came to *save* the world, and he will come to *judge* the world. Children, you neither saw the first day, nor the second, but you will see the third. In the prospect of that day, present the following prayer :—

> " O may I stand before the Judge,
> When earth and seas are fled,
> And hear the Judge pronounce my name,
> With blessings on my head."

May the Holy Spirit answer this prayer!

In speaking to you of this day, I will show you what will take place in the *morning* of the day, what will take place in the *principal part* of the day, and what will happen at the *end* of the day.

What shall happen in the morning of the day.

A *trumpet* shall be sounded. " In a moment, in the twinkling of an eye, at

the last trump; for the trumpet shall
sound." 1 Cor. xv, 52. "For the Lord
himself shall descend from heaven with a
shout, with the voice of the archangel, and
with the trump of God." 1 Thess. iv, 16.
An archangel will blow this trumpet. He
will sound the trumpet so loudly that all
the inhabitants of the earth shall hear it.
At one instant all who are alive shall hear
it and all the dead in their graves, and those
who are in the bottom of the ocean, shall
hear it. The powerful sound of this trumpet shall pierce through mountains, and
shall enter into the deepest tombs of the
dead.

The Judge shall appear. He shall
come in the clouds.

> " Behold, on flying clouds He comes ;
> The saints shall bless the day ;
> While they that pierced him sadly mourn
> In anguish and dismay."

The Judge shall come *suddenly*, and
when no one is expecting him. While
men shall be engaged in their usual em-
ployments—while the gardener is employed among his trees and flowers, and

the husbandman in cultivating the fields, and the tradesman in his business, and the merchant in his counting-house, and the king sitting among his nobles—then, in a moment, shall the Judge appear.

The Judge shall come *honorably attended*. His holy angels shall attend him. "When the Son of man shall come in his glory, and all the holy angels with him, then shall he sit upon the throne of his glory." Matt. xxv, 31. He shall be attended by his saints. "Behold, the Lord cometh with ten thousand of his saints, to execute judgment upon all." Jude 14.

The dead shall *be raised*. On the morning of the day of judgment the resurrection of the dead shall take place. When the assizes are held, the prisoners who are to appear before the judge to be tried are all in a state of readiness in the morning of the day. So it will be on the morning of the judgment-day.

In speaking of the resurrection, the following things are very important to be remembered.

God *can* raise the dead. He is almighty.

With greater ease than I can lift a rose from the ground, God can raise the dead from their cold graves. God can as easily awake the dead in their tombs as a mother can awake her babe in its cradle. Besides, God has shown that he can raise the dead, for he has done it already in several instances. He raised to life the son of the Shunamite, he raised to life the body of a man who was buried in the grave of Elisha, he raised the son of the widow of Nain, he raised the body of Lazarus, and he brought to life the deceased Dorcas.

God *will* raise the dead at the last day. He has given us his word that he will do it, and his word cannot fail. Hear what he has said: "Many of them that sleep in the dust of the earth shall awake, some to everlasting life, and some to shame and everlasting contempt." Dan. xii, 2. As God has spoken in the Old Testament, he has also spoken in the New: "The hour is coming, in the which all that are in the graves shall hear his voice, and shall come forth; they that have done good, unto the resurrection of life; and they that have done evil, to the resurrection of damnation." John v, 28, 29. The *righteous* shall rise first. Saith an apostle, "The dead in Christ shall rise first." We know not how long before the wicked they will rise. On earth the wicked are often first, they stand before the righteous. Yes, and they look upon them with disdain. At the day of judgment matters will be completely changed. The righteous shall be first, and the wicked shall be last. The righteous beggar shall be first, and the wicked king shall be last. O what a change!

The righteous will rise with *great glory*. They will shine brighter than the stars for ever and ever. How amazing: the bodies of the righteous will come out of the dark tomb shining like glorious suns. Very different will it be with the wicked. They will rise covered with the defilements of sin. We cannot conceive how shocking they will appear.

The righteous will rise with *great joy*. Their faces will be joyful like the countenances of angels. The wicked will rise with great sorrow. Anguish will be painted in their mournful looks. The righteous will rise with singing. "Awake and sing, ye that dwell in the dust." The music of angels will awake them from the bed of death, and as soon as they awake the righteous will begin to sing the praises of God and the Lamb. How different with the wicked: they will awake with sighing, weeping, and groans. Their crying will pierce the skies. My dear children, may God deliver you from so dreadful a doom. See with what confidence and delight the righteous shall rise, and with what trembling and horror the wicked shall come out of their graves. No wonder, for the righteous shall rise to meet their Saviour, and the wicked to meet an avenging God. Think of this, my young friends. Happy, happy will you be, if, in the prospect of this, you shall be able to sing—

> "Arrayed in glorious grace,
>   Shall our vile bodies shine;
> And every shape, and every face,
>   Look heavenly and divine."

In the prospect of that joyful morning,

pious children may lift up their voices, and sing—

> " How loud shall our glad voices sing,
> When Christ his risen saints shall bring,
> From beds of dust and sleeping clay,
> To realms of everlasting day.

> " Hasten, dear Lord, the glorious day,
> And this delightful scene display ;
> When all the saints from death shall rise, ·
> Raptured in bliss beyond the skies.
> Soon shall the trumpet sound, and we
> Shall rise to immortality."

We now proceed to show what will take place during *the principal part* of the judgment-day.

Five things will take place. The Judge will appear ; angels and men shall appear before him ; the books will be opened ; all shall be judged according to their works ; and just sentences will be pronounced.

O, while I speak to you of these things, may Jesus deeply affect your young hearts!

The Judge will appear. Jesus Christ shall be the Judge. He who was ordained to be the Saviour of men, is appointed to be the Judge of men. "The Father hath committed all judgment unto the Son." Perhaps none of you ever saw a king sitting upon his throne. But all of you shall see Christ seated upon his throne of judgment. "Every eye shall see him." O the millions of millions who shall look upon him when he is seated on his glorious throne! No man or angel can tell how glorious this throne will be. Great is the glory of the rainbow in the sky; but compared with the glory of the throne of judgment, it is no more than one single dew-drop upon the blade of grass. We must not even speak of the majesty of an earthly king upon his throne. Compared with Christ upon the throne of judgment, it is no more than the enthroning of a worm or a winged insect. We know not where this throne will be placed; but it will be where all the vast assembly shall see it. So glorious and bright shall the appearance of the Judge be, that he shall, like the sun, seem equally near every individual who shall be placed before his tribunal.

How shall Christ appear on the throne

of judgment? St. John saw Christ in his glory, and thus speaks of him : " His head and his hairs were white like wool, as white as snow ; and his eyes were as a flame of fire ; and his feet like unto fine brass, as if they burned in a furnace ; and his voice as the sound of many waters. And he had in his right hand seven stars ; and out of his mouth went a sharp two-edged sword ; and his countenance was as the sun shineth in his strength." Rev. i, 14–16. In the following manner this apostle speaks of the terror with which the appearance of Christ the Judge shall strike his enemies : " And the kings of the earth, and the great men, and the rich men, and the chief captains, and the mighty men, and every bondman, and every freeman, hid themselves in the dens, and in the rocks of the mountains ; and said to the mountains and rocks, Fall on us, and hide us from the face of Him that sitteth on the throne, and from the wrath of the Lamb : for the great day of his wrath is come ; and who shall be able to stand?" Rev. vi, 15–17.

When shall the Judge appear? This question we cannot answer. "Of that day and hour knoweth no man; no, not the angels of heaven, but my Father only." Great and blessed changes must take place before that day arrives. The Jews will be converted to Jesus. That is a blessed event yet to come. The Gospel must be preached in all lands. That blessed event is yet to come. Jesus shall wonderfully reign a thousand years on earth, when, like a mighty ocean, knowledge, love, and holiness shall overspread the earth. That blessed event is yet to come. All these things must take place before Christ shall appear in the clouds as the Judge of all.

Angels and men shall appear before him. Good angels shall attend him, and bad angels shall be dragged before him in everlasting chains. "God spared not the angels that sinned, but cast them down to hell, and delivered them into chains of darkness, to be reserved unto judgment." 2 Peter ii, 4. "And the angels which kept not their first estate, but left their

own habitation, he hath reserved in everlasting chains under darkness unto the
judgment of the great day." Jude 6.

> " Down headlong from their native skies
>   The rebel angels fell :
> And Christ, when seated on the throne,
>   Shall cast them into hell."

CHILDREN IN HEAVEN.

It is well with the child.—2 Kings iv, 26.

WHAT a glorious, what a blessed place is
heaven! Some have called the starry sky
the portico, or porch, or gate of the heavenly palace. If the gate be so glorious,
what must the palace itself be? What a
difference there is between this world and
heaven! Great is the difference between
a desert and a garden beautified with the
loveliest flowers; far greater the difference
between earth and heaven. Great is the
difference between the sky at night, with
its twinkling stars, and the sky at noonday,
filled with the brightness of the meridian

sun; far greater the difference between
earth and heaven. Great is the difference
between a prison and the abodes of princes;
far greater the difference between earth
and heaven. Heaven is so glorious, so
pure, so happy, so blessed, that the most
eloquent tongue cannot describe its purity,
its happiness, its glory, its blessedness:
even the heart cannot conceive its excellence. If the starry heavens were a million of times more glorious than they are,
even then they would be unworthy to be
compared with the heaven of heavens, into
which holy children are taken when they
die. Once St. Paul was taken to heaven,
and returned again to this world. Then
he told his holy and pious friends that what
he heard he could not utter, and what he
saw he could not describe, 1 Cor. ii, 9:
"Eye hath not seen, nor ear heard, neither
have entered into the heart of man, the
things which God hath prepared for them
that love him." Is this the case? Then
how glorious must heaven be! The same
holy apostle saith, 2 Cor. xii, 4: "How
that he was caught up into paradise, and

heard unspeakable words which it is not lawful" (that is, *possible*) "for a man to utter." Is this the case? Then how glorious must heaven be!

My dear little children who love Christ, who believe in Christ, who serve Christ, what good, what welcome news I have to tell you—that heaven shall be your home. It is prepared for you, and Jesus is preparing you for it.

> "There is beyond the starry sky
> A heav'n of joy and love;
> And holy children when they die
> Go to that world above."

Methinks I hear some pious child say, "O, I long to be there!"

> "Haste, my beloved, bear my soul
> Up to thy bless'd abode:
> Fly, for my spirit longs to see
> My Saviour and my God."

By the assistance of the Holy Spirit I propose to show the blessedness of pious children in heaven. "Holy Spirit, give thy gracious aid!" In one moment, when the body draws its last breath, pious children are made perfect in holiness, in wisdom, and in happiness. They are removed from suffering, from sorrow, and from death. They are taken far beyond the reach of temptation, of sin, of Satan, and of the wicked. They enjoy in heaven the fellowship of saints, of angels, and of the Father, Son, and Holy Ghost, one God. And, to crown all, they are employed in singing the sweetest songs of praise to their Saviour and their God.

1. They must be blessed, for they are *perfect in holiness.* What is it to be perfectly holy? It is to be completely free from sin : it is to possess in perfection every grace. The dear child on entering heaven is made pure as angels are pure, and holy as God is holy. That holiness is the perfection of loveliness. The beauty of the morning sky is nothing compared with this loveliness :—

> " These children are beloved of God,
> Wash'd are their robes in Jesus' blood ;
> More spotless than the purest white,
> They shine in uncreated light."

2. At death, pious children are made perfect in *knowledge* and *wisdom.* Therefore, they must be blessed. The first

moment they enter heaven they know
more of God, of creation, of providence,
and redemption, than the whole Church
of God on earth. O, how wonderful!
"Here, they saw through a glass darkly;
in heaven, they see face to face. Here,
they know in part; in heaven they know
even as they are known." 1 Cor. xiii, 12.

3. At death, pious children are made
perfect in *happiness.* The more sin there
is, the more misery. The more there is of
holiness, there is the more of happiness.
The most sinful man on earth is the most
miserable man; and the holiest man on
earth is the most happy man. What, then,
must the happiness of heaven be, where
spotless holiness in all its glory reigns?

> "There streams of endless pleasure flow;
>   And full discoveries of thy grace,
> Which we but tasted here below,
>   Spread heavenly joys through all the place."

4. At death, pious children are forever
removed from *suffering, sorrow,* and *death.*
No book could contain an account of the
suffering and sorrows which are felt at
this moment by young and old on the face

of the earth. And death is a mighty, terrible king, reigning over all nations. O, how blessed we shall be if we enter that heaven, of which it is said, Rev. xxi, 4: " And God shall wipe away all tears from their eyes; and there shall be no more death, neither sorrow, nor crying, neither shall there be any more pain: for the former things are passed away."

> " His own soft hand shall wipe the tears
>   From ev'ry weeping eye;
> And pains, and groans, and griefs, and fears,
>   And death itself shall die."

5. At death, pious children are forever removed from the presence of the wicked. The pious child on earth has sometimes a wicked, graceless, swearing, drunken, cruel father; or he has a wicked, lying, unkind brother, neglecting the Bible, and profaning the Sabbath. We cannot tell how much the pious child suffers by such a father or such a brother. It would grieve you to hear his sighs, and to see his tears. At death he is relieved from all this misery; he is taken from the presence of a wicked father, or of a wicked brother, and

he is admitted to the joyful, blessed presence of his divine Father, and of his brethren and kindred in heaven. In the hopes of such a separation from wicked relatives on earth, and of being admitted into the company of such a blessed society of friends in heaven, he could say—

> " My soul doth long for heaven still,
> While life or breath remains;
> There my best friends, my kindred dwell,
> There God my Saviour reigns."

6. At death, pious children enjoy the *fellowship of saints and angels.* Therefore, how happy they must be! A person living *alone* in the loveliest part of the world, or in the noblest palace that was ever reared, or even in heaven itself, could not be happy. We cannot be happy without society; but if society is not good, it cannot give happiness. Spotless saints in heaven are perfectly happy. O, how happy shall holy children be, when they mingle with such holy, spotless saints! I feel persuaded that all the saints in heaven are known to each other. If we enter that holy, happy place, we shall not

need to ask, Who is Adam, or Noah, or
Moses, or Paul, or John? otherwise, the
holy child would be a stranger in the
heavenly world. And how sweet must
be the society of the saints in heaven, for
their love is perfect! Society, without
love, can never give pleasure; but where
there is perfect love, there is perfect bliss.

Lastly. The blessedness of pious children
in heaven appears from the sweet songs
they sing to their Saviour's praise. On
earth our hearts are not always in tune to
praise our Lord; here, tears are mingled
with songs, and sighs with praise. Here,
we often sing in the *minor key*, and feelings of sorrow are mingled with feelings
of joy. How different the praises beyond
the sky! "The ransomed of the Lord return and come to Zion with songs and
everlasting joy upon their heads; they
obtain joy and gladness, and sorrow and
sighing have forever fled away." Isaiah
xxxv, 10.

THE END.

CPSIA information can be obtained at www.ICGtesting.com
Printed in the USA
LVOW032302101111

254488LV00002B/2/P

9 781599 252575